Literary Lives

General Editor: **Richard Dutton**, Professor of English, Lancaster University

This series offers stimulating accounts of the literary careers of the most admired and influential English-language authors. Volumes follow the outline of the writers' working lives, not in the spirit of traditional biography, but aiming to trace the professional, publishing and social contexts which shaped their writing.

Published titles include:

Cedric C. Brown
JOHN MILTON

Peter Davison
GEORGE ORWELL

Linda Wagner-Martin
SYLVIA PLATH

Felicity Rosslyn
ALEXANDER POPE

Richard Dutton
WILLIAM SHAKESPEARE

John Williams
MARY SHELLEY

Michael O'Neill
PERCY BYSSHE SHELLEY

Gary Waller
EDMUND SPENSER

Tony Sharpe
WALLACE STEVENS

William Gray
ROBERT LOUIS STEVENSON

Joseph McMinn
JONATHAN SWIFT

Leonée Ormond
ALFRED TENNYSON

Peter Shillingsburg
WILLIAM MAKEPEACE THACKERAY

David Wykes
EVELYN WAUGH

John Mepham
VIRGINIA WOOLF

John Williams
WILLIAM WORDSWORTH

Alasdair D. F. Macrae
W.B. YEATS

Literary Lives
Series Standing Order ISBN 0–333–71486–5 hardcover
Series Standing Order ISBN 0–333–80334–5 paperback
(*outside North America only*)

You can receive future titles in this series as they are published by placing a standing order. Please contact your bookseller or, in case of difficulty, write to us at the address below with your name and address, the title of the series and one of the ISBNs quoted above.

Customer Services Department, Macmillan Distribution Ltd, Houndmills, Basingstoke, Hampshire RG21 6XS, England

Robert Louis Stevenson

A Literary Life

William Gray

First published 2004 by
PALGRAVE MACMILLAN
Houndmills, Basingstoke, Hampshire RG21 6XS and
175 Fifth Avenue, New York, N.Y. 10010
Companies and representatives throughout the world

PALGRAVE MACMILLAN is the global academic imprint of the Palgrave
Macmillan division of St. Martin's Press, LLC and of Palgrave Macmillan Ltd.
Macmillan® is a registered trademark in the United States, United Kingdom
and other countries. Palgrave is a registered trademark in the European
Union and other countries.

ISBN 0–333–98400–5 hardback
ISBN 0–333–98401–3 paperback

This book is printed on paper suitable for recycling and made from fully
managed and sustained forest sources.

A catalogue record for this book is available from the British Library.

Library of Congress Cataloging-in-Publication Data
Gray, William, 1952–
    Robert Louis Stevenson : a literary life / William Gray
        p.   cm. — (Literary lives)
    Includes bibliographical references and index.
    ISBN 0–333–98400–5 — ISBN (invalid) 0–339–98401–3 (pbk.)
    1. Stevenson, Robert Louis, 1850–1894. 2. Authors, Scottish—
    19th century—Biography. I. Title. II. Literary lives
    (Palgrave Macmillan (Firm))

    PR5493.G668 2004
    828'.809—dc22   2003070192

10   9   8   7   6   5   4   3   2   1
13 12 11 10 09 08 07 06 05 04

Printed and bound in Great Britain by
Antony Rowe Ltd, Chippenham and Eastbourne

In memory of my father, whose rendition of Blind Pew scared the living daylights out of me

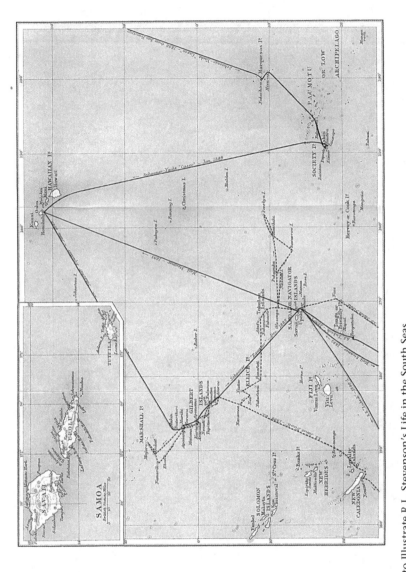

Map to Illustrate R.L. Stevenson's Life in the South Seas

Source: Robert Louis Stevenson, *In the South Seas* (The Edinburgh Geographical Institute 1894–6). © John Bartholomew & Son Ltd.

Contents

Acknowledgements

I would like to express my sincere thanks to the following: the Library and the English Department at University College Chichester (and especially Isla Duncan, with whom I shared the Acting Headship during interesting times); Chichester Library; Richard Dutton, the series editor, for his support and constructive criticism; Elaine Greig of the Writers' Museum, Edinburgh, for her help, especially in providing the cover picture; Yale University Press for permission to quote from *The Letters of Robert Louis Stevenson*; Stanford University Press for permission to quote from Barry Menikoff's *Robert Louis Stevenson and 'The Beach of Falesá'*; Iain G. Brown of the Scottish National Library; M. Henri Corbeille of Grez-sur-Loing; Jonathan Gray; John McFie of 17 Heriot Row; Anna Fleming, whose mother's godmother was Anna (Boyle) Henley, and who lent me copies of the Henley papers she inherited (now held by the Beinecke Rare Book and Manuscript Library, Yale University); Professor Rory Watson; and, above all, Lorna, for walking to Grez in the summer heat, making time to read various drafts, and generally welcoming 'Lou' into our marriage.

List of Abbreviations

B = Graham Balfour, *The Life of Robert Louis Stevenson (One Volume Edition)* (London: Methuen, 1906)

L 1–8 = Booth, Bradford A. and Mehew, Ernest (eds), *The Letters of Robert Louis Stevenson*, 8 vols (New Haven and London: Yale University Press, 1994–95)

M = Maixner, Paul (ed.), *Robert Louis Stevenson: The Critical Heritage* (Lonon: Routledge, 1971)

S = Swearingen, Roger G., *The Prose Writings of Robert Louis Stevenson* (London: Macmillan – now Palgrave Macmillan, 1980)

T 1–35 = The Tusitala Edition of *The Works of Robert Louis Stevenson* in 35 vols (London: Heinemann, 1924)

T1	*New Arabian Nights*
T2	*Treasure Island*
T3	*The Dynamiter*
T4	*Prince Otto*
T5	*Dr Jekyll and Mr Hyde. Fables*
T6	*Kidnapped*
T7	*Catriona*
T8	*The Merry Men and Other Tales*
T9	*The Black Arrow*
T10	*The Master of Ballantrae*
T11	*The Wrong Box. The Body-Snatcher*
T12	*The Wrecker*
T13	*Island Nights' Entertainments.*
T14	*The Ebb-Tide. The Story of a Lie*
T15	*St Ives*
T16	*Weir of Hermiston & Some Unfinished Stories*
T17	*An Inland Voyage. Travels with a Donkey*
T18	*The Amateur Emigrant. The Silverado Squatters*
T19	*Memoir of Fleeming Jenkin. Records of a Family of Engineers*
T20	*In the South Seas*
T21	*Vailima Papers*
T22	*Poems I (A Child's Garden of Verses, Underwoods, Songs of Travel)*
T23	*Poems II (Ballads, New Poems)*
T24	*Plays*

Introduction and Chronology

Introduction

In [my biography of] my Grandfather, I've had... to give up the temporal order almost entirely; doubtless the temporal order is the great foe of the biographer; it is so tempting, so easy...[1]

Perhaps more than most writers, Robert Louis Stevenson may require a *Literary* Life. As Henry James put it on reading Graham Balfour's *Life of Robert Louis Stevenson*: 'Louis... has *superseded*, personally, his books, and this last replacement of himself so *en scène* (so largely by his own aid, too) has *killed* the literary baggage.'[2] While serious critical attention to Stevenson's literary works languished for most of last century, the 'Life of Stevenson' increasingly flourished, becoming almost a minor literary genre in its own right.[3] For a résumé of Stevenson's life, the reader is directed to the Chronology below. However, the version of Stevenson's literary life in the following chapters does not foreground linear chronology in the way that most biographies of Stevenson do. The present study is in some respects more of an exercise in literary geography than in literary history, in the sense that its structure is defined by reference to the different geographical and cultural contexts in which Stevenson lived and worked.

This attempt to contextualize Stevenson primarily in terms of place rather than time by no means implies an abandonment of an historical perspective. The sequence of different geographical and cultural contexts discussed below follows roughly the chronological sequence of Stevenson's life, except that the chapter on Scotland has been located at the heart of the book. The decision to position the chapter on Stevenson and Scotland at the centre of the book, rather than at the beginning, may seem strange. Partly it was taken with the intention precisely of 'making strange' the familiar story of Stevenson's life; my (to some extent) non-linear narrative would then be, in terms of the Russian Formalist theory of defamiliarization, a particular 'plot' (*sjuzet*) constructed out of the 'story' (*fabula*) contained in the Chronology. It is also arguable that, in an imaginative and emotional sense, Stevenson never really left Scotland at all; it informs his writings from start to finish. The placing of Scotland at the heart of the book is then a kind of metaphor for the idea that Stevenson's Scottishness lay at the very core of his being both as a man and as a writer. To have begun with Scotland would certainly have emphasized its priority in a temporal sense. For Stevenson, however, Scotland came first in more than a merely temporal sense. Therefore I have begun to some extent *in medias res*, with the chapter on 'The English Scene', which describes Stevenson's sustained engagement with English life and letters, from his early visits to Suffolk, through his 'piratical descents' on London, to his final letters to the likes of Edmund Gosse and George Meredith, written after he had abandoned any hope of ever visiting England again. This chapter will, I hope, convey a sense of the literary context within which Stevenson came to develop his distinctive style and status as a Scottish writer.

Stevenson's stays in England, France, America, the South Seas and finally Samoa (where he stayed in the Scottish sense of 'made his home') are looked at in more or less chronological order, although there are inevitable overlaps, particularly during the periods spent in England and in France. Should any confusion arise, the reader is asked to consult the Chronology. Although the occasional chronological awkwardness may result, the experiment of structuring an account of Stevenson's literary life primarily in terms of place rather than time does permit a more sustained focus on each of the different geographical and cultural contexts which shaped him as a writer.

One *mea culpa*, though hopefully a pardonable, and even a happy fault: I have erred on the side of letting Stevenson speak in his own words as much as possible, and have risked interrupting the flow of the narrative by always giving a reference. This citing of chapter and verse is not only to acknowledge my indebtedness to Stevenson (books on Stevenson can sometimes be remarkably well written); it is also to give directions to any readers new to Stevensoniana, and particularly to Booth and Mehew's splendid eight-volume edition of *The Letters of Robert Louis Stevenson*, published by Yale University Press.

Chronology

1850   Robert Lewis Balfour Stevenson born on 13 November in Edinburgh to Thomas Stevenson (of the 'Lighthouse' Stevensons) and Margaret, daughter of Lewis Balfour, minister of Colinton church.

1857   The Stevensons move to 17 Heriot Row, in Edinburgh's prestigious New Town.

1858–67   Irregular attendance (due to poor health) at a variety of schools, but mainly private tuition.

1862–3   Visits to Germany, Italy and the South of France with his parents.

1866   Stevenson's first publication, *The Pentland Rising* (an historical account of an insurrection by 'Covenanters'⁴), appears anonymously in a limited edition at his father's expense.

1867   Goes to Edinburgh University to study engineering, but has poor attendance record, figuring as 'an idler'.

1868–70   Stays in various locations on Scottish coastline, including Earraid, as part of his training as engineer. Around this time the spelling of his name (though not its pronunciation) is changed from 'Lewis' to 'Louis'. This change is purportedly due to a family dislike of someone named Lewis, though another probable motive is the Francophilia which is *de rigueur* for the Bohemian the young Stevenson aspires to be.

1871   Decides to abandon engineering and study law.

1873   The tension between Stevenson's religious agnosticism and the orthodox Protestantism of his devout parents reaches crisis-point. Stevenson's health breaks down. In July he escapes to relatives in Suffolk, where he meets Fanny Sitwell (with whom he falls in love) and Sidney Colvin. After a brief return to Edinburgh, he goes south again, first to London, and then (under doctor's orders) to Mentone in the South of France. December sees his first paid publication, 'Roads', signed L.S. Stoneven, in *The Portfolio*.

1874   Returns to Edinburgh. 'Ordered South', Stevenson's first paid publication under his own name, appears in *Macmillan's Magazine* in May, to be followed in August by 'Victor Hugo's Romances' in the *Cornhill Magazine*. Resumption of his legal studies.

1875   Called to the Scottish Bar, but does not practise. Meets W.E. Henley in Edinburgh Infirmary. Joins his cousin Bob in Paris, Barbizon and Grez.

1876   Visits France in the spring, and again in late summer when he and Walter Simpson make the canoe trip recorded in *An Inland Voyage*. In Grez he meets Fanny Osbourne, a married woman with two children, Sam (later Lloyd) and Belle.

1877   From Edinburgh, Stevenson visits London, as well as Paris and Grez, where he and Fanny Osbourne become lovers. 'On Falling in Love' and essay on Villon appear in the *Cornhill*.

Stevenson's first published fiction, 'A Lodging for the Night', appears in the *Temple Bar*.

1878 In August, Fanny Osbourne returns with her children to her husband in California. Stevenson travels with a donkey in the Cévennes. Publication of *An Inland Voyage, Edinburgh: Picturesque Notes*, and various essays and short stories in the *Cornhill*, the *New Quarterly Review* and *London*.

1879 Stevenson ill in Edinburgh in March/April; recuperates at Gareloch, and later visits London and Paris. In August he sets off on the gruelling journey to California described in *The Amateur Emigrant*. Fanny's divorce from Sam Osbourne agreed. Essays published in the *Cornhill*, and 'The Story of a Lie' in the *New Quarterly Review*.

1880 Louis and Fanny marry in San Francisco in May. After a 'honeymoon' in the mountains of Northern California (the basis for *The Silverado Squatters*), they travel to Scotland. In October they go to London, where Stevenson is advised to winter in Davos in Switzerland. Copyright edition of the play *Deacon Brodie* (with W.E. Henley).

1881 In May Louis, Fanny and Lloyd return to Scotland, staying at Pitlochry and Braemar. Stevenson writes *Treasure Island*, which is completed in October in Davos, where they winter again. *Treasure Island* serialized in *Young Folks* from October, under the name of Captain George North. Publication of *Virginibus Puerisque*, and of 'Thrawn Janet' in *Cornhill*.

1882 Summer spent in Scotland, winter in various locations in the South of France. Publication of *Familiar Studies of Men and Books* and *New Arabian Nights*, and essays in *Cornhill* and *Longman's*.

1883 In March the Stevensons move to Hyères, their home until July 1884. Publication of *Treasure Island* (in book form, under Stevenson's own name) and *The Silverado Squatters*. 'Across the Plains' appears in *Longman's*. Stevenson writes poetry (some of which will appear in *A Child's Garden of Verses*), *Prince Otto*, and *The Black Arrow*, which is serialized in *Young Folks* under the name of Captain George North. 'A Note on Realism' appears in *Magazine of Art*.

1884 Stevenson seriously ill. The Stevensons move to Bournemouth in July, their home for next three years. Private printing of plays *Admiral Guinea* and *Beau Austin*, co-written with Henley, a frequent visitor. Essays (including 'A Humble Remonstrance') in *Longman's* and *Magazine of Art*.

1885	Move to 'Skerryvore', where Henry James is a frequent visitor. Publication of *Prince Otto, A Child's Garden of Verses, The Dynamiter* (with Fanny Stevenson), as well as 'Olalla' and 'On Some Technical Elements of Style in Literature'. Stevenson writes *Strange Case of Dr Jekyll and Mr Hyde*, which is published in January 1886.
1886	Publication of *Kidnapped* in book form after a run in *Young Folks* under Stevenson's own name. Letter to *The Times* about Rodin and Zola.
1887	Thomas Stevenson dies in May. In August Louis sails for America with Fanny, his mother, and Lloyd; they settle for health reasons at Saranac Lake in the Adirondack Mountains. Publication of *The Merry Men and Other Tales, Memories and Portraits, A Memoir of Fleeming Jenkin* and *Underwoods*, a volume of poetry.
1888	Quarrel with Henley. A deal with S.S. McClure for a series of travel articles for newspaper syndication enables Stevenson to charter the yacht *Casco* for a cruise in the Pacific with his family. They visit the Marquesas, the Paumotus, Tahiti and Hawaii. A series of twelve monthly essays (including 'A Chapter on Dreams') appears in *Scribner's Magazine*, where monthly instalments of *The Master of Ballantrae* also begin in November. Publication of *The Black Arrow* in book form.
1889	Visit to leper colony on Molokai. In June the Stevenson party (including his son-in-law Joe Strong, but minus his mother, who returns to Scotland) cruise on the trading schooner the *Equator* through the Gilbert Islands, reaching Samoa in December. Stevenson already at work on *A Footnote to History*, and begins series of letters to *The Times* about the situation in Samoa. Publication of *The Wrong Box* (with Lloyd Osbourne), and *The Master of Ballantrae* in book form.
1890	Purchase of estate, and construction of house begun, at Vailima near Apia on Samoan island of Opolu. Visit to Sydney, where Stevenson writes and publishes *Father Damien: An Open Letter to Reverend Doctor Hyde*. Further illness leads Stevenson to take another cruise, on the trading steamer *Janet Nicoll*, though a variety of South Sea islands. Lloyd leaves for England. In autumn the Stevensons settle at Vailima, and the *Vailima Letters* to Colvin begin. Publication of *Ballads*.
1891	Stevenson meets his mother and Lloyd in Sydney and accompanies them to Vailima. Serial publication of *In the*

South Seas in the New York *Sun* and in *Black and White*, where 'The Bottle Imp' also appears in serial form.

1892   Increasing involvement in Samoan politics, leading in December to the issue by the British High Commissioner of the Sedition (Samoa) Regulation, which seems designed to gag Stevenson. Publication of *A Footnote to History*, *Across the Plains*, *The Wrecker* (with Lloyd Osbourne) and *Three Plays by W.E. Henley and R.L. Stevenson*. 'The Beach of Falesá' serialized in *Illustrated London News*.

1893   His mother returns to Scotland. War in Samoa. Louis visits Honolulu, where he falls ill. Publication of *Catriona* and *Island Nights' Entertainments*. *The Ebb-Tide* (with Lloyd Osbourne) begins serial publication in Jerome K. Jerome's *To-day*.

1894   Maggie Stevenson returns to Vailima. Order restored in Samoa. Followers of Mataafa build 'The Road of Loving Hearts' in gratitude for Stevenson's support during their imprisonment; he gives an 'Address to the Chiefs' at its opening. Publication of *The Ebb-Tide* in book form. Stevenson working on *St Ives* and *Weir of Hermiston*. He dies of a cerebral haemorrhage on 3 December, and is buried on top of Mount Vaea, above Vailima.

1
The English Scene

There was something of a pose in Robert Louis Stevenson's claim to feel out of place in England. The demands of geography and of social class meant that he was bound to become familiar at least with London, which lay on the route from Edinburgh to the Continent. In August 1863 the 12-year-old Stevenson was sent for a term to the Burlington Lodge Academy, Spring Grove, Isleworth, near London. Two of his uncles, Lewis and Mackintosh Balfour, were then living in Spring Grove, and three of the latter's sons attended the school. Also staying at 'Uncle Mack's' was another cousin, Jane Wilson, the future grandmother of Graham Greene (*L1* 99); it was Jane's marriage to the Revd Carleton Greene in October 1870 that was first to bring Stevenson to the Suffolk village of Cockfield, the scene of his fateful meetings three years later with Fanny Sitwell and Sidney Colvin. After a term at Spring Grove (on which he drew for 'A Foreigner at Home'), Louis was taken to join his mother in Mentone in the Riviera for the first part of 1864. Torquay was to succeed Mentone as the Stevensons' preferred health resort in subsequent years.

From 1867 Louis went unwillingly to Edinburgh University to study engineering, and subsequently, as a compromise, law. His cousin Bob Stevenson, by contrast, had the previous year gone south to Sidney Sussex College, Cambridge. In his extensive correspondence with Bob at this period, Louis participated vicariously in this 'ideal world of gardens' and 'the semi-scenic life, costumed, disciplined, and drilled by proctors', which contrasted with his own 'greatly different experience of crowded class-rooms, of a gaunt quadrangle, of a bell hourly booming over the traffic of the city', as he later wrote in 'A Foreigner at Home' (*T29* 8). To Louis's lasting benefit as a writer, Edinburgh University offered 'no quiet clique of the exclusive, studious and cultured; no rotten

1

borough of the arts'; rather, 'all classes rub shoulders on the greasy benches' (ibid.). While Bob was being initiated into Hegelian philosophy (*L1* 142), Louis was, relatively speaking, roughing it in Edinburgh's Old College and in a variety of locations around the Scottish coastline where he was sent to get some 'hands on' experience of engineering. He was, however, to taste the exclusive Cambridge environment in 1870 when visiting his cousin Maud, wife of the Revd Churchill Babington, formerly a Fellow of St John's College, who had taken the college living of Cockfield, near Bury St Edmunds (*B* 111). Babington was the Disney Professor of Archeology at Cambridge (and, as Louis confided to his mother, irritatingly snobbish about Carlyle's academic credentials (*L1* 205)). Louis delighted in walking through the Suffolk countryside with his mother's cousin, Graham Balfour, whose son was later to be Stevenson's biographer.

Stevenson's delight in the English landscape, which he celebrated in 'A Foreigner at Home', is also apparent in an unfinished essay he wrote about a visit to Cumberland in 1871 (*B* 104). In 'Cockermouth and Keswick' Stevenson introduced the theme of the mutual strangeness of Scotland and England. He returned to this theme in an essay he planned, but did not complete, for the *Portfolio* in 1875 (*L2* 107), and finally wrote up in 'A Foreigner at Home'. The essay describing the Cumbrian trip of 1871 begins:

> it flashed upon me that I was in England; the evening sun lit up English houses, English faces, an English conformation of street as it were, an English atmosphere blew against my face. There is nothing perhaps more puzzling...than the great gulf that is set between England and Scotland – a gulf so easy in appearance, in reality so difficult to traverse. I was as much in a new country as if I had been walking out of the Hotel St. Antoine at Antwerp (*T30* 58).

This extract prefigures the declaration in 'A Foreigner at Home', written ten years later by a much more widely travelled Stevenson, that: 'A Scotsman may tramp the better part of Europe and the United States, and never again receive so vivid an impression of foreign travel and strange lands and manners as on his first excursion into England. The change from a hilly to a level country strikes him with delighted wonder. Along the flat horizon there arise the frequent venerable towers of churches. He sees at the end of airy vistas the revolution of the wind-mill sails. He may go where he pleases in the future; he may see Alps, and Pyramids, and lions; but it will be hard to beat the pleasure of that moment' (*T29* 4). Stevenson's discrimination of the differences between Scotland and England moves from scenery and architecture to the trickier terrain of culture and society, and becomes considerably more provocative when he opines: 'The dull, neglected peasant, sunk in matter, insolent, gross and servile, makes a startling contrast with our own long-legged, long-headed, thoughtful, Bible-quoting ploughman. A week or two in a place like Suffolk leaves the Scotsman gasping' (*T29* 6). Doubtless with an admixture of personal experience, Stevenson continues: 'A Scotsman is vain, interested in himself and others, eager for sympathy, setting forth his thoughts and experience in the best light. The egoism of the Englishman is self-contained. He does not seek to proselytise. He takes no interest in Scotland or the Scots, and, what is the unkindest cut of all, he does not care to justify his indifference' (ibid.). In the end, something like a national inferiority complex seems to emerge when Stevenson complains that, even though a Scot's interest in 'John Bull' may attest a livelier mind, 'it still puts you in the attitude of a suitor and a poor relation. Thus even the lowest class of the educated English towers over a Scotsman by the head and shoulders' (*T29* 6–7).

When Stevenson returned to Suffolk in July 1873, his first letter home from Cockfield Rectory recorded his 'astonishment ... at the hopeless gulph [sic] that there is between England and Scotland, and English and Scotch', adding that the unexpected unfamiliarity of everything made him feel 'as strange and outlandish here, as I do in France or Germany' (*L1* 283). The 'beautiful old English towns' seemed unreal to him, with 'great screens of trees that seem twice as high as trees should seem, and everything else what ought to be in a novel, and what one never expects to see in reality' (ibid.). These feelings of defamiliarization may have been exaggerated by Stevenson's state of mind when he revisited Suffolk. His second visit to Cockfield was in fact a flight from Edinburgh, where a long-running conflict with his parents over religious belief had rumbled on through most of 1873.

Already in February 1873 he had written to Charles Baxter: 'I think if Cambridge can be managed, it would be the best thing. A little absence is the only chance' (*L1* 274). This letter had begun: 'My dear Baxter, The thunderbolt has fallen with a vengeance now. You know the aspect of a house in which somebody is awaiting burial – the quiet step – the hushed voices and rare conversation – the religious literature that holds a temporary monopoly – the grim, wretched faces; all is here reproduced in this family circle in honour of my (what is it?) atheism or blasphemy' (*L1* 273). Louis Stevenson had grown up in an intensely religious atmosphere which as a child he had imbibed deeply, even playing at being a minister like his maternal grandfather Lewis Balfour. In his later teens he had begun to break away from the traditional Christian beliefs which his mother embraced rather emotionally, and his father adhered to in their harshly dogmatic Calvinistic form with a scrupulous intellectual rigour, reading obscure theologians in the original Latin and even publishing his own book *Christianity Confirmed by Jewish and Heathen Testimony and the Deduction from Physical Science* (*L1* 32). The influence of Louis's cousin Bob was blamed for his lapse from faith, leading to a climactic confrontation between Thomas Stevenson and Bob in which the latter declared with exasperated sarcasm 'that he didn't know where [Louis] had found out that the Christian religion was not true, but that *he* hadn't told [him]' (*L1* 295).

Louis, however, was quite capable of losing his faith – at least the orthodox Christian beliefs of his parents – all on his own. As early as 1867 he had recommended to Bob a review of Walt Whitman's unorthodox gospel (*L1* 119); five years later he was reading the radical evolutionary speculations of Herbert Spencer 'very hard', and offering papers to the exclusive Speculative Society, housed in Edinburgh University's Old College, on such topics as 'Christ's teaching and modern Christianity' and 'the authority of the New Testament' (*L1* 259 and n.13). With Baxter and few others from 'the Spec.', and under the charismatic leadership of Bob, back in Edinburgh at the School of Art, they formed the *L.J.R.* (Liberty, Justice and Reverence), a secret society (or drinking club) whose constitution advocated freedom of religious thought and the abolition of the House of Lords (*L1* 225 and n.7). As Baxter and Stevenson were to recall in their correspondence almost twenty years later, there had been hell to pay when Thomas Stevenson had discovered the *L.J.R.* constitution, probably in the early months of 1873 (*L7* 192 n.6; *L1* 273 n.1).

From 'the real Hell' generated by Louis's refusal to lie about his religious agnosticism when questioned by his father (*L1* 273), there seemed no escape. In July 1873 he was driven to pour out his soul to a Miss Elizabeth Crosby, daughter of a London solicitor and a family friend. To Miss Crosby, who had obviously written to Louis in a fit of *Weltschmerz*, he replied: 'There is no door of escape from this ennui. I try to evade it by constant change; by science, law, literature, perfect sunshine idleness when the weather permits, science again, law again, literature again, and perhaps a little, at the end of the cycle, of what has been mendaciously called "life". But leap as I may from one to the other, disgust is always at my back' (*L1* 277). Stevenson hoped to see Miss Crosby when he came down to England in July or August (*L1* 278).

When he finally did escape to England, Louis found the confidante he so desperately needed, but it was not Miss Crosby. On his arrival at Cockfield Rectory on 26 July 1873 he met Mrs Frances Jane Sitwell, a beautiful woman almost twelve years his senior, who was estranged but not yet separated from her husband, the Revd Albert Sitwell. Fanny Sitwell had recently lost her elder son, and was staying with her close friend Maud Babington at the Rectory. That Louis fell in love with Fanny Sitwell that August in Suffolk is evident from the letter he wrote her on the evening of his return to Edinburgh: 'Do you know, I think that yesterday and the day before were the two happiest days of my life. . . . I had to get supper and the streets were wonderfully cool and dark, . . . and I could not help fancying as I went along all sorts of foolish things – *chansons* – about showing you all these places to you, Claire,[1] some other night; which is not to be. Dear, I would not have missed last month for eternity' (*L1* 288). Louis was to pour out his soul to Fanny Sitwell for the next two years. Although physically he may have been in Edinburgh, emotionally he was still in Suffolk, reliving that golden August. On 9 September he wrote from Heriot Row: 'the sound of the wind and leaves comes in to me through the windows, and if I shut my eyes I might fancy myself some hundred miles away under a certain tree. And that is a consolation, too: these things *have been*' (*L1* 296). A month later, in an Edinburgh where it was raining pitilessly, he described a 'wonderful rehabilitation of the past' in which 'large tracts of one's memory seem lit up with a sudden burst of sunshine. I have been living in Cockfield garden all morning; coming and going in the shrubberies; . . . Every place is sacred' (*L1* 338). The drift into religious imagery seems inevitable. In an earlier letter he confessed that he had been 'reckoning the beads of my rosary of recollection, very piously', and declared to his *Madonna*:[2] 'Remember always that you are my Faith' (*L1* 321–2). There is an irony in Stevenson's use of Catholic discourse, given that much of the content of his letters to Fanny Sitwell concerned his continuing conflict with his fiercely Protestant parents about questions of religious belief. His letters are also saturated with German phrases and quotations, particularly from Heine and Goethe (Stevenson had briefly visited Germany with Walter Simpson the previous year). He frequently refers to Goethe's *Werther*, both in the general sense of '*Werthering*' (i.e. moping or suffering from 'the blue devils'), and in the more specific sense of being hopelessly and impossibly in love with someone else's wife. Even Stevenson realized that some of this must have appeared over the top. After making another quasi-religious declaration to Fanny ('I hope more in the strong inspiration of your sympathy than ever Christian hoped out of his deity'), he added: 'I hope you do not think that I am phrasing [Scots for 'using flowery, gushing language'[3]; if I am phrasing, it is because... "it is my nature to"....*Don't* think it phrasing!' (*L1* 291). Yet there *was* something rather stagy about the whole affair. Writing from an Edinburgh shrouded in haar, where 'the poor...look so helplessly chill and dripping', Stevenson mused: 'And to look back out all this at Cockfield! If I were as unscrupulous as Goethe, I believe I could write a book about some events in my life that would rather tickle the long ears' (*L1* 302). In fact Stevenson did attempt to make a book out his affair with Fanny Sitwell. The name 'Claire', which so misled earlier biographers of Stevenson, was not only a nickname for Fanny, but also the title for an abortive work-in-progress for which Stevenson unabashedly recycled his letters to Fanny. To Fanny herself he admitted: '[I] have just stopped to make my first addition to Claire. I have added a few sentences out of this letter, making the meaning clearer of course and trying to better the loose expression one uses in *really* writing to dear friends' (*L1* 338). He paid 'Claire' the rather backhanded compliment of citing her as a reason for not making progress with *Claire*: 'I have not been going on with Claire: I have been out of heart for that; and besides it is difficult to act before the reality. Footlights will not do with the sun; the stage moon and the real, lucid moon of one's dark life, look strangely on each other' (*L1* 319). Stevenson evidently found it hard to resist the temptation to 'phrase'.

In much of Stevenson's correspondence around this time there is indeed something rather contrived and self-conscious. He was consciously writing for posterity. Obviously his adoring mother, the recipient of by far the largest number of his letters, was going to hoard them. But to his cousin Bob, his greatest confidant before Fanny Sitwell, he proposed in November 1868, days after his eighteenth birthday:

> If you keep my letters and I keep yours, what a curious retrospect it will be for us. My letters to you would form a history of myself, which, as I am too indolent to write a diary, I should like to have for future instruction and amusement. Perhaps you who know my weakness, too pitiable only to be ludicrous, may guess at another reason, too contemptible, too *small* for me...to put in black and white (*L1* 169).

This other reason had already been divulged to Bob in a letter the previous month: 'Did I ever become great, this letter would figure in my life. Strange how my mind runs on this idea. Becoming great, becoming great, becoming great. A heart burned out with the lust of this world's approbation: a hideous disease to have ...' (*L1* 143). At least he realized, he later wrote to Bob:

> What an egotistical brute I am! self! self! self! That is the tune, the burthen, the fable, the moral. Self! self! Well you must take me as you find me. I have no confidant, and ... with the exception of my father to whom such matters would be a subject for scolding, no *friend* to whom I can speak; ... My daily life is one repression from beginning to end, and my letters to you are the safety valve (*L1* 169).

Louis's letters to Bob, and indeed to just about everyone else, dried up after Fanny Sitwell took over as his great soul mate and confidante. The only exception is another new friend Stevenson made at Cockfield, Sidney Colvin. Colvin was a Fellow of Trinity College Cambridge, and the newly elected Slade Professor of Fine Art at Cambridge. What made the young Stevenson hero-worship Colvin, whom he met at Cockfield Station with 'great agitation', was the fact that he was an established contributor to the *Fortnightly Review* and other magazines (*T29* 164–5). Stevenson admitted in his fragmentary 'Memoirs of Himself' that probably he and Colvin would not naturally have taken to each other, but Fanny Sitwell had done her work to set up this encounter between 'the ready worshipper' and 'the ready patron' (ibid.). She had urged her admirer Colvin to bring forward his promised visit to Cockfield in order to meet what she called 'a real young genius'.[4] The man whom Stevenson awaited at Cockfield Station 'as the Messiah',[5] did indeed have an impressive track record. Five years older than Stevenson, he had been made a Fellow of Trinity in 1868, and the following year elected to the New Club, which included among its members Walter Pater, as well as the editors of the *Fortnightly Review*, the *Pall Mall Gazette*, and the *Cornhill Magazine* (respectively, John Morley, Frederick Greenwood, and Leslie Stephen). In 1871 the New Club became the Savile Club, with Colvin the Honorary Secretary. Among his friends he counted Burne-Jones and Rossetti; Ruskin had been a family friend and a hero, though Colvin had turned against him after Ruskin had not supported Colvin's candidature for the Professorship of Fine Arts at Cambridge.[6] It is certain, according to Michel Le Bris, that, whether or not he was conscious of his homosexual feelings, Colvin fell in love with Stevenson that first day (but then Le Bris also claims that it is '*certain*' that Louis and Fanny Sitwell slept together, which most other biographers have denied).[7]

A further insinuation that Le Bris was not the first to make, and which Colvin would have strongly refuted, was that he was in some sense 'on the make' in his discovery of the young Stevenson. Hindsight, and Stevenson's later, sometimes bitter, comments, may portray Colvin as a predatory figure, feeding on the younger man's creative genius. But if Fanny Sitwell was to fulfil all of Louis's emotional (if not physical) needs, then Colvin was just what the young Stevenson needed to help him in chosen career as a writer. Stevenson later acknowledged his debt to Colvin: 'If I am what I am and where I am, if I have done anything at all or anything well, his is the credit. It was he who paved my way in letters' (*T29* 166). When he first met Colvin in August 1873, Stevenson had to his literary credit a handful of pieces (the fragment on 'Cockermouth and Keswick', and early versions of his essays on Whitman and on John Knox), though none of them had been published. His first publication for which he was paid was the essay 'Roads'; it appeared in the *Portfolio*, signed L.S. Stoneven, in December 1873. It had been planned during walks with Colvin around Cockfield, and the Suffolk countryside is evoked in the essay, with references to 'the wonderful life-giving speed of windmill sails above the stationary country', and 'the occurrence and recurrence of the same church tower at the end of one long vista after another' (*T25* 185). Predictably, there is a quotation from Whitman about 'the gay, fresh sentiment of the road', and a long quotation from Goethe's *Werther*, the latter introduced both to illustrate the *Sehnsucht* evoked by the Suffolk countryside, and to impress (not least Fanny Sitwell) (*T25* 188–9).

After Cockfield, Louis spent some days in London at the end of August 1873, staying with Colvin in his cottage in Norwood, and also apparently with the Sitwells. If the latter arrangement smacks somewhat of the *ménage à trois*, the relationship between Louis, Fanny Sitwell and Colvin seems also to have been some kind of bizarre variation on that theme. From a psychoanalytical perspective, the Louis/Fanny/Colvin triangle seems to be a more productive version of the destructive Edinburgh *ménage à trois* of Louis, Maggie and Thomas. With the restrained and disciplined Colvin replacing the violently emotional Thomas Stevenson, and the calmly nurturing Fanny replacing the hysterical Maggie, Louis was eventually able – quoting Poe's lines: 'You who are *more than a mother unto me/And fill my heart of hearts*' – to tell his "mother of election", Fanny Sitwell, of the insight he had only just gained: 'my mother is my father's wife; the children of lovers are orphans' (*L2* 96; 102–3). Whatever social and economic pressures may have forbidden the fulfilment of Louis's desire for Fanny Sitwell, at a deeper psychological level it may have been necessary for him first to identify her as his overwhelmingly sexualized 'second Mother, first Wife',[8] so as then to learn to relinquish her, and develop a positive working relationship with her partner and husband-to-be, Sidney Colvin. Perhaps Stevenson had to discover and/or create the therapeutic context in which he could work out his emotional salvation (there had certainly been a rehearsal for the Cockfield scenario in Louis's relationship with Professor Fleeming Jenkin and his wife Anne back in Edinburgh).

The first surviving letter from Stevenson to Colvin is dated 16 September 1873; it inaugurated a regular correspondence which was to last over 21 years. In the opening paragraph Stevenson laments his inability to communicate with his father: 'Always the gulf over which no man can go, always a great hell between people' (*L1* 308). Immediately, however, he draws back, and apologizes, as if realizing that unburdening himself emotionally should be restricted to his letters to Fanny Sitwell. To the latter he agonized that he had written to Colvin 'with a heart so full of bitterness that it flowed slaveringly over upon my beard' (the fact that he had slavered, and moreover hadn't a beard, obviously undermined his right to be in the company of Victorian gentlemen) (*L1* 309). But Colvin showed the young Stevenson how a literary gentleman should acquit himself, writing back six sides of advice and reassuring him that his 'little paper' – 'Roads' – 'would do', all of which left Louis quite speechless with gratitude (ibid.). In his next letter to Fanny, Louis commented on: '[H]ow strangely well and long, Colvin manages to write. He doesn't seem to give way either, ... [and] seems always to remember where he is and which side is uppermost. I wish I could learn to do the like' (*L1* 315). However, Colvin's influence did not extend to securing Louis's little paper publication in his favoured organ, *The Fortnightly Review*; the latter declined 'Roads', which was subsequently accepted by P.G Hamerton's *Portfolio*.

By late October 1873, the two months since Stevenson had been in London seemed like two years, he told Fanny Sitwell, and Cockfield seemed 'in a former existence' (*L1* 345). However, there had been a promising development: the Lord Advocate, the principal law officer of the Crown in Scotland, had advised Louis to go to the English bar (*L1* 342). On 16 October Stevenson wrote to Colvin asking him to organize the two barristers required for his petition to join the English bar. On 24 October, without telling his parents, he set off for London. Once there, he seemed in such a state of ill-health and nervous exhaustion, largely caused by rows with his father about religion, that Colvin and Fanny Sitwell insisted he see Dr Andrew Clark, a fashionable specialist in lung diseases, and a member of the Savile Club. Dr Clark obligingly ordered Louis not to take the law exam, not to return to Scotland, and to go south; by 'south' he meant the French Riviera, and definitely not Torquay with his mother (*L1* 354–5).

Stevenson's return to Mentone, described in his essay 'Ordered South', is discussed in the next chapter. On 23 April 1874 Stevenson was back in London, and three days later in Edinburgh, dividing his time between Heriot Row and Swanston Cottage, a rented house near Edinburgh, in a secluded spot at the foot of the Pentland Hills. But by June he had returned to London, staying with Colvin in lodgings in Hampstead. Stevenson was beginning to mix with a variety of literary people, including Charles Appleton, founder and editor of the *Academy*; Charles Grove, editor of *Macmillan's Magazine*; Andrew Lang; and Leslie Stephen, who tried in vain to get Stevenson an introduction to a crotchety old Thomas Carlyle (*L2* 26 n.2). It appears that during this stay in London there was some kind of crisis in his relationship with Fanny Sitwell; presumably she had made clear to him (*pace* Le Bris) the impossibility of any physical relationship. In late June Stevenson wrote to Fanny from Hampstead: 'Looking back upon some of my past in continuation of my humour of the last two or three days, I am filled with shame. ... Try to set some of it down, as I do to myself, to my shaken health' (*L2* 25). Writing from Swanston in July he promised: 'I do think the passion is over; I would not be too sanguine to fancy there would never be any momentary relapse; but in the meantime, I am quite strong and satisfied. Another thing you will be glad to learn, and that is what I feel for S.C. ... I like so much to be with him' (*L2* 32). It is difficult to resist the feeling that some Oedipal corner has been turned.

That some kind of 'relapse' occurred may be inferred from the fact that the first page of a letter dated August 1874 (and edited by Colvin) is missing, leaving only the words: '...to be unworthy of yourself' (*L2* 38). The fragment continues:

Ten years ago, does it seem to you? To me it seems a whole long lifetime. I have crossed such a dizzy chasm that I do not yet dare to look back; ... The storm is over. ... I am not sad nor angry, nor regretful. I am fully content and fear nothing, nor death, nor weakness, nor any falling away from my own high standard and yours. ... I see more clearly by how much I still fall short of the mark of our high calling; in how much I am still selfish and peevish and a spoiled child. You will see that I am writing out of a great blackness' (ibid.).

The tension in Stevenson between his 'own high standard', and the selfish, peevish and spoiled child within, points forward not only to Freud's likely story of the Superego and the Id, but also to Stevenson's own *Strange Case of Dr Jekyll and Mr Hyde*.[9] The storm referred to in the letter was literal as well as emotional. Stevenson was writing on board the yacht *Heron* somewhere between Oban and Portree, from where he took the boat home after a yacht cruise up the West coast of Scotland with Walter Simpson. In September Stevenson was back in England, admiring the beauty of 'my dear Cumberland country', and staying in Chester with his parents *en route* for a holiday in Wales. In a letter to Fanny Sitwell he reverts to his theme of the differences between Scotland and England, in this case comparing the jollity of the English pub with Scottish bars 'where we drink solemnly among bare tables or, if we garnish the liquor at all, garnish it with political talk' (*L2* 49). After the Welsh holiday, his parents returned to Edinburgh, while Louis continued south to London. He stayed again at Hampstead, this time with Colvin's friend Basil Champneys, whose book *A Quiet Corner of England*, a study of Winchelsea, Rye and the Romney Marsh, Stevenson reviewed in the December issue of *The Academy*. Stevenson himself was to produce another essay about the English landscape in the next weeks. From Hampstead he went to stay with Andrew Lang at Merton College, Oxford; thence he took a walking tour in Buckinghamshire, where, as he had written to his mother from Hampstead, there were 'certain beech woods' of which he had heard 'great things' (*L2* 57). These beech woods provided the subject matter of 'An Autumn Effect', published in the *Portfolio* in April and May 1875. His walk from High Wycombe to Tring is endowed by Stevenson with a high degree of cultural capital for the *Portfolio*. The essay opens with an epigraph in French from an article in the *Revue des Deux Mondes*, glimpsed on a friend's table, which Stevenson expects his readers will peruse, if they have not already done so. Anticipating his later essays on the French countryside, Stevenson says cleverly that: 'The whole scene had an indefinable look of being painted, the colour was so abstract and correct, and there was something so sketchy and merely impressional about these distant single trees on the horizon that one was forced to think of it all as a clever French landscape. For it is rather in nature that we see resemblance to art, than in art to nature' (*T30* 69–70). The essay as a whole prefigures Stevenson's subsequent French travel writing, with its mixture of deft landscape sketches, anecdotes, and even the appearance of a donkey who holds centre stage for a page or so.

Stevenson had met Lang at Mentone the previous February, when they had been mutually unimpressed. 'Good-looking, delicate, boyish,

Oxfordish etc He did not impress me unfavourably; nor deeply in any way,' wrote Stevenson to his mother of Lang (*L1* 483). The latter wrote later of his first encounter with Stevenson: 'He looked...more like a lass than a lad, with a rather long, smooth oval face, brown hair worn at greater length than is common, large lucid eyes....He was like nobody else whom I ever met....I shall not deny that my first impression was not wholly favourable. "Here," I thought, "is one of your aesthetic young men, though a clever one." '[10] On reading 'Ordered South', however, Lang was converted: 'Here was a new writer, a writer indeed; one who could do what none of us, *nous autres*, could rival, or approach. I was instantly "sealed in the tribe of Louis," an admirer, a devotee, a fanatic.'[11] Stevenson and 'Pretty-well Lang', as Louis wrote to Colvin, dined together a good deal at Mentone, and Lang was one of those who supported Louis's election, proposed by Colvin, to the Savile Club in June 1874. This did not stop Stevenson from sending up Lang in a piece of doggerel intended for a satirical piece to be called *Diogenes at the Savile Club*, ending with the refrain: 'Am I not/A lady-dady Oxford kind of Scot' (*L3* 241). Other targets in this projected spoof on the most literary of the London clubs included Thomas Hardy who 'had looked in to lay down the normal of the Vulgar Woman', Oscar Wilde 'to buy a statuette from Pater', and Gilbert and Sullivan 'to submit a song with toothcomb accompaniment' (*T5* 196). Diogenes is introduced to the composite figure of Besant-and-Rice, the best-selling (but now forgotten) literary partnership of Walter Besant and James Rice; Besant, who subsequently went solo, would later form a literary link between Stevenson and Henry James.[12] Stevenson and Henry James first met at lunch with Andrew Lang and Edmund Gosse in 1879. James was initially unimpressed by Stevenson: 'a shirt-collarless Bohemian and a great deal (in an inoffensive way) of a *poseur*' (*L3* 159 n2). Stevenson's revenge was to come in the verses on James intended for *Diogenes*, which included the lines:

> A bland colossus, mark me stride,
>   From land to land, the sea,
> And patronise on every side
>   Far better men than me (*L3* 245).

Stevenson's friendship with Edmund Gosse had also begun in the Savile Club when they had been introduced by Colvin sometime in the mid-1870s.[13] According to Gosse's *Critical Kit-Kats*, he and Stevenson lunched together, and then spent most of the day getting acquainted: 'The fountains of talk had been unsealed, and they drowned the conversations. I came home dazzled with my new friend, saying, as Constance does of Arthur, "Was ever such a gracious creature born?" '[14] Gosse describes how in the late 1870s Stevenson would make 'sudden piratical descents' on London, 'staying for a few days or weeks, and melting into air again'.[15] On these forays to London Stevenson would usually stay at the Savile Club, which, Gosse said, he 'pervaded', being its 'most affable and chatty member'.[16]

It was not until some years later, when he had returned from France to settle in Bournemouth in the mid-1880s, that Stevenson got to know two of the greatest literary lions associated with the Savile Club, Thomas Hardy and Henry James. However, already in the 1870s Stevenson had developed a close friendship with W.E. Henley, a lesser but not inconsiderable literary lion (though Henley he was not formally elected to the Savile Club until 1887). Leslie Stephen had in 1875 introduced Stevenson to Henley, a fellow contributor to the *Cornhill*, while Henley was a patient of the pioneering Joseph Lister at Edinburgh Infirmary. Henley had travelled to Edinburgh in an attempt to save his right foot from tuberculosis – he had already lost his left leg through amputation (a handicap bequeathed to Long John Silver, who was modelled on Henley's 'maimed strength' (*L4* 129)). Henley's experience in Edinburgh Infirmary is vividly evoked in his poem-sequence *In Hospital*, which contains the famous description of the young Stevenson in 'Apparition'. The concluding lines:

> Valiant in velvet, light in ragged luck,
> Most vain, most generous, sternly critical,
> Buffoon and poet, lover and sensualist:
> A deal of Ariel, just a streak of Puck,
> Much Antony, of Hamlet most of all,
> And something of the Shorter-Catechist.

were to be controversial from the beginning to the end of Stevenson's and Henley's relationship. The final phrase was to be central to Henley's notoriously hostile review in 1901 of Balfour's *Life*,[17] while in 1876 the poem's references to Stevenson's vanity and sensuality offended his mother (who was otherwise 'much pleased' by the poem), and left his uncle and aunt Balfour 'simply speechless with indignation'.[18] After a spell working in Edinburgh for the *Encyclopaedia Britannica*, when he became part of the circle around Stevenson (and even let Stevenson move temporarily, and secretly, into his lodgings[19]) Henley moved in

1877 to London, where he lived in a variety of lodgings in Shepherd's Bush. From late October to December 1878, after his travels with a donkey in the Cévennes, Stevenson stayed in London, splitting his time between the Savile Club and Shepherd's Bush, with a flying visit to Colvin's rooms in Trinity College, Cambridge. He and Henley were working closely together at this time, not only on the play *Deacon Brodie*, but also on the production of *London*, the short-lived journal edited by Henley.

It was in *London* that Stevenson's tales subsequently published as *New Arabian Nights* first appeared in serial form in between June and October 1878. The first and most famous of these 'Latter-Day Arabian Nights', entitled 'The Suicide Club', opens with a preposterous scene in an Oyster Bar off Leicester Square, where an eccentric young man is distributing cream tarts to all and sundry, before baring his soul to Prince Florizel of Bohemia (a.k.a. Theophilus Godall) and Colonel Geraldine (a.k.a. Major Alfred Hammersmith) (*T1* 1–5). While some of the action of these bizarre tales takes place in Paris, they are also set in London, with one of the characters, the unfortunate Bartholomew Malthus, living at 16 Chepstow Place (the Sitwells lived at number 15). The stories are very 'knowing', rather camp, and full of in-jokes – one of the characters is reading the *Fortnightly Review*. Other work that Stevenson produced for *London* included 'A Plea for Gas Lamps', 'Pan's Pipes' and 'El Dorado' (appearing in April and May 1878, and later in *Virginibus Puerisque*), and 'Providence and the Guitar', which appeared in November 1878. When Stevenson began 'The Pavilion on the Links' in November 1878, he intended it for *London*, but it was still unfinished when he left for America in August 1879. Meanwhile *London* had expired in the spring of that year, and the piece was accepted, to Stevenson's surprise, by Leslie Stephen for the *Cornhill*; its publication was delayed, according to Swearingen (*S* 38), partly on account of Stephen's expectation of a novel from George Meredith requiring immediate serialization.[20]

George Meredith was one of the figures in the English literary scene who had the greatest influence on Stevenson. Travelling up to London from Box Hill in Surrey, Meredith was a member of the Garrick Club, rather than the Savile. Stevenson had first met him in March 1878 when he and his mother stayed at the Burford Bridge Inn, close to Flint Cottage, Meredith's home at Box Hill. The only surviving letter written by Stevenson during this visit was to Walter Crane, urging him, at the behest of Kegan Paul, to expedite his frontispiece for *An Inland Voyage*; the letter does not mention Meredith. However, at this time Meredith was working on *The Egoist*, to be published in October 1879 by Kegan

Paul, and it is likely that, among other common interests, the character of 'the vile Paul' would have been discussed at this first meeting between Stevenson and Meredith; it certainly was when Stevenson again visited Meredith the following June. On the latter occasion, Stevenson wrote to his mother, 'Meredith and I had great fun about Paul who was diplomatising with both of us.' (*L2* 322) Of *The Egoist*, Stevenson was later to write in a 1887 piece for the *British Weekly* entitled 'Books Which Have Influenced Me': 'I should never forgive myself if I forgot *The Egoist*.... [F]rom all the novels I have read (and I have read thousands) [it] stands in a place by itself' (*T28* 66). Stevenson tells how a young friend of Meredith's had accused the author of taking him as the model for Willoughby, the central character of *The Egoist*; Meredith had replied: 'No, my dear fellow, he is all of us.' Despite having read *The Egoist* five or six times, Stevenson intended to reread it, he claimed, because, like the young man in the anecdote, he thought that Willoughby was 'an unmanly but a very serviceable exposure of myself' (*T28* 67). If Stevenson's recognition of himself in Willoughby was due to a universal quality in the latter, there is a much more specific resemblance between the young Stevenson and Gower Woodseer in Meredith's *The Amazing Marriage*, published in 1895, but already underway in 1879, Meredith later told Stevenson (*L8* 163 n.1). The similarity between Stevenson and Gower Woodseer was spotted by an early reviewer,[21] who did not, however, foreground Meredith's mockery of the idealistic young Woodseer, perching injured in the Alps like 'the insanest of mortals', and prompting the snobbish Chillon Kirby to comment: 'These freaks give us a bad name on the Continent.'[22]

Stevenson admired Meredith greatly – 'the only man of genius of my acquaintance', he wrote to Henley in April 1882 (*L3* 321). A month later Stevenson again visited Meredith at Box Hill. It was inevitable that Stevenson's admiration for Meredith would influence his writing. In 1880 Stevenson had written to Henley: 'You need not be alarmed that I am going to imitate Meredith' (*L3* 56); however, there is little doubt that *Prince Otto*, an early version of which Stevenson mentions in the same letter, was indeed significantly influenced by his admiration of Meredith. The origins of *Prince Otto* are in a tragedy entitled *Semiramis* which Stevenson lists among his juvenilia in 'A College Magazine' (*T29* 30). That *Prince Otto* was beginning to take shape in Stevenson's mind is clear from the letter to Henley just cited; but it was in the summer of 1882, shortly after his visit to Meredith in May, that Stevenson wrote the first chapter. The bulk of the novel was written the following year at Hyères (*S* 82).

When *Prince Otto* was finally published in book form in November 1885, its debt to Meredith was noted. In an unsigned review in the *Pall Mall Gazette* Andrew Lang said he was frequently reminded of Meredith (if Stevenson does not take us to Meredith's heights, Lang opined, 'at least we are spared the rough places of descent' (*M* 182)). *Prince Otto* also reminded Henley of Meredith. In an unsigned review in the *Atheneum*, he criticized the 'notes of blank verse which afflict the reader' (*M* 186), a fault he had already detected in the manuscript version of *Prince Otto*. 'It beats too often with the iambic pulse; it feels too often a little Stevensonian, a little mannered and dry', Henley wrote to Stevenson in April 1885 (*M* 179). Nevertheless, in this letter Henley also commended the style of what he later called in the *Atheneum* review 'an essay in pure literature',[23] particularly praising the evocations of landscape. Curiously, the very chapter ('Princess Cinderella') singled out for praise by Henley in the *Atheneum*, and Lang in the *Pall Mall Gazette*, is the one which Gosse, in a letter to Stevenson in November 1885, condemned: 'I don't know whether you have already been upbraided for this piece of fine writing. ... It is a wilful and monstrous sacrifice on the altar of George Meredith, whose errors you should be the last to imitate and exaggerate' (*M* 189). Gosse complained that readers of *Prince Otto*, entranced by the narrative, have forgotten about the author until they read this chapter, and are 'amazed to find you so offensively clever and original' (ibid.). However, the letter that mattered most to Stevenson was from the master himself. Meredith's letter to Stevenson about *Prince Otto* has disappeared, but Stevenson told Henley about it in tones which would not be out of place in James's 'The Figure in the Carpet': 'I had a letter yesterday from George Meredith, which was one of the events of my life. He cottoned (for one thing), though with differences, to Otto; cottoned more than my rosiest visions had inspired me to hope; said things that (from him) I would blush to quote' (*B* 228; *L5* 154).

   That he, like many of his contemporaries (and especially those least conscious of it), owed a debt of gratitude to Meredith, Stevenson later acknowledged in a letter of February 1890, in which he tentatively agreed to edit a volume of Meredith's uncollected short stories (*L6* 368–9). Stevenson wished to delay a final decision on this project until he could meet Meredith himself when he made the journey from the South Seas back to Europe in June 1890. However, neither the planned visit, nor the book proposal, ever materialized. The poetry of Meredith also had an impact on Stevenson. It was while he was writing up *Prince Otto* during 1883 in Hyères that he received a copy of Meredith's *Poems and Lyrics of the Joy of Earth*, published that year. One of the poems in this collection, 'Love in the Valley', gave him one of his three greatest experiences with poetry, he later told W.B. Yeats; the other works which similarly intoxicated him were Swinburne's *Poems and Ballads*, and Yeats's own 'The Lake Isle of Innisfree' (*L8* 262). Three days after writing this letter to Yeats in April 1894, Stevenson wrote to Meredith for the last time, praising the young writer Lysaght, who had visited Vailima with a letter of introduction from Meredith, and news of Box Hill. Stevenson told Meredith he looked forward to seeing the portrait of himself, aged 25, in the figure of Gower Woodseer. *The Amazing Marriage* did not finally appear, however, until a month after Stevenson's death (*L8* 262 and n.4).

The last time Stevenson visited Meredith at Box Hill was in August 1886, from Bournemouth (*L5* 297 and n.1). The previous August he had visited another English novelist who dominated the end of the nineteenth century, Thomas Hardy. *En route* from Bournemouth to Dartmoor, the Stevensons had stayed overnight at the King's Arms, Dorchester, and had taken the opportunity to call on Hardy in his new house at Max Gate. Fanny Stevenson had felt 'an instinctive tenderness' for this 'pale, gentle frightened little man' with an ugly wife, and commented, apparently without a trace of self-conscious irony: 'What very strange marriages literary men seem to make' (*L5* 125 n.1). Stevenson himself was more professional in his attitude. Having made Hardy's acquaintance, he took the opportunity the following May to propose a dramatization of the recently published *Mayor of Casterbridge*, which he had read with 'sincere admiration': 'Dorchester is touched in with the hand of a master' (*L5* 259). In his reply from the Savile Club, Hardy warmly welcomed Stevenson's proposal, but, although he accepted Stevenson's invitation to dine at Colvin's home in the British Museum shortly afterwards, nothing further came of the project (*L5* 259 n.1). When Stevenson left England for the last time in August 1887, Gosse had to 'scour London' to find a copy of Hardy's latest novel, *The Woodlanders*, for Stevenson to take with him (*L6* 1). What Stevenson made of *The Woodlanders* is not recorded. However, of *Tess of the D'Urbervilles*, published in 1891, he was highly critical. In a sentence which Colvin tactfully excised from the *Vailima Letters*, Stevenson called *Tess*: 'as false a thing as ever I perused, unworthy of Hardy and untrue to all I know of life' (*L7* 284). His criticisms of *Tess* continued in letters to J.M. Barrie and Henley, and culminated in a letter to Henry James:

Tess is one of the worst, weakest, least sane... books I have yet read....
it seems to me... to have no earthly connexion with human life or

human nature; and to be merely the unconscious portrait of a weakish man under a vow to appear clever, or a rickety schoolchild setting up to be naughty and not knowing how.... I could never finish it ... but so far as I read, James, it was (in one word) damnable. *Not alive, not true,* was my continual comment as I read; and at last – *not even honest!* (*L7* 450).

The vehemence of Stevenson's criticisms of *Tess* may be in some measure due to its *succès de scandale* in an area in which he himself had had problems: the representation of sexuality in the context of Victorian publishing. In a less vitriolic mood, Stevenson was willing to compare the cuts that 'The Beach of Falesá' and *Tess* had suffered at the hands of magazine editors, concluding; 'I wish we could afford to do without serial publication altogether' (*L7* 413).

The other dominant figure in English letters with whom Stevenson developed a close relationship was Henry James; though he was American, James had settled in London in 1876 (finally being naturalized a British subject in 1915). Five years after their unpromising first meeting in 1879, Stevenson and James encountered each other again, this time in the medium of the printed word. In 1884 Walter Besant performed the two acts for which he is probably now best remembered: he founded the Society of Authors; and delivered a lecture at the Royal Institution on 'The Art of Fiction'. When the latter was published as a pamphlet, it prompted the famous reply by Henry James, bearing the same title, in *Longman's Magazine* in September 1884. That same month, Stevenson, who had recently moved to Bournemouth where he was living under the constant threat of lung haemorrhages, wrote: 'I must write stupidly, dear 'Coggie' [Ferrier], for I am full of the vilest drugs.... In spite of blood and silence, Henley and I have finished two plays.[24] I am now busy on an answer to Henry James and Besant. (Did you see the former in *Longman* – dreadful nonsense admirably said, and with the friendliest compliment to me.)' (*L5* 8–9). James had disarmed Stevenson's initial scepticism by complimenting him on 'the delightful story of *Treasure Island*', which seemed to James 'to have succeeded wonderfully in what it attempts'.[25] James was in fact only using *Treasure Island* as an example to illustrate the diversity of the novel; it is as much a novel as de Goncourt's *Chérie*, James claimed, since 'the moral consciousness of a child is as much a part of life as the islands of the Spanish Main, and the one sort of geography seems to me to have those "surprises" of which Mr. Besant speaks quite as much as the other'.[26] James's preference for *Treasure Island* was on grounds of literary technique, since, all things being equal, he confessed to feeling much more at home exploring the moral consciousness of a child: 'I have been a child, but I have never been on a quest for buried treasure.'[27] But if James had never been on a quest for buried treasure, Stevenson was to respond, apparently assuming (unlike James) that the child in question was *male*, 'it can be demonstrated that he has never been a child. There never was a child (unless Master James) but has hunted gold, and been a pirate, and a military commander, and a bandit of the mountains . . .'.[28] Stevenson's introduction of the topic of the imaginative experience of childhood was to turn the exchange with James into a path which Stevenson had already explored in his essay 'Child's Play', published in 1878 in the *Cornhill*, and reprinted in *Virginibus Puerisque* (1881).

In turning James's essay to his own advantage, Stevenson was continuing the pattern of repetition and displacement which seems to haunt James's work. James himself was using Besant's piece as what has been called a 'target-of-opportunity'[29] in order to publish his own 'Art of Fiction', just as, in a postscript to his first letter to James, Stevenson confessed that: 'I took your paper merely as a pin to hang my own remarks upon' (*L5* 43). Stevenson invited James to continue the chain by publishing a reply to his remarks ('what fine remarks can you not hang on mine! (ibid.)), though publicly nothing came of this. James's essay has been deemed a significant document in the history of literary theory, not least by linking Coleridge's *Biographia Literaria* and the American New Critics in its emphasis on the novel as 'a living thing, all one and continuous, like every other organism'.[30] Stevenson's essay, by contrast, only figures in a footnote to *The Norton Anthology of Theory and Criticism*, though the fact that, as a result of Stevenson's intervention, James changed his original contention that the novel '*does* compete with life' to the substantially lesser claim that it 'does attempt to represent life',[31] might seem to warrant further attention to 'A Humble Remonstrance', as Stevenson entitled his reply to James in the December edition of *Longman's*. Stevenson's starting point is that the basic concept which both Besant and James seem to take as given, 'the art of fiction', is problematic; it is 'both too ample and too scanty' (*T29* 133). Instead, Stevenson proposed to specify the topic more precisely. What Besant and James were really attempting to discuss, according to Stevenson, was 'the art of narrative', and even more precisely, 'the art of *fictitious* narrative *in prose*' (ibid). The latter qualification is added because certain works in verse from *The Odyssey to Paradise Lost* are clearly narrative; the former qualification is made because of Stevenson's awareness of an issue that was to be raised a century later by the likes of Hayden White:[32]

The art of narrative, in fact, is the same, whether it is applied to the selection and illustration of a real series of events or of an imaginary series. Boswell's *Life of Johnson* (a work of cunning and inimitable art) owes its success to the same technical manoeuvres as (let us say) *Tom Jones*: the clear conception of certain characters of man, the choice and presentation of certain incidents out of a great number that offered, and the invention (yes, invention) and preservation of a certain key in dialogue.... [B]ut it is not only in Boswell, it is in every biography with any salt of life, it is in every history where events and men, rather than ideas, are presented – in Tacitus, in Carlyle, in Michelet, in Macauley – that the novelist will find many of his own methods most conspicuously and adroitly handled (*T29* 134).

Stevenson also strikes a (post)modern note when he suggests that the word 'truth' will seem 'on a more careful examination ... of very dubious propriety, not only for the labours of the novelist, but for those of the historian. No art – to use the daring phrase of Mr James – can successfully "compete with life"' (ibid.). In what almost reads like an anticipation of the Lacanian 'real', Stevenson evokes the pre-linguistic flux which no art can ever adequately represent, let alone 'compete with': 'Life goes before us, infinite in complication; attended by the most various and surprising meteors; appealing at once to the eye, to the ear, to the mind – the seat of wonder, to the touch – so thrillingly delicate, and to the belly – so imperious when starved' (*T29* 134–5). Life, Stevenson continues, 'is monstrous, infinite, illogical, abrupt and poignant; a work of art, in comparison, is neat, finite, self-contained, rational, flowing and emasculate. Life imposes by brute energy, like inarticulate thunder; art catches by the ear, among the far louder noises of experience, like an air artificially made by a discreet musician. A proposition of geometry does not compete with life; and a proposition of geometry is a fair and luminous parallel for a work of art' (*T29* 136) Such an anti-mimetic formalism recalls *l'art pour l'art* aesthetics, as well as suggesting the characteristically modernist gesture of 'flinging representation to the winds'.[33] James wrote privately in response to 'A Humble Remonstrance', offering, he said, 'not words of discussion, dissent, retort or remonstrance, but of hearty sympathy of everything you write. It's a luxury ... to encounter some one who *does* write – who is really acquainted with that lovely art.'[34] He praised Stevenson's style which 'floats pearls and diamonds', and, in response to Stevenson's invitation to continue the debate in print, added teasingly that his essay was 'only half of what I had to say, and some day

I shall try and express the remainder. Then I shall tickle you a little affectionately as I pass'.[35]

It was four months later that James, visiting his invalid sister Alice in Bournemouth, accepted Stevenson's invitation and called on the Stevensons in their new house of Skerryvore. On this first visit James was mistaken for a carpet-layer and shown to the tradesmen's entrance. However, he soon charmed the Stevensons, especially his countrywoman Fanny Stevenson who thought he looked like the Prince of Wales (*L5* 104). For ten weeks James visited the Stevensons regularly, even joining them for dinner on their wedding anniversary. On his departure Fanny Stevenson wrote to Colvin: 'After ten weeks of Henry James the evenings seem very empty, though the room is always full of people' (*L5* 120). A particular chair that had belonged to Louis's grandfather became 'Henry James's chair'; it figures in the famous portrait of the Stevensons by John Singer Sargent, with Fanny seated on it in an Indian dress. In October 1885 Stevenson pleaded with James to return and occupy 'his' chair, which stood 'gaping': 'Now, my dear James, come – come – come' (*L5* 144). There is no record that James returned to Skerryvore, though in February 1886 he sent the Stevensons a mirror, 'a magic mirror,' wrote Fanny in her letter of thanks, 'which seems to reflect not only our own plain faces, but the kindly one of a friend entwined in the midst of all sorts of pleasant memories' (*L5* 210). Louis's response to the mirror was to sign himself absent-mindedly 'Henry', and in due course to write a poem, 'The Mirror Speaks', ending with the hope that 'the Prince of Men,/Henry James, shall come again' (*L5* 223). Whatever other meetings with James there may have been in London,[36] the final meeting was in the South Place Hotel, Finsbury, where James, recently returned from eight months in Italy, came like other London literati to see the Stevensons before they sailed for America in August 1887 (*L6* 1). James had two parting gifts: a crate of champagne for the voyage; and a literary portrait of Stevenson, eventually published in *Century Magazine* in April 1888. In this lengthy appreciation, James praised Stevenson as above all 'a writer with a style', though he rejected William Archer's claim that Stevenson wanted his readers to 'look in the first place to his manner and only in the second place to his matter'.[37] The message which, according to James, runs through the range of Stevenson's very dissimilar literary productions ('It is just because he has no speciality that Mr. Stevenson is an individual') is 'the direct expression of the love of youth. . . . Mingled with his almost equal love of a literary surface it represents a real originality.'[38] Apart from *Prince Otto*, which is 'an experiment in style, conceived one summer's day, when the author had given the reins to his high appreciation of Mr. George Meredith', and *Jekyll and Hyde*, 'an experiment in mystification' which has 'the stamp of a really imaginative production, that we may take it in different ways',[39] everything Stevenson has written is a direct apology for, or rhapsody on, boyhood.[40] James reserved his greatest praise for *Kidnapped*, and paid Stevenson a high compliment when, alluding to their exchange on 'The Art of Fiction', he claimed that the 'Flight in the Heather' chapter is 'signal proof of what the novel can do at its best and what nothing else can do so well.... It is capable of a rare transparency – it can illuminate human affairs in cases so delicate and complicated that any other vehicle would be clumsy. To those who love the art that Mr. Stevenson practises he will appear ... not only to have won a particular triumph, but to have given a delightful pledge.'[41]

James's essay, borrowed from *Century Magazine* in advance of publication, was read with delight in the Stevenson household, Stevenson wrote to James from America in October 1887 (*L6* 16). This was the beginning of a faithful, if intermittent, correspondence between Stevenson, writing from a variety of addresses ranging from Sydney to Honolulu, and James, writing almost always from 34 De Vere Gardens, Kensington. Even James's American geography was, from 'long alienation', vague; yet he promised to follow the Stevensons' Pacific cruise 'with an aching wing, an inadequate geography and an ineradicable hope', signing himself 'Ever, my dear Louis, yours, to the last snub – Henry James'.[42] He missed Stevenson 'shockingly', he said; yet 'London is more peopled to me by your living in Samoa than by the residence of almost anybody else in Kensington and Chelsea.'[43] Unlike some of Stevenson's other literary friends, James did not resent and patronize the exiled Stevenson. Having chosen for himself 'the English scene', James was nevertheless free from the kind of parochialism and snobbery revealed by Edmund Gosse when he wrote, after reading *In the South Seas*: 'The fact seems to be that it is very nice to *live* in Samoa, but not healthy to *write* there. Within a three-mile radius of Charing Cross is the literary atmosphere, I suspect.'[44] If Stevenson had begun his literary career by inserting himself into the heart of the English literary establishment, he increasingly felt compelled, as he found his own voice as a writer, to break with that narrow 'English scene' epitomized by Gosse. Both literally and literarily, Stevenson would always be too much of a nomad (and – perhaps not coincidentally – a Scot) to feel altogether comfortable in England.

2
The French Connection

'The complete Gaul': so Stevenson described himself in a letter to Sidney Colvin in February 1874 (*L1* 477), anticipating Lloyd Osbourne's later assertion in his introduction to *New Arabian Nights* that: 'mentally he [Stevenson] was half a Frenchman; in taste, habits, and prepossessions he was almost wholly French. Not only did he speak French admirably and read it like his mother-tongue, but he loved both country and people, and was really more at home in France than anywhere else' (*T1* xx). Osbourne's introduction provides a vivid evocation of the first meeting of Fanny, Belle and Sam (later Lloyd) Osbourne with Louis Stevenson on the latter's eagerly awaited arrival in Grez-sur-Loing, sometime in the summer or early autumn of 1876.[1] Grez, Barbizon and the neighbouring towns and villages of the Fontainebleau forest, which served as summer quarters for the art students of Paris, were to figure significantly in Stevenson's writings. Stevenson began really to know the French and their language, however, in Mentone in the Riviera. It was to Mentone he was sent (or 'ordered') in 1873 by Dr Clark, to recover from the 'breakdown' partly caused by the tension between himself and his parents over his religious agnosticism (*L1* 415; 448; 451). However, Stevenson's earliest experiences of Mentone had been in 1863 and 1864 when he had visited his convalescent mother there. When he arrived in Mentone in November 1873, he was thus returning to familiar territory, and much of his correspondence home is taken up with the 'safe' topic of the changes in Mentone since his previous visits.

The letters Stevenson sent during his journey to Mentone (via Paris, Lyons, Orange, Avignon and Marseilles) could be seen as the first examples of his French travel writing. Despite his disclaimer: 'I cannot write while I am travelling; *c'est un défaut*; but so it is', Stevenson sent Fanny Sitwell a vivid evocation of Avignon (*L1* 359). His complaint of an inability to write persisted at Mentone: 'My dear Mother, Beautiful weather, perfect weather; sun, pleasant cooling winds; health very good: only incapacity to write' (*L1* 497). It was accompanied by an incapacity to *feel*. 'Being sent to the South,' he wrote to Fanny Sitwell, 'is not much good unless you take your soul with you, you see; and my soul is rarely with me here. I don't see much beauty. I have lost the key; I can only be placid and inert, and see the bright days go past uselessly one after the other (*L1* 374). Of such a 'numbness of spirit', such a 'sense of want, and disenchantment of the world and life' (*T25* 68), Stevenson was nevertheless able to write, not only in his letters, but also in the essay 'Ordered South', completed by 11 February 1874 (*L1* 481). Here he describes how, despite 'the eternal magnificence' of the Riviera scenery, the invalid:

> has only a cold head-knowledge that is divorced from enjoyment. He recognises with his intelligence that this thing and that thing are beautiful, while in his heart of hearts he has to confess that it is not beautiful for him....The world is disenchanted for him. He seems to himself to touch things with muffled hands, and to see them through a veil (*T25* 63–4).

Yet in the midst of what might be seen as a case of depression following a breakdown, there is still the occasional flash of feeling, which 'penetrates vividly into [the] numbed spirit', and brings with it a joy that is all the more poignant for its very rarity' (*T25* 64). Such tiny epiphanies may spring from very trivial sources, Stevenson wrote, quoting a friend's saying that 'the "spirit of delight" comes often on very small wings', and when we least expect it; conversely, 'when we expect it most certainly', it leaves us 'to gape joylessly for days together' (*T25* 65). In 'Ordered South' Stevenson mentions some examples of Wordsworthian 'spots of time'[2] when a particular place, by some strange alchemy, is transfigured and 'stands forth in a certain splendour of reality' (*T25* 65).

It is possible to correlate some of the examples in the essay of what Stevenson called 'the glad moment', with descriptions in his letters, most obviously perhaps in the case of the day when 'the invalid' of the essay finds his first violet, and is 'lost in pleasant wonder'. This corresponds to Stevenson's letter of 7 December 1873 to Fanny Sitwell which began:

> The first violet. There is more secret trouble for the heart in the breath of this small flower, than in all the wines of all the vineyards of Europe....I am quite drunken at heart....The first breath, veiled

and timid as it seems, maddens and transfigures and transports you out of yourself.... It is like a wind blowing out of fairyland. – No one need tell me that the phrase is exaggerated, if I say that this violet *sings* (*L1* 401).

This is not altogether empty 'phrasing', since the violet symbolized the young Stevenson's passion for Fanny Sitwell (he had actually swallowed one of the violets she sent him (*L1* 305)). Even so, Stevenson felt the need to offer an (overblown) apology for his overblown diction: 'I beg pardon for this rhapsody. The violet has turned my whole mind out of doors; and my brain is swept and garnished, an empty house full of nothing but perfume and love' (ibid.). It was not just the violet, and his love for Fanny, that had turned his mind 'out of doors', however; in a letter to Fanny the following day, he admitted that he had been 'under the influence of opium' (*L1* 402).[3]

Yet Stevenson's life at Mentone was far from being that of an outsider cultivating his *disponibilité* to rare aesthetic and spiritual experiences. He was socially much involved with the variety of British residents in Mentone (a popular resort for British convalescents), as well as with its more exotic denizens such as the Russian sisters Mesdames Garschine and Zassetsky. In an increasingly flirtatious relationship with the former of these, at least fifteen years his senior, the young Stevenson found that he was getting out of his depth, as is clear from his letters to Fanny Sitwell (*L1* 445–9). That he should speak so openly of this flirtation to Fanny, almost twelve years his senior, and with whom he was supposedly in love, creates another arabesque in the complex pattern of mother/wife/lover substitutions that constituted Stevenson's erotic life. This pattern was given a further Oedipal twist by the arrival in Mentone of Sidney Colvin, Fanny Sitwell's 'intended' and Louis's father-figure. Together they visited Monaco and Monte Carlo, where in a mood of mild hysteria they produced a spoof bilingual hotel advertisement for the GRAND HOTEL GODAM (or THE GREAT GOD-DAMN HOTEL) PLACE DU PARADIS-ALCIBIADE KROMESKY with (in the 'English' version) 'All the agreements of hihg-life ... Specialitys of roasbeef, rhum-punch, Pekoë tea, porterbeer, wischkey, old Thom, and other consummations in the britisch taste. – One speaks all the languages'.[4] For Louis 'the sun of Jink', as he put it to Bob, had not yet set ('Jink' was the Stevenson cousins' word for the elaborate practical jokes they used to perpetrate back in Edinburgh (*L1* 414, n.1)).

Louis had always had a taste for French literature. Already in 1866 he had written to Bob (*L1* 112) about Alexandre Dumas's *Le Vicomte de*

Bragelonne, which he was later to rank as his favourite novel. He had first made its acquaintance (indirectly) in a hotel in Nice in 1863 through his study of 'certain illustrated dessert plates' bearing the name d'Artagnan (*T29* 111). Writing from Mentone in January 1874 Stevenson asked Colvin to send him a copy of Baudelaire's *Petits Poèmes en Prose* (*L1* 470), which he would later use as a model for his own prose poems;[5] that he was already familiar with Baudelaire's work is shown by his letter, itself almost a prose poem, to Bob Stevenson in March 1870 (*L1* 192–4). It was to Bob's sister, Katherine de Mattos, herself an aspiring writer, that Stevenson recommended as a model 'those specimens of consummate polished perfection', Baudelaire's *Petits Poèmes en Prose*; though he added, in a phrase that indicates the limits of his Francophilia, that she should 'study also a far greater man, Thackeray' (*L2* 63). The great literary discovery of Stevenson's stay in Mentone was the novels of George Sand. He wrote in almost identical terms to Bob, and to Elizabeth Crosby: 'At present, I do nothing but read George Sand and sit in the sun by the sea shore' (*L1* 389; 399). Although Stevenson enthused to his cousin Bob that George Sand's *Consuelo* contains 'some of the best passages in the way of literary workmanship in the world' (*L1* 389), the pleasure which Stevenson derived from these texts probably had more to do with their 'readerly' than their 'writerly' qualities. As he wrote to Fanny Sitwell: 'I go from one novel to another and think the last I have read the most sympathetic and friendly in tone, until I have read another. It is life in a dreamland' (*L1* 385). The fact that Sand's novels fed into his own fantasy life – one of the novels is 'strangely like your own story', he wrote to Fanny Sitwell (ibid.), and another (*Consuelo*) provided him with one of his most enduring pet names for Fanny (ibid.) – was no doubt part of their attraction.

Another giant of nineteenth century French literature whose works were familiar to Stevenson was Victor Hugo, a snatch of whose verse he was wont to drop into his correspondence (*L1* 374, 447). Stevenson's first published piece of literary criticism was his essay 'Victor Hugo's Romances', which appeared in the *Cornhill* in August 1874. Colvin had passed on to Stevenson a commission from Leslie Stephen for an article on Hugo's novels, since Stevenson, according to Colvin, was already working on an essay on Hugo when Colvin visited him in Monaco (*S* 13). Writing from Paris on his way home from Mentone, Stevenson told Fanny Sitwell: 'Bob wrote to my dictation three or four pages of 'V. Hugo's Romances': it is d-----d nonsense, but to have a *brouillon* is already a great thing' (*L1* 501). Several of his letters from Paris in April 1874 refer to his difficulty in finishing the Hugo essay. He even begged

Colvin to find him a cheap English translation of *L'Homme Qui Rit* [*The Laughing Man*] 'so that I may finish this article while I'm in the vein...I'm just a thought weary of V. Hugo just now' (*L1* 503) – and this from the man who insisted that Dumas should read in the original French rather than any 'blackguard travesty of a translation' (*T29* 114–15). In May 1874 the finished essay went off to Stephen, who accepted it, sending Stevenson a much fuller critical response than he usually gave to his contributors.[6] The essay, which appeared unsigned in August 1874, was mistakenly attributed to Stephen himself by an anonymous critic in the *Spectator*, and, in a case of misplaced sycophancy which Stevenson later recounted with some merriment, was described as 'masterly' (*S* 14). Stevenson's essay tries to position Hugo in terms of the development of the novel, placing him on a trajectory running from Fielding through Scott – though Stevenson's theorizing about the history of the novel struck Stephen as 'doubtful, as at least to require qualification' (*T31* 161). More resonant with modern critical interest in ideology, post Althusser and Macherey, is the way that Stevenson traces the subsumption of the individual under transpersonal forces, 'those more general relations that are so strangely invisible to the average man in ordinary moods', and to the consciousness of which art can awaken us (*T28* 22).

The essay on Victor Hugo was completed in Edinburgh. It was almost a year before Stevenson could visit France again. In a letter of November 1874 he announced to his cousin Katherine de Mattos the dispatch of the long-promised volume of Baudelaire's *Petits Poèmes en Prose*, and regretted being unable to visit her brother Bob in Paris; he was, as he told Bob a few weeks later, too 'bloody uncoiny' (*L2* 79–80, 85). However, around 10 March 1875 Louis wrote asking Bob to rig up a mattress in his studio in the Boulevard Mont Parnasse (*L2* 124); on 29 March he wrote to his mother from the Café du Sénat, Près du Luxembourg, announcing his departure for Barbizon (*L2* 126). Louis's arrival in Paris is described by Will Low in *A Chronicle of Friendships*, which recounts how he and Bob met Louis off the Calais train at the Gare St Lazare. After the inevitable *flânerie* through the streets of Paris, they took a cab from the Pont des Arts to Lavenue's restaurant in Montparnasse. After Louis had drunk a tumblerful of chartreuse or curaçoa in order to *épater* whatever *bourgeois* happened to be watching, they sauntered home via the Boulevard St. Michel, pausing at the famous Bal Bullier 'which we surveyed philosophically, as prudent youths taking their pleasure otherwise, and having small interest in the riotous scenes enacted there'.[7] On the day after 'the morning after', having spent a day 'in a gross slumber', as Louis wrote to his mother, attributing his lethargy to the journey rather than to the chartreuse (*L2* 126), the Stevenson cousins left Paris for Barbizon. Much of this episode was later used in *The Wrecker* where Bob and Louis appear as 'the brothers Sennis, – Stennis-*aîné* and Stennis-*frère*, as they used to figure on their accounts in Barbizon – a pair of hare-brained Scots'(*T12* 53). On 2 April 1875 Stevenson wrote to his mother from Barbizon: 'And in the forest it is still, and one can sit out. I shall make a nice article out of it I think...' (*L2* 127). The article he made out of it was 'Forest Notes', written up during the summer of 1875. It included material about Louis's first trip to Grez during a second visit he made to the Fontainebleau forest in August of that year, and was published in the *Cornhill* in May 1876. 'Forest Notes' opens with a description of the Gâtinais plain, which borders the Fontainebleau forest:

> The sun goes down, a swollen orange, as it were into the sea. A blue-clad peasant rides home, with a harrow smoking behind him in the dry clods. Another still works with his wife in their little strip. An immense shadow fills the plain; these people stand in it up to their shoulders; and their heads, as they stoop over their work and rise again, are relieved from time to time against the golden sky (*T30* 117).

This is a Millet, a homage to the great painter who had died shortly before Stevenson's first visit to Barbizon (*T30* 107). Stevenson quite explicitly attempts to make word-pictures in 'Forest Notes'. Describing a scene in which he himself is being painted, seated under a beech-tree, by an artist friend, he talks of the need 'out of emulation with the painter, [to] get ready your own palette, and lay out the colour for a woodland scene in words' (*T30* 126). In 'Forest Notes' Stevenson painted a flattering picture of Grez (later a haunt of the painter John Lavery and the 'Glasgow Boys', as well as the home of the composer Frederick Delius). He described it in a letter to his mother: 'I have been at a place called Grez, a pretty and very melancholy village on the plain. A low bridge of many arches choked with sedge; great fields of white and yellow water lilies; poplars and willows innumerable; and about it all such an atmosphere of sadness and slackness, one could do nothing but get into the boat and out of it again, and yawn for bed time' (*L2* 156). Grez also figures in his later essay 'Fontainebleau: village communities of painters', written in 1883 in Hyères. As Stevenson put it in his letter proposing this Fontainebleau essay – or 'Fonty', as it was nicknamed (*L4* 136, 142) – to Henley's *Magazine of Art*: 'I have already written on the subject a good while since; but I should now treat it differently, with an eye to artistic education in (*L4 130*). Apart from the more poised and polished style of the later essay, its main interest lies in what Stevenson has to say about 'artistic education', not only for its own sake, but also for the light his remarks shed on *literary* theory. He writes that despite the foolishness and pretension of this 'purely artistic society', it is 'still excellent for the young artist' because of its very French preoccupation with *style*, the love of which 'the very air of France' communicates (*T30* 103). These young artists are 'mostly fools':

> they hold the latest orthodoxy in all its crudeness; they are at that stage of education ... when a man [sic][8] too much occupied with style to be aware of the necessity for any matter; and this, above all for the Englishman, is excellent. ... Here, in England, too many painters and writers dwell dispersed, unshielded, among the intelligent bourgeois. These, when they are not merely indifferent, prate to him about the lofty aims of art. And this is the lad's ruin. For art is, first of all, a trade. The love of words and not a desire to publish new discoveries, the love of words and not a novel reading of historical events, mark the vocation of the writer and the painter. The arabesque, properly speaking, and even in literature, is the first fancy of the artist; he first plays with his material as child plays with a kaleidoscope; and he is already in a second stage when he begins to use his pretty counters for the end of representation (*T30* 102).

This approaches a manifesto for *l'art pour l'art*, and anticipates the anti-mimetic aesthetic which Stevenson would develop the following year in 'A Humble Remonstrance'.[9]

Stevenson was again in Barbizon in the spring of 1876 (*L2* 173), and back in Edinburgh by 18 May 1876 (*L2* 174 n.1). There is some disagreement among Stevenson's biographers about the date of his return to Grez later that year, and his first meeting with Fanny Osbourne. More recent Stevenson biographers such as Calder (1980), McGlynn (1993) and Le Bris (1994; 2000) continue the tradition of Furnas (1952)[10] that the first (admittedly brief) encounter in Grez between Stevenson and Fanny Osbourne was in July 1876, *before* the former's departure with Walter Simpson for the canoe trip through Northern France described in *An Inland Voyage*. Ernest Mehew claims, however, that it is only the older version of events given by Balfour, according to which Fanny and Louis met *after* the 'inland voyage', that fits the available evidence (*L2* 183 n.1). In the Preface to the Tusitala edition of *An Inland Voyage* Lloyd Osbourne wrote:

It was at the old inn at Grez-sur-Loing that I first saw Robert Louis Stevenson.... [A]fter the meal when we all trooped down to the riverside to see the "Cigarette" and the "Arethusa" – the two canoes that had just finished the "Inland Voyage" – the stranger allowed me to sit in his, and even went to the trouble of setting up the little masts and sails for my amusement (*T17* ix).

The famous anecdote about RLS vaulting in through the window of the Hotel Chevillon at Grez (*T1* xii), which is sometimes conflated with the arrival scene just given, actually comes from Osbourne's Introduction to *New Arabian Nights* in the first volume of the Tusitala edition. This version does mention Stevenson's canoeing exploits, though not any actual canoes; these, according to *An Inland Voyage*, had been drawn out of the river Oise at Pontoise, north of Paris (*T17* 110).

Whether or not Stevenson's meeting with Fanny Osbourne after the 'inland voyage' was their first, and whether it (or indeed the prior meeting, if there was one) was a *coup de foudre*, is presumably forever lost in a romantic mist. We do know that, after ending the canoe trip at Pontoise and before travelling on to Grez, Stevenson had spent about a week in Paris, in order, he told his mother, to slake his 'considerable thirst for the [Théâtre] Français and a town after all this wild work in the rain' (*L2* 190–1). For the weather during the canoe trip was 'deplorable' (*L2* 189) – 'the worst weather I ever saw in France', as Stevenson wrote to Henley from Chauny (*L2* 188). Against 'incessant, pitiless beating rain', Stevenson and Simpson fought on, until one lunchtime at Pimprez, 'in a steam of vapour' caused by the landlady's unaccustomed step of lighting 'a few sticks in the chimney for our comfort', the innocent, but unconsciously ironical, question 'These gentlemen travel for their pleasure?' proved 'too much' (*T17* 83). Stevenson continues: 'The scales fell from our eyes. Another wet day... and we put the boats into the train' (ibid.). Fortunately 'the weather took the hint' (ibid.), and the voyage concluded in tolerable weather. The incident at Pimprez is mentioned in a letter to his mother from Compiègne, and Stevenson comments: 'Indeed, I do not know that I would have stuck to it as I have done, if it had not been for professional purposes; for an easy book may be written and sold, with mighty little brains about it, where the journey is of a certain seriousness and can be named. I mean a book about a journey from York to London must be clever; a book about the Caucasus may be what you will' (*L2* 189). The precedents in the genre of travel writing that Stevenson may have had in mind include: Sterne's *Sentimental Journey*, to which an unsigned review in *London* (probably by Henley) flatteringly compared *An Inland Voyage* (*M* 48; *L2* 254); 'The Log of the "Isis" and "Nautilus" Canoes' in Sweden, a bland if prettily illustrated piece published in the *Cornhill* in 1870, alongside the serialization of Meredith's *Adventures of Harry Richmond*; and finally, bearing a resemblance close enough to worry Colvin, J.L Molloy's *Our Autumn Holiday on French Rivers*. The latter, according to Balfour, seems to have suggested the idea of an inland voyage to Stevenson in the first place (*B* 143), though Stevenson was defensive about this to Colvin, claiming that his real intertext was the much more literary *Reisebilder* of Heine (*L2* 231–2, and notes 3–4).

Despite Stevenson's view that a travel book 'where the journey is of a certain seriousness and can be named' does not need to be 'clever', some of the contemporary reviewers did feel that Stevenson's first book was trying a bit too hard. One reviewer commented: 'The making of bricks without straw is weariness to the flesh, and this is what Mr Stevenson has essayed', though he did concede that Stevenson wrote 'pretty, rippling English' (*M* 52–3). According to a more acerbic review: 'Mr Stevenson, like the sailor's famous parrot, has an unfathomable profundity of thought; and he has devoted most painstaking study to perverted ingenuities of expression.... [A] little of his mannerism goes a long way' (ibid.). This reviewer, who would not have been surprised by Stevenson's famous confession that he had 'played the sedulous ape' to the flower of English letters (*T29* 29), found it reprehensible (in an age which had not yet attained to the postmodern taste for 'aping' and parrotry) that the style of *An Inland Voyage* was 'a compound of styles' (ibid.). Nevertheless there were 'flashes of unaffected liveliness' when 'he dashes off telling little sketches of character, and has graceful touches of vivid landscape painting'; he also had the ability, the reviewer remarked with some prescience, of making himself 'thoroughly at home with the natives' (ibid.). This anonymous reviewer had hit upon the enduring if modest claims which Stevenson's first book makes upon the reader. To pick a descriptive passage almost at random:

> It was a fine, green, fat landscape, or rather a mere green water-lane going on from village to village. Things had a settled look, as in places long lived in. Crop-headed children spat upon us from the bridges as we went below, with a true conservative feeling (*T17* 10).

The nostalgia of such evocations of a seemingly timeless rural setting is intensified by our knowledge that the area which Stevenson and Simpson traversed was to be devastated forty years later in the Great War, a possibility which Stevenson dimly foresaw at Landrecies: 'even this place was a point in the great warfaring system of Europe, and might on some future day be ringed about with cannon smoke and thunder' (*T17* 41).[11]

It is ironical that the first book of a writer who came to be known for his ruthlessly spare depictions of action,[12] should be, as the anonymous reviewer in the *Saturday Review* put it, 'more full of moralizing than of incident' (*M* 52). Nevertheless some of the moralizing reflection is not without interest, not least because the experience of being 'unhoused', even if only temporarily and by choice, was real enough:

> You may have a head knowledge that other people live more poorly than yourself, but it is not agreeable... to sit at the same table and pick your own superior diet from among their crusts.... Thus the poor man, camping out in life, sees it as it is, and knows that every mouthful he puts in his belly has been wrenched out of the fingers of the hungry (*T17* 30).

Stevenson may only ever have flirted with radical politics, but he possessed an acute sense of the injustice of his society, and a real generosity (as opposed to any kind of 'charity'), that derived from his ability to identify, literally as well as imaginatively, with the poor. He was also familiar with the experience of alienation, both literally and metaphysically. Literally, Stevenson seems to have had difficulty in convincing foreign officials of his status as a British subject: 'If he [Stevenson] travels without a passport, he is cast... into noisome dungeons: if his papers are in order, he is suffered to go his way indeed, but not until he has been humiliated by a general incredulity. He is a born British subject, yet he has never succeeded in persuading a single official of his nationality' (*T17* 17). His status as a psychological or metaphysical subject was also problematized during the 'inland voyage' when he experienced a sense of alienation or depersonalisation which he named 'the Apotheosis of Stupidity', and described as follows: 'the central bureau of nerves, what in some moods we call Ourselves, enjoyed its holiday without disturbance, like a Government Office. The great wheels of intelligence turned idly in the head, like fly-wheels, grinding no grist' (*T17* 93). Stevenson continued his musings on this state of 'ecstatic stupor' (or what the *Saturday Review* called 'the dreamy mysticism of his philosophical speculations' (*M* 53)):

> What philosophers call *me* and *not-me*, *ego* and *non ego*, preoccupied me whether I would or no. There was less *me* and more *not-me* than

I was accustomed to expect. I looked upon somebody else, who managed the paddling; ... my own body seemed to have no more intimate relation to myself than the canoe, or the river, or the river banks. ... Something inside my mind, a part of my brain, a province of my proper being, had thrown off allegiance and set up for itself, or perhaps for the somebody else who did the paddling. I had dwindled into quite a little thing in a corner of myself. I was isolated in my own skull. ... I was about as near Nirvana as would be convenient in practical life (*T17* 93–4).

Or: '*Je est un autre*', as Rimbaud famously wrote,[13] at roughly the same time, and in roughly the same place, though in a much less genteel fashion.

If Rimbaud pushed to its extreme limit the idea of the privileged status of the artist as seer, there is in *An Inland Voyage* a more modest, genteel, and almost burlesque version of the claim that the artistic vocation enjoys a special dignity. At Précy, Stevenson and Simpson came across a performance by a man with marionettes, which prompted Stevenson to reflect on his great love for (especially French) 'strollers': 'I ... have always found them singularly pleasing. Any stroller must be dear to the right-thinking heart; if it were only as a living protest against offices and the mercantile spirit' (*T17* 103). He continued:

[I]f a man is only so much of an actor that he can stumble through a farce, he is made free of a new order of thoughts. He has something else to think about beside the money-box. He has a pride of his own, and, what is of far more importance, he has an aim before him that he can never quite attain. He has gone upon a pilgrimage that will last him his life long, because there is no end to it short of perfection. (*T17* 104)

To be an artist is to be marked out: 'To be even one of the outskirters of art leaves a fine stamp on a man's countenance' (ibid.). If this was vanity, then it was a kind of vanity which deeply appealed to Stevenson. He tells an anecdote of an old stroller in the aftermath of a wretched performance: 'The vanity of an artist! That is the kind of thing that reconciles me to life: a ragged, tippling, incompetent old rogue, with the manners of a gentleman and the vanity of an artist, to keep up his self-respect!' (*T17* 105) Another 'man after my own heart', he says, is a M. de Vauversin who had been an actor in Paris, but because of a 'nervous affection' caused by the heat and glare of the footlights, had taken up instead the life of a strolling artist. When his partner, a Mlle. Ferrario, had admitted to an inclination to a more settled existence, 'with a million of money down', M. de Vauversin had magnificently replied:

> *Eh bien, moi non*; – not I! If anyone is a failure in this world, is it not I? I must go about the country gathering coppers and singing nonsense. Do you think I regret my life? Do you think I would rather be a fat burgess...? Not I! I have had moments when I have been applauded on the boards: I think nothing of that; but I have known in my own mind sometimes, when I have not had a clap from the whole house, that I had found a true intonation, or an exact and speaking gesture; and then, messieurs, I have known what pleasure was, what it was to do a thing well, what it was to be an artist. And to know what art is, is to have an interest forever, such as no burgess can find in his petty concerns. *Tenez, messieurs, je vais vous le dire*, – it is like a religion. (*T17* 107–8)

M. de Vauversin's philosophy echoes the Bohemian aesthetic of Bob and Louis Stevenson at this time, and is strongly reminiscent of the aesthetic attitude struck by M. Berthelini in 'Providence and the Guitar',[14] a short story based on Stevenson's encounter with a strolling French actor and his wife at Grez. Like Stevenson's other French novellas, and the *New Arabian Nights* stories[15] with which they were published, and like the Paris section of *The Wrecker* (written years later), 'Providence and the Guitar' is a satire on the pretensions of *la vie de Bohème* to which Stevenson was so deeply attracted. Le Bris has dramatized the tension between Stevenson the writer of novels of action, and Stevenson the aesthete, the subtle artificer of delicate arabesques, so that, in order to become the former kind of writer, Stevenson had decisively to reject 'ses années bohémiennes' and 'kill in himself his cousin Bob',[16] 'le brilliantissime prince des nuits de Saint-Germain-des-Près'. This process of self-destruction is evident in the pages of *New Arabian Nights* where the satire of Stevenson, the self-proclaimed Bohemian [bohémien affiché] and aesthete, devours itself in 'a frenzy of self-destruction' [un vertige d'autodestruction].[17] If Stevenson finds it impossible to maintain the comic detachment inherent in the genre of satire, says Le Bris, it is because he feels obliged:

> to include himself in the thrust of his criticism: the literary affectation, the posturing, the fascination with death, the blatant dilettantism, the temptation to a voyeuristic withdrawal from the world, the

amorality, and the cowardice when confronted with the need for action; these are not just faults which he denounces in others, they are temptations against which he struggles, a part of himself which he ridicules for page after page.[18]

The Frenchness of the *New Arabian Nights* volume is apparent firstly in the subject matter of the stories. Not only are the last three ('Providence and the Guitar'; the Villon story 'A Lodging for the Night'; and 'The Sire de Malétroit's Door') all explicitly French (the latter two apparently deriving from Théodore de Banville's 'Gringoire' (*M* 122)), but also the *New Arabian Nights* story sequences ('The Suicide Club' and 'The Rajah's Diamond') are themselves frequently set in vividly evoked Parisian locations: the Latin Quarter and the Bullier Ball Rooms; Montmartre; and the Boulevards. The form also has French inspiration. The style is Gallic to a fault – 'one pervading affectation being the use of French idioms literally translated into English' (*M* 118). Several reviewers refer to Dumas *père*, to whom, according to one review, Stevenson bore more resemblance 'than to any English author' (*M* 117). However in Dumas 'the intensity of writing is stronger, and the excitement of the reader far more stimulated, than in the slighter sketches of the *New Arabian Nights*. We can imagine Dumas losing himself in his characters, and believing in his stories, while Mr Stevenson gives us the impression of being outside both. He is the stage manager skilfully directing his actors, while he never ceases to regard them from the point of view of pure art. He has the advantage, however, of Dumas in the subtle humour which pervades everything he writes' (ibid.). It is the humour, both its nature ('cold at times and rarely mirthful'[19]) and its uncertain object (probably the reader), which seems to have been so unsettling to the Victorian reader. One Victorian reviewer describes the experience of reading Stevenson as follows:

He juggles with his readers and with his characters. He dresses up a puppet and tells you it is a man, and you believe it, and hold your breath when the sword is at the puppet's breast. Then he holds up the stripped manikin and smiles maliciously. With him, men and ideas are but literary properties, to be used as he sees fit, for this or that effect (*M* 121).

Such a playing with the 'reality-effect'[20] may be familiar enough to readers of modern and postmodern fiction, but it could come as something of a shock to the Victorian system. Before Stevenson became celebrated

(and relegated) as a so-called 'children's author', he made his name
(and his first serious money (*S* 78)) as a writer of avant-garde experimental
texts. Gurus of postmodernism such as Borges and Baudrillard have referred
respectfully to Stevenson.[21] In its own literary context, Stevenson's *New
Arabian Nights* was ranked by George Saintsbury, in an unsigned review
in the *Pall Mall Gazette*, 'very high indeed, almost *hors concours*, among
the fiction of the present day' (*M* 108).

Meanwhile Stevenson's work as a literary historian-cum-critic continued. In 1877, the same year as he was writing the novella 'A Lodging
for the Night: A Story of François Villon', his first piece of fiction to be
published, he was also composing his essay 'François Villon, Student, Poet,
Housebreaker'. The former piece in fact derived from the latter. Stevenson
wrote to Colvin that 'while I was full of Villon, I wrote a little
story...about him' (*L2* 211), and in the Villon essay itself he rather
archly tells us, after having described the murder which is also the central
action in the novella: 'If time had only spared us some particulars,
might not this last have furnished us with the matter of a grisly winter's
tale?' (*T27* 130). Stevenson's first published tale anticipates not only his
later 'Winter's Tale', *The Master of Ballantrae*, but also his later fiction
generally, in that it gives a vivid depiction of murder and a flight
through a hostile, if picturesque, environment. The dramatic impetus of
the tale is not sustained, however, and it becomes more of a dramatized
debate between Villon and the aged nobleman who gives him lodging
for the night. This debate turns on the question of the relation between
morality and social milieu. If there is a modern ring to this topic, such
a contemporization of Villon in the tale is also evident in the Villon
essay, which boldly connects the medieval poet with the context of
nineteenth century France: 'Paris now is not so different from the Paris
of then; and the whole of the doings of Bohemia are not written in the
sugar-candy pastorals of Murger' (*T27* 126). Indeed, in one of the grand
generalizations to which Stevenson the literary historian was prone,
Villon is linked via Rabelais to the controversies surrounding the French
literature of Stevenson's own immediate context. Stevenson wrote of
Villon in the essay: 'Not only his style, but his callous pertinent way of
looking upon the sordid and ugly sides of life, becomes every day
a more specific feature in the literature of France' (*T27* 141). In the
'Preface, by Way of Criticism', written later for *Familiar Studies of Men
and Books*, Stevenson even more specifically linked 'the spirit of Villon'
with Zola, the Goncourts, and 'the infinitely greater Flaubert', all of
whom, despite a similarity in ugliness, Villon 'surpasses...in native
power' (*T27* xx). Even if Stevenson was tempted (only tempted, mind)

to regret having written on an author of whom he so heartily – he would have us believe – disapproved, nevertheless he admired the style with which Villon executed subjects perhaps better not treated at all. In a comment which applies equally, one suspects, to at least Flaubert among modern French authors, Stevenson conceded that 'the pleasure we take in the author's skill... reconciles us to the baseness of his attitude' (ibid.).

Villon also appears in 'Charles of Orleans', another essay in literary history which Stevenson had written a year or so previously. As in other such essays by Stevenson, history figures rather more than literature in 'Charles of Orleans', though history à la Stevenson is far from the kind which is 'deplorably adulterated and defaced, fitted to very vague and pompous words, and strained through many men's minds of everything personal and precise'(*T27* 152). On the contrary, Charles of Orleans is brought before the reader as one 'of those who have... survived themselves most completely, left a sort of personal seduction behind them in the world, and retained after death, the art of making friends' (*T27* 146). It takes one, they say, to know one. It is by no means unlikely, Stevenson speculated, that Villon himself, 'the greatest ballade-maker of all time', might have visited the court of Charles at Blois (*T27* 169). In contrast to Villon, who 'was almost more of a modern than de Banville himself' (*T27* 177),[22] Charles saw 'literature was an object rather than a mean', and 'loved bandying words for its own sake' (*T27* 175). If, however, 'we are pleased to find... obvious sentiments stated without affectation', there is in the rondels of Charles 'a genuine pathos in these simple words, and the lines go with a lilt, and sing themselves to music of their own' (*T27* 178). The qualities Stevenson found in Charles's verse are not unlike those of his own, which at times, partly under the influence of Charles, played with the rondel form.[23]

The attitude of Charles of Orleans could hardly be more different from that of another French poet, Béranger, on whom Stevenson wrote in a short essay in 1875 for the ninth edition of *The Encyclopedia Britannica*. This brief essay on Béranger emphasized the poet's 'strong sense of political responsibility' and his higher estimation of the public interest than 'any private passion or favour' (*T28* 177); Béranger was critical of *l'art pour l'art* and of the absence of any motive of 'public usefulness'. Despite sharing with Villon and Charles of Orleans the experience of imprisonment, he differed sharply from them in his lack of self-pity. Stevenson's fascination with writers who had been imprisoned is not without biographical significance; he often used the metaphor of imprisonment in relation to his own experience, whether of illness or of parental oppression (for the latter he also used the metaphor of the gyve or fetter in his fable 'The House of Eld').

He later wrote up the farce his own brief imprisonment in 1875 at Châtillon-sur-Loire on suspicion of being Prussian spy, with the confiscation of his knapsack containing, appropriately enough, two volumes of the *Poésies de Charles d' Orléans* and Stevenson's own 'remarkable English roundels...to this day unpublished' (*T17* 117–20). The reality of imprisonment was not conducive to further roundels.

It was at Le Monastier in the Haute Loire in September 1878 that Stevenson completed the *New Arabian Nights* stories, or 'Araby the Damned', as he put it in a letter to Henley, predicting that these hated 'Arabians' would be the death of him (*L2* 265–6). Stevenson felt under intense pressure because he was simultaneously writing *New Arabian Nights* and *Edinburgh: Picturesque Notes*, as well as 'A Mountain Town in France', the essay celebrating Le Monastier which was intended as the first chapter of *Travels with a Donkey in the Cevennes*.[24] Such a heavy writing schedule led Stevenson to explode with rage (only partially mock, one suspects) at a letter from Henley which awaited him at Alais [Alès] at the end of his walking tour through the Cévennes. In response to the accusation of neglecting *Deacon Brodie*, the play they were co-writing, Stevenson expostulated:

> *Par exemple*, I find you a hell of a fine fellow to complain of my idleness with this cursed *Deacon*. Idleness! *parbleu!* I have just finished the Arabians and *Edinburgh*; I go on a tour on my two feet, goading a she ass before my face, pass most of the Cevennes, traverse a good distance, write about 24,000 words of a Journal; and on my arrival, I find you complaining of my idleness! (*L2* 279).

Such a strongly defensive response to the suggestion of idleness may seem rather odd coming from one who only two years previously had written so eloquent 'An Apology for Idlers'. However, there is in Stevenson a complex and paradoxical relation between work and play, between the bourgeois or 'belly-god Burgess' with his Protestant work ethic (*T25* 174), and the Bohemian playing the role of the vagabond or gypsy. Stevenson's ambivalence about active engagement in life, as opposed to passive withdrawal, is also expressed in 'Will o' the Mill', published in the *Cornhill* in January 1878; this tale is ambiguous on every level, including its genre. In 'An Apology for Idlers' Stevenson included among those we might nowadays call workaholics 'scribblers who keep scribbling at little articles', irrespective of whether they publish three or thirty articles a year (*T25* 59–60). In his retrospective 'A College Magazine' Stevenson confessed that, although he was 'known and pointed out for the pattern of an idler' (*T29* 28), nevertheless during the 'full, vivid instructive hours of truantry' which he celebrated in 'An Apology for Idlers', he always kept two books in his pocket: 'one to read, one to write in' (ibid.). The famous Stevensonian claim in *Travels with a Donkey* that: 'For my part, I travel not to go anywhere, but to go. I travel for travel's sake' (*T17* 178) can be seen for a pose, even without the benefit of *The Cevennes Journal* (Stevenson's original journal, finally published in 1978) which includes the following line omitted from *Travels with a Donkey*: '[I travel for travel's sake.] And to write about it afterwards, if only the public will be so condescending as to read.'[25] Though Stevenson would later have to travel for his health's sake, in the 1870s he travelled largely for the sake of copy.

The message of 'travel for travel's sake' (echoing the Bohemian *l'art pour l'art* ideal and its denunciations of bourgeois philistinism) continues as follows: 'The great affair is to move; to feel the needs and hitches of our life more nearly; to come down off this feather-bed of civilization, and find the globe granite underfoot and strewn with cutting flints' (*T17* 178). Even the generally favourable reviewer in *Fraser's Magazine* found such posturing hard to take. 'In our day' he wrote, 'hardships were not voluntary. We had them without the asking. What a thing it is to be young, to be super-refined, to load up a donkey with all one's belongings, and to start out upon the barest of hill-sides ... This is the last whim of exquisite youth' (*M* 67). More positively, the reviewer wrote appreciatively of the author's 'quite exceptional gift of literary expression' and his 'graceful art of writing about nothing'; for 'nothing particular happens to the traveller ... but he tells us that nothing in detail, hour by hour of his not very long journey, with a happy grace of narrative' (*M* 68). There is something almost Flaubertian in writing a book about nothing, *un livre sur rien*, purely for the sake of style. If the anonymous reviewer of *Fraser's Magazine* did not make such French connections, then Grant Allen, writing in the *Fortnightly Review*, did: '[Mr. Stevenson's] "Inland Voyage" struck the key-note of his literary gamut; and the new volume of travel ... has the self-same happy ring, the self-same light and graceful touch, as if Mr. Stevenson were rather a Frenchman born out of due place, than a Scotsman of the Scots.... Mr. Stevenson is a stylist who lays himself out for the mastery of style' (*M* 65).

It is not entirely true, however, to say that *Travels with a Donkey* is a book about nothing. The verdict on *An Inland Voyage* which Stevenson himself gave in a letter to his mother from Le Monastier, three days before setting off with Modestine into the Cévennes – 'It is not badly written, thin, mildly cheery, and strained. *Selon moi'* (*L2* 276) – hardly applies to *Travels with a Donkey*. The religious reflections of the earlier book continue (especially in the section 'Our Lady of the Snows'), and there are much thicker descriptions both of the (after all more interesting) countryside and of its historical significance (Stevenson was deeply interested in the history of the Camisards, the 'French Covenanters'[26]). And the book is informed, deeply if not explicitly, by his personal life. As Stevenson wrote in the Dedication to Colvin: 'Every book is, in an intimate sense, a circular letter to the friends of him who writes it. They alone take his meaning; they find private messages, assurances of love, and expressions of gratitude dropped for them at every corner' (*T17* 129). The 'private messages' were above all for Fanny Osbourne, who the previous month had returned to her husband in California. This 'parting without prospect of return' had left 'all ... dark before them', according to Balfour (*B* 114). Probably the most memorable chapter of the book, 'A Night among the Pines', has at its heart a declaration to Fanny:

> The outer world, from which we cower in our houses, seemed after all a gentle habitable place; and night after night a man's bed, it seemed, was laid and waiting for him in the fields. ... And yet even while I was exulting in my solitude I became aware of a strange lack. I wished a companion to lie near me in the starlight, silent and not moving, but ever within touch. For there is a fellowship more quiet even than solitude, and which, rightly understood, is solitude made perfect. And to live out of doors with the woman a man loves is of all lives the most complete and free (*T17* 208).

If Fanny's absence haunts *Travels with a Donkey*, 'the female' is allegedly present in the form of an obsession with women that an anonymous reviewer in *The Spectator* claimed to detect (*M* 69–74). Stevenson himself referred to 'that delicious article in which the *Spectator* represented me as going about the Cevennes roaring for women, and only disquieted at the monastery because it was not a bawdy house ...' (*L3* 96). 'She' is also present in the form, shocking to modern readers, of the presumably unconscious figuring of Modestine as a woman. Stevenson's literal treatment of Modestine qua donkey was shocking even to some nineteenth century readers (*M* 71–2). However offensive we may find Stevenson's treatment of Modestine, both literally, and *a fortiori* in her figuration as a woman, there is nevertheless some pathos at the end of the book as the grief, and sense of bereavement, which Stevenson must have felt (but did not show[27]) at the departure of Fanny Osbourne, is displaced, somewhat bizarrely, onto Modestine:

> She was patient, elegant in form, ... and inimitably small. Her faults were those of her race and sex; her virtues were her own. Farewell ... Father Adam wept when he sold her to me; after I had sold her in my turn, I was tempted to follow his example; and being alone with a stage driver and four or five agreeable young men, I did not hesitate to yield to my emotion (*T17* 253).

In the difficult year between Fanny Osbourne's departure for California in August 1878, and Stevenson's setting out to join her the following August, he also spent June 1879 in France. It is perhaps significant that he did not stay at Grez, but in Cernay-la-Ville, where Bob had worked the previous year (*L2* 288–9). There Stevenson seems mostly to have been struggling to complete 'this thing for Kegan Paul' (*L2* 321), presumably 'The Story of a Lie'; he completed it on board the *Devonia* shortly before arriving in New York, *en route* for San Francisco.

* * *

The next time Stevenson visited France, he was a married man. On the way back to Scotland from the Swiss health resort of Davos, where they had spent the winter of 1880–81, Louis and Fanny Stevenson spent a 'delicious' week Chez Siron in Barbizon, and a less enjoyable time in Paris, that 'temple of stenches' and 'the most putrid city in the universe' (*L3* 177, 175). Apart from travelling through France on the way to and from Davos, the Stevensons' next, and most extended, stay in France was from October 1882 until June 1884. Once again, and by the same Dr Clark as in 1873, Louis was 'ordered South'. This time the destination was Montpellier, though the Stevensons planned to move as soon as possible to Hyères. In fact they ended up at Campagne Defli, St Marcel, near Marseille, where they stayed until an outbreak of fever, possibly typhus, forced them to leave. In February 1883 they moved east along the coast to Hyères, where they found the chalet 'La Solitude' This tiny Swiss chalet was a souvenir from the Paris Exposition of 1878, from where their landlord had transported it back to Hyères. There, perched on a cliff, it made, according to Fanny's prefatory note to *The Dynamiter*, an incongruous spectacle; yet it was here that Stevenson said he spent the happiest period in his life (*T3* vii).

While living in the South of France, Stevenson kept abreast of literary affairs back in England. In particular, he tried to send to Henley as regularly as he was able what he called 'the monthly cricket'; that is, an article-by-article review of the monthly *Magazine of Art* edited by Henley. It was in the *Magazine of Art* that Stevenson's own critical essay, 'A Note on Realism', appeared in November 1883. Stevenson had (initially at least) a less happy relationship with another editor, James Payn, who in 1883 had succeeded Leslie Stephen at the *Cornhill*. In a note to *New Arabian Nights* Stevenson had made what he on reflection considered to be an ill-judged pleasantry about an unnamed author who had 'borrowed' the idea of one of his stories. The anonymous author was named by a journalist as James Payn, the author of now largely unread novels, but in Stevenson's day a man of letters to be reckoned with. Stevenson tried to cover himself by writing appeasing letters both to the *New York Tribune* and to the *Atheneum* (*L4* 10–11). Whether or not Payn's judgement was clouded by non-literary considerations, as the new editor of the *Cornhill* he rejected Stevenson's story, 'The Treasure of Franchard', on the grounds that part of it was 'not suitable to British proprieties' (*L4* 39 n.1). The novella was subsequently accepted by *Longman's Magazine* for the April and May issues of 1883. Begun in Kingussie and completed at St Marcel, 'The Treasure of Franchard' has been regarded as a small masterpiece (though also condemned as a 'Kailyard' novel set in France[28]). Contemporary reviewers praised it on its publication in the collection entitled *The Merry Men* in 1887. 'No man without the most definite genius could have written this tale', wrote the anonymous reviewer in the *Spectator* (*M* 254), while the review in the *Nation* picks out 'The Treasure of Franchard' as a model for aspiring writers: 'The mere technical art of all these stories is so obvious that comment is superfluous. But we cannot refrain from commending the last ['The Treasure of Franchard'] to aspiring writers' (*M* 257).

What these reviewers do not mention is the extent to which the style and handling of this story is influenced by French models. Part of the pleasure which this text yields is derived from Stevenson's playing with his reader's awareness of the French 'originals' lying just below the surface of the text (in a fashion not dissimilar to the way Julian Barnes plays with his reader's knowledge of Flaubert's style in *Flaubert's Parrot*). One reviewer criticized Stevenson's residual 'affectation' (*M* 252), though he was arguably missing the point of Stevenson's deliberately allusive and slightly 'camp' style. 'The Treasure of Franchard' is, to use Stevenson's phrase from the Dedication of *Travels with a Donkey*, a 'circular letter' to his friends, and full of 'private messages'. The friend he had particularly in mind was his cousin Bob, to whom he asked Henley to send a copy of the original magazine version. Bob's wife had just given birth to a daughter, and Stevenson wrote: 'I should like him, as he now smiles upon his kid, to smile upon himself and Anthony in Chevillon's, the captives of debt' (*L4* 117). For 'The Treasure of Franchard' is a kind of jokey and nostalgic recreation of the lost youth of the Stevensons. It is set in Grez, particularly in Chevillon's inn (renamed Tentaillon's), and manages to include a brief history of Grez, as well as some evocative descriptions of the village (the detail of the 'most furious barking' on arrival at Grez will probably strike a chord with any visitor who has arrived at Grez on foot). The appearance in the story of Bob (a ploy later to be used in *The Wrecker*) as one of the English boarders, 'prisoners for lack of remittance', who 'spoke French pretty fluently' and who was 'a humorous, agile-minded fellow' (*T8* 230), is given an ironical twist by the fact that he and his compatriot are suspected of the theft of the treasure. After all, '[t]hey are painters, therefore they are continually lounging in the forest. They are painters, therefore they are not unlikely to have some smattering of education. Lastly, because they are painters, they are probably immoral' (*T8* 216). Thus speaks Doctor Desprez, in the resounding periods which the reader has come to expect of him; he is a man capable of 'archly scanning the syllables' of his utterances (*T8* 211). Stevenson's technique of rendering into English almost literally the cadences and expressions of spoken French is endearingly comic. Desprez, like a benign version of Flaubert's M.Homais, addresses his wife as 'my cherished one' and 'my beautiful', and in a moment of crisis delivers the line: 'Why, madame, a blow like this would set a frog into a transpiration' (*T8* 214). Given Stevenson's willingness to render French expressions literally into English, the very few expressions actually in French stand out: Desprez's first word in the story is: '*Sapristi!*'; and the novella ends with another French expletive: ' "*Tiens!*" said Casimir.' Stevenson was taken to task for ending the novella in this way by a young correspondent, A.Trevor Haddon. In reply to this nineteen year old art student, Stevenson agreed (perhaps too graciously) that the ending was weak:

When I made Casimir say '*Tiens*' at the end, I made a blunder. I thought it was what Casimir would have said and put it down. As your question shows, it should have been left out. It was a 'patch' of realism, and an anti-climax. Beware of realism; it is the devil: it is one of the means of art, and now they make it the end! And such is the farce of the age in which a man lives, that we all, even those who most detest it, sin by realism (*L4* 141).

In September 1883, two months after this letter to Haddon, Stevenson was discussing with Henley the proofs of his essay 'A Note on Realism', to which he also referred in two lengthy letters to his cousin Bob written later that month, and at the beginning of the next (*L4* 153 n.3, 168–171, 180–2). His target both in the essay, and in his letters to Bob, was the hegemony in contemporary French literature and painting of Realism, 'the genial error of the present French teaching' (*L4* 169). He saw in both painting and literature a tension between 'idealism', which focuses on 'the main concept' of a work of art, and is content to use 'languid conventions to fill up the field' (*L4* 180); and 'realism', which fills, or more often swamps, the field with details drawn from nature. In painting, doing studies from nature is all very well, Stevenson thought; but 'studio work is the real touch' (*L4* 169). Realism is a *technique* or a *method*, which may be legitimately used to 'fill up the field'; it can indeed be an improvement on the stale conventionality of some traditional art (whether literature or painting). The problem with the modern French theory and practice was that the *method* of realism had become the *raison d'être* of the work of art; they had forgotten that the most crucial gift of the artist is the ability to omit. Writing to Bob about Balzac's realism, Louis wound himself up into a passionate artistic *cri de coeur*: 'He would leave nothing undeveloped, and thus drowned out of sight of land amid the multitude of crying and incongruous details. Jesus, there is but one art: to omit! O if I knew how to omit, I would ask no other knowledge. A man who knew how to omit would make an *Iliad* of a daily paper' (*L4* 169). The artist should therefore cultivate being 'partly blind', for 'artistic sight is judicious blindness' (ibid.). Looking at nature, a mature artist sees 'not the scene, but the water colour sketch' (ibid.); and it is only in the studio that he learns this:

> He goes to nature for facts, relations, values – material; as a man, before writing a historical novel, reads up memoirs. But it is not by reading memoirs, that he has learned the selective criterion. He has learned that in the practice of his art; and he will never learn it well, but when disengaged from the ardent struggle of immediate representation, of realistic and *ex facto* art. He learns it in the crystallisation of daydreams; in changing not in copying fact; in the pursuit of an ideal, not in the study of nature (*L4* 169–70).

The writer who developed realism to the limit was of course not Balzac, but Zola, who became something of a *bête noire* for Stevenson. The latter wrote in 'A Note on Realism': 'A man of the unquestionable force of

M. Zola spends himself on technical successes. To afford a popular flavour and attract the mob, he adds a steady current of what I may be allowed to call the rancid. That is exciting to the moralist; but what more particularly interests the artist is this tendency to the extreme of detail, when followed as a principle, to degenerate into mere *feux-de-joie* of literary tricking' (*T18* 70). It was therefore like a red rag to a bull when, in 1886, in defence of the Royal Academy's decision to reject a sculpture by Stevenson's much admired friend Rodin, Edward Armitage wrote that Rodin was 'the Zola of sculpture', and that his work is 'too realistic and coarse even for the strong stomach of the French public' (*L5* 311 n.1). In response to Armitage, Stevenson wrote to *The Times* that: 'M. Zola is a man of a personal and a forceful talent, approaching genius, but of diseased ideals . . . [he] presents us with a picture, to no detail of which we can take grounded exception. It is only on the whole that it is false. Hence we call his work realistic in the evil sense, meaning that it is dead to the ideal, and speaks only to the senses. M. Rodin's work is the clean contrary of this' (*L5* 311–12).

Although Stevenson championed Rodin, the latter was never able to make a bust of him, as he did of Henley. A bust of Stevenson had been planned, but when Henley went to Paris for the modelling, Stevenson was too ill to accompany him (*L4* 240 n.1). In May 1884 he suffered the worst haemorrhage he had ever experienced. Stevenson seems to have been dangerously ill for some weeks, though it is not entirely clear how seriously ill he actually was, and how much his illness was exaggerated by Fanny's alleged tendency to 'alarmism'; the relevant correspondence is distorted by the various writers' need for self-justification, as well as by the need to shield Stevenson from his over-anxious parents. What can be said with some certainty is that during the year and a half that Stevenson stayed at Hyères, he enjoyed at best indifferent health. His work-rate suffered from this, as it did from his grief over the death of his 'oldest friend except Bob' (*L4* 155), James Walter Ferrier, in memory of whom he wrote 'Old Mortality' (*T29* 19–27). Stevenson seems to have been deeply shaken by his first experience of bereavement: 'after love it is the one great surprise that life preserves for us' (*L4* 163).

The quantity and quality of the work that Stevenson did produce in Hyères was inevitably affected by his precarious state of health. When he was below par, he worked on less demanding material, such as, under his *nom de plume* of Captain George North, a serial for *Young Folks* entitled *The Black Arrow* – a piece of 'tushery', Stevenson told Henley (*L4* 128–9). Stevenson himself thought so little of *The Black Arrow* that during the process of writing he actually forgot what had happened to several of the principal characters (*M* 83–4). He and Fanny collaborated on *More New Arabian Nights*, or *The Dynamiter*, as it is better known. According to Fanny's Prefatory Note to the Tusitala edition, *The Dynamiter* is based on stories she made up to divert Louis when she was unable even to read to him when his sick room had to be darkened because of his ophthalmia (on top of sciatica, and the ever-present threat of a haemorrhage) (*T3* xi). Fanny claimed that these stories were not written up until they had moved to Bournemouth in the summer of 1884, although Stevenson's letters from Hyères earlier in the year do suggest that he was already at work on them. He wrote, for example, to Bob mid-April: 'I am now, having been ill with fever, and my new Arabians interrupted, writing a lot of sort of dickering verse; of no interest to you ... but a great diversion to myself. I sent one shitty thing to Low ... and I have another on female underclothes which is my own favourite, as that is about the deepest poetry I have' (*L4* 269).[29] He was also writing many of the poems that were eventually to appear in *A Child's Garden of Verses*. This collection was known in the Hyères period as *Penny Whistles*, and Stevenson had a number of copies printed privately to circulate among his friends to gauge their response. But his main business during this period was *Prince Otto*, which he referred to as his 'chief o' works' (*L4* 245), and to which he devoted as much care and effort as his health would allow. According to Fanny in her Prefatory Note to *Prince Otto*: 'The labour that went into the making of the book was greater than he ever expended over any other novel, either before or after' (*T4* xiii). The book is difficult to place in any definite genre. Stevenson insisted in a letter to Will Low of early December 1883 that it was a romance, 'not a novel – a romance, my lad' (*L4* 211), though an earlier letter to Henley catches more of the ambiguity of the work: 'It is queer and a little, little bit free; ... the whole thing is not a romance, nor yet a comedy; nor yet a romantic comedy; but a kind of preparation of some of the elements of all three in a glass jar' (*L4* 194).

Prince Otto was in many respects a putting into practice of the aesthetic ideals Stevenson had expressed in 'A Note on Realism' and in his letters to Bob. In February 1886 Louis wrote to Charles Warren Stoddard, then teaching literature at Notre Dame, Indiana, and suggested he put *Prince Otto* on the reading list, as 'a strange example of the difficulty in being ideal in an age of realism' (*L5* 203). Stevenson also suggested as secondary reading his own 'A Note on Realism' and other of his essays on literature, including 'A Humble Remonstrance' (which he misnamed 'Humble Apology'), where he had developed some of the ideas announced in 'A Note on Realism'. Henley, who edited the *Magazine of Art* where the

'Realism' essay was published, also noticed the connections between the theory of the essay and the practice of the novel. On *Prince Otto's* publication in November 1885, by which time Stevenson had left France for Bournemouth, Henley wrote in an unsigned review in the *Atheneum*:

Mr. Stevenson's new book is so plainly an essay in pure literature that to the average reader it may be something of a disappointment. It has none of the qualities of an ordinary novel.... The ordinary material of the novel he throws aside; in half a dozen sentences he gives the results of a whole volume of realism; he goes straight to the quick of things, and concerns himself with none but essentials.... it may be taken as a model by anybody with an understanding of art in its severer and more rigid sense, and a desire to excel in the higher ranges of literary achievement. (*M* 185)

But in a letter to Henley of November 1885 Stevenson wrote of his resentment at being damned, as he saw it, with faint praise in this review, and not least by its patronizing comparisons with Dumas and Musset[30] (*L5* 156–7). Nevertheless he was never to repeat the experiment in 'pure literature' of *Prince Otto*, which on his own admission was 'pitched pretty high and stilted' (*L4* 110).

The Stevensons moved from Hyères to Bournemouth in 1884. Apart from a brief visit ashore when the *S.S. Ludgate Hill*, bound for New York, called at Le Havre in August 1887, the last time Stevenson visited France was in August 1886, when he and Fanny stayed for a week with the Lows in Paris. This was not, however, to be Stevenson's last contact with the French language and culture, since many of the ports of call on his Pacific voyages were in French colonies.[31] In July 1890 Stevenson visited Noumea, capital of the French colony of New Caledonia, and notorious for its convict settlement. It was here that Stevenson read Zola's *La Bête Humaine*,[32] as he wrote to Henry James on 19 August 1890. On the same day Stevenson also wrote to Marcel Schwob, a young French writer who had sent Stevenson several admiring letters. Stevenson and Schwob shared a common interest in Villon, on whom Schwob had recently given learned papers.[33] Stevenson's fiction had come as a revelation to Schwob, and seemed to offer a way out of the impasse in which the contemporary French novel found itself, 'squeezed between naturalism and psychological analysis "*à la française*"'.[34] Schwob had asked Stevenson's permission to translate *The Black Arrow*, which Stevenson granted, only regretting that Schwob had not chosen a book Stevenson himself admired. He told Schwob: 'Comprehend how I have lived much of my time in France, and loved your country, and many of its people, and all the time was learning that which your country has to teach – breathing in rather that atmosphere of art which only there can be breathed; and all the time knew – and raged to know – that I might write with the pen of angels or of heroes, and no Frenchman be the least wiser! And now steps in M. Marcel Schwob...' (*L6* 401) Although they would probably never meet in the flesh, Stevenson acknowledged, his step-son Lloyd Osborne might shortly be in Paris and would give Schwob news. Lloyd, however, did not find time to go to Paris, Stevenson told Schwob in a letter of January 1981, in which he gave him permission to translate whichever of his works he preferred (*L7* 70). In July 1894, in what was to be his final letter to Schwob, Stevenson praised the latter's *Mimes*, warning the young writer that it was a promising début rather than 'a thing final in itself', for 'life is a series of farewells, even in art; even our proficiencies are deciduous and evanescent.' (*L8* 316–17) In 1899, five years after Stevenson's death, Schwob's translation of 'Will o' the Mill' finally appeared in *La Vogue*.[35] Two years later, in 1901–02, Schwob made a pilgrimage to Samoa, but was too ill to visit Stevenson's grave; he died, aged 38, in 1905.

3
Forever Scotland

'I am a Scotsman, touch me and you will find the thistle.'[1]

While it is hardly necessary these days to insist upon Stevenson's credentials as a Scottish writer,[2] it is worth recalling that not only his first publication, *The Pentland Rising*[3] (appearing in a limited edition at his father's expense in 1866), but also the books he was working at the time of his death, *Weir of Hermiston* and *St Ives*,[4] were deeply enmeshed in the history and landscape of Scotland. And particularly of Southern Scotland, it might be added, for although Stevenson's fiction ventures into the Scottish Highlands and Islands, and although he proposed to write a history of the Highlands,[5] nevertheless his deepest roots were in the culture and traditions of Presbyterian Lowland Scotland. The most powerful and enduring influences on (or intertexts for) Stevenson's literary life were arguably the Biblical and Covenanting stories he learned first at the knee of his nurse 'Cummy' [Alison Cunningham], and later in the histories of the Covenanters by the likes of Walker, Wodrow and Kirkton.[6] Stevenson himself claimed in a letter to J.M. Barrie that, *pace* the critics who 'know so much better what we are than we do ourselves': 'My style is from the Covenanting writers.' (*L8* 205) To George Saintsbury he wrote of the 'common devotion' he shared with James Hogg, author of *Confessions of a Justified Sinner*, to 'the Covenanting literature – of which I read more when young than you could dream', and of which 'quaint, unwholesome authors' he had gathered 'quite a library' (*L7* 126). In 1868–69, a couple of years or so after the *The Pentland Rising*, and the related fiction[7] he wrote about the same time, Stevenson was planning *A Covenanting Story-Book* which was to comprise up to ten stories, of which perhaps five, including 'The Curate of Anstruther's Bottle, and

'The Devil on Crammond Sands' seem to have been written, but only one, 'The Story of Thrawn Janet', ever published (*L1* 416n; 436n; *S* 6–7). By the time Stevenson finally got round to writing up 'Thrawn Janet' in 1881, the title of the projected collection of stories had changed to *The Black Man and Other Tales*. The 'black man', who intervenes so terrifyingly in 'Thrawn Janet', and appears, rather differently, at the end of 'The Merry Men', is, according to Scottish tradition and especially the 'quaint, unwholesome authors' mentioned above, a manifestation of the devil himself. A story entitled 'The Wreck of the *Susanna*', mentioned in the projected contents of *The Black Man*, is probably an early version of 'The Merry Men'. 'The Body Snatchers', another story planned for the projected collection, was started at this period, and eventually appeared as 'The Body Snatcher' in the *Pall Mall Christmas 'Extra'* of 1884, though not in book form during Stevenson's lifetime. 'Thrawn Janet' and 'The Merry Men' were published in the *Cornhill* in 1881 and 1882 respectively, and, with revisions to 'The Merry Men', in *The Merry Men and Other Tales* in 1887. In the book version of 'The Merry Men', 'the black man' is represented not as a demonic figure (though he does so appear to the narrator's deranged uncle), but as some 'fallen king', the narrator imagines, a noble savage whose dignified silence is sharply contrasted with the 'ranting incongruities' of the 'incurable and dismal lunatic' Uncle Gordon (*T8* 49–50). The narrator says patronizingly of 'the black' (doubtless at some ironical distance from the author): 'Respect came upon me and grew stronger, the more I observed him; I saw he had a powerful mind and a sober and severe character, such as I loved to commune with; and before we reached the house of Aros I had almost forgotten, and wholly forgiven him, his uncanny colour' (*T8* 51). Thus the apparently Other 'really' represents what is rational and universal. In contrast, the truly uncanny is much closer to home; it lurks in the fanaticism of Uncle Gordon, 'plainly bred up in a country place among Cameronians [extreme Covenanters]' (*T8* 11), whose obsession with the sea as 'the muckle yett [gate] to hell', created not by the Lord but by 'the muckle black deil [devil]' (*T8* 14–15), is precisely an obsession with *sin*. 'If it wasna sin, I dinna ken that I would care for 't', he says, as he identifies himself with the destructive ecstasy symbolized by the eponymous "Merry Men": "I'm a deil, I ken't. . . . I'm wi' the sea, I'm just like ane o' her ain Merry Men" ' (*T8* 46). 'The Merry Men' derives in an obvious sense from Stevenson's own family background. 'Aros' is Earraid, 'the islet' later to appear in *Kidnapped*, where Stevenson stayed with his father in 1870 during the construction of the Dhu Heartach lighthouse. 'Aros roost [tidal race]' seems to be based on Sir Walter Scott's descriptions in

Voyage in the Lighthouse Yacht, and also in *The Pirate*, of Sumburgh Roost in the Shetlands which he visited with Stevenson's grandfather Robert Stevenson in 1814. The phrase 'Merry Men' itself appears in a poem quoted by Scott in his introduction to *The Pirate*, where he recalls this tour of the Scottish islands with Robert Stevenson.[8] The tale also derives from a broader and deeper cultural background in which there is an obsession with evil that is characteristic of Presbyterian Lowland Scotland,[9] with the revelation of the uncanny amidst the canniest of peoples.

There is a crucial difference in narrative standpoint between 'The Merry Men' and 'Thrawn Janet'. While the former is narrated by the young Charles Darnaway, like his uncle of 'an unmixed Lowland stock' (*T8* 3), and a student of Edinburgh University at the zenith of the Scottish Enlightenment, the latter tale is told by an unnamed local 'over his third tumbler' (*T8* 110). From the perspective of Charles Darnaway, Uncle Gordon, who 'used to remind me of one of the hill-preachers in the killing times before the Revolution'[10] (*T8* 12), is simply deranged, and projects onto the 'black man' the obsessive fears generated by what Charles considers his fanatical religion (whereas Charles projects onto the 'black man' the fantasies of his own Enlightened religion). By contrast, the narrator of 'Thrawn Janet' is sceptical of the 'college professors' and believes that 'the lads that went to study wi' them wad hae done mair an' better sittin' in a peat-bog, like their forebears of the persecution, wi' a Bible under their oxter [armpit] an' a speerit o' prayer in their heart' (*T8* 111). 'The Merry Men', with its elements of adventure and suspense, is a kind of case history with a secure narrative position outside of the madness it portrays. 'Thrawn Janet', by contrast, sucks the reader into the horror it evokes. Fanny Stevenson recalled how when Louis first read the tale to her in Kinnaird Cottage at Pitlochry in the summer of 1881 it 'sent a "cauld grue [shudder]" along my bones' and 'fairly frightened' Stevenson himself.[11] If Uncle Gordon's demented outburst about 'the horror – the horror o' the sea!' leaves the narrator and his companions 'somewhat staggered' (*T8* 16), in 'Thrawn Janet' we are confronted by 'the Horror' itself, and it is an act of God, rather than any 'book learnin', that saves Mr Soulis. The black man in 'The Merry Men' is a real human being who dies as a result of Uncle Gordon's madness; the Black Man in 'Thrawn Janet' is the devil himself who has taken possession of Janet's corpse, and who goes elsewhere when her corpse is miraculously struck by lightning. Soulis's enlightened treatment of Janet, and his rational explanation of her hideous appearance as the result of a stroke caused by mistreatment by the locals, is shown to be self-deceiving; the superstitious fears of the parishioners of Balweary are vindicated. Enlightened humanistic rationalism never expunged Stevenson's sense of the reality of evil, which he imbibed from his nurse 'Cummy', a Fifer steeped in Covenanting lore. Not only is the Balweary of 'Thrawn Janet' presumably based on the 'ruinous tower of Balwearie' in Fife, home to the magician Michael Scott;[12] there are also some uncanny verbal echoes of the conclusion of 'Thrawn Janet' in the famous stanzas entitled 'Shadow March'[13] published in *A Child's Garden of Verses*, which Stevenson also began to write in the summer of 1881, and dedicated to Alison Cunningham.

The triumph of irrational demonic forces over rational Enlightenment values is also portrayed 'The Body Snatcher', another tale written at Pitlochry in 1881; it was intended for the *Black Man* collection, but only ever appeared in periodical form during Stevenson's lifetime. Like the the story of Thrawn Janet, this is a tale told over a tumbler, by the drunken Scotsman Fettes in the George at Debenham. Fettes has been jolted out of his customary state of 'melancholy alcoholic saturation' (*T11* 183) by the appearance at the inn of Dr. Wolfe Macfarlane, a figure from Fettes's distant past as a medical student in Edinburgh. Macfarlane had been the class assistant of 'Mr. K---', clearly the notorious Robert Knox of the anatomical school at Edinburgh University, and the chief customer of the 'resurrectionists' including Burke and Hare. Fettes's scruples about the murderous origins of the 'subjects' acquired for Mr K--- had been overcome by Macfarlane, who had persuaded Fettes that he was 'a man of the world' with a contempt for 'all cant' such as 'Hell, God, Devil, right, wrong, sin, crime, and all the old gallery of curiosities' (*T11* 200). Such bold talk had, however, been annihilated one terrifying night when the corpse which Fettes and Macfarlane were bringing back to Edinburgh from Glencorse kirkyard was miraculously transformed from the female body they had exhumed, into the body of Gray, an acquaintance, and already 'long-dissected' victim, of Macfarlane. Like Mr Soulis, Fettes never really recovers from his encounter with the supernatural, though there is sense of justice in his chastening which is harder to see in the former case. Fettes is a kind of Deacon Brodie figure,[14] who for his 'unimpeachable eye-service to his employer Mr. K---…indemnified himself by nights of roaring blackguardly enjoyment' (*T11* 189). This doubleness of life, which is even more pronounced in the suave Macfarlane, points forward to Dr Jekyll, who, like Dr Macfarlane, manages to keep up a highly successful front despite his dark and diabolical secret life.

Written in Bournemouth in 1885, in circumstances as open to question as the tale itself,[15] *Strange Case of Dr Jekyll and Mr Hyde* betrays its

Edinburgh origins in both its topography[16] and its atmosphere of medical research in the laboratory and dissecting room. It is also profoundly Scottish in its central themes of doubleness and obsession with evil. Stevenson was aware of the similarity of his own *Jekyll and Hyde* to Hogg's *Confessions of a Justified Sinner*, which he read 'in black, pouring weather on Tweedside' (*L7* 125), probably during his stay in 1882 at Stobo Manse, with its grim churchyard. He speculated in a letter to George Saintsbury that he may perhaps have been told the story of Hogg's *Confessions* as a child (a strange, if apparently not untypical, choice for story-time in the Stevenson nursery). Certainly, he continued, he had been exercised by a similar idea for some time before his reading of Hogg's dark tale for himself 'damped out' his own idea, 'though perhaps unconsciously it came again in a new frm' (*L7* 126). Presumably Stevenson is here referring to *Jekyll and Hyde*, whose genesis, Stevenson himself tells us in 'A Chapter on Dreams', was partly unconscious or, as he puts it, the work of his 'Brownies...who do one-half my work for me while I am fast asleep, and in all human likelihood, do the rest for me as well, when I am wide awake and fondly suppose I do it for myself' (*T30* 50). The idea which Stevenson had being trying for some time to embody in narrative form was 'that strong sense of man's double being which must at time come in upon and overwhelm the mind of every thinking creature'(*T30* 51) – though particularly a mind steeped in the theological tradition running from St. Paul's awareness of 'a different law at work in my body' (Romans 7.23) through Augustine to Calvin and the Calvinist tradition which exerted such a dominant influence on Scottish culture. Justification by grace and faith alone, and not by 'works', and the apparent corollary of Predestination, had been the watchwords of this Calvinist theological tradition, whose distortion led with a terrifying logical precision to the excesses depicted by Hogg in his masterpiece. It is in part this tradition that Stevenson is alluding to when he suggests that, whatever conscious or unconscious influence Hogg's tale may have had on him, he shares with Hogg 'a common devotion to the Covenanting literature' (*L7* 126).

However susceptible *Jekyll and Hyde* may be to a Freudian reading, it can also (and not incompatibly) be read as a kind of theological fable. In Freudian terms, Jekyll's problem is not so much caused by his 'badness' (his Id) as by his excessive desire to be good, his 'imperious desire to carry my head high', to live up to 'the high views that I had set before me' (*T5* 57). This last phrase is ambiguous; who exactly is doing the setting here? Is it Jekyll himself? Or is it some other authority figure, archetypally the Father? Is it the Father *in* Jekyll, i.e. the Superego, as

Freud would say? In classically Freudian terms, the disorder in Henry Jekyll is actually *generated* by a Superego (that is, an internalized Father-figure or conscience) that is overactive and (to use Jekyll's own word) 'exacting' (ibid.). To switch discourses (or myths), Jekyll's problem – like that of Robert Wringhim in Hogg's *Confessions* – is spiritual *pride*, his 'imperious desire to carry my head high'. The fatally split self which is dramatized in *Jekyll and Hyde* is due not so much to some inherent dualism in human nature (for example, between spirit and flesh), as to the repressive action of a spiritual pride which seeks to be more god-like than it is possible for human beings to be. The Original Sin (Jekyll's 'original evil') which dominates Calvinist theology, which in turn dominated Scottish culture for centuries, is precisely spiritual pride. In the Biblical myth of the Fall the serpent tempts Adam and Eve to eat the forbidden fruit by saying: 'You will be like God'. Henry Jekyll's problem is that he wants to be entirely good, and not a mixture of good and evil. But according to Christian teaching: 'There is only One who is good' (Matthew 19:17). The specifically protestant or Calvinist doctrine, classically articulated in the doctrine of the justified sinner, is that human beings are saved by *grace*, not because they are good; they are saved or 'justified' *despite* being sinners, and are therefore *simul justus et peccator* – paradoxically *both* 'justified' *and* sinful. A haunting sense of the danger of forgetting the power and the ineradicable nature of evil pervades *Strange Case of Dr Jekyll and Mr Hyde* as well as the stories intended for *Black Man* collection. This sense of evil as a mystery at once terrifying and fascinating is central to the Covenanting tradition which had been inculcated in Stevenson from childhood, and which, it could be argued, formed the bedrock of his conscious and unconscious life.

Besides the tales of the Covenanting 'martyrs', which obsessed Stevenson from the beginning to the end of his literary life, the other great romance of Scottish history is, in a paradox typical of Scottish culture,[17] that of the Jacobite Rising of 1745. Politically and culturally, Covenanters and Jacobites could hardly be more different – Presbyterian Lowland Whigs versus Gaelic-speaking, Catholic or Episcopalian Highland clans. What the 'wild clans, and hunted Covenanters', as Stevenson put in his essay 'The Foreigner at Home' (*T29* 9), had in common, besides offering resistance to any middle-class accommodation with the status quo as defined by the English establishment, was an ability to split and dislocate the Scottish people and the Scottish psyche. Above all in *Kidnapped* and in *The Master of Ballantrae* Stevenson portrays a Scottish identity divided against itself. In *Kidnapped* particularly there is a literal crossing of the (Highland) line when David Balfour is knocked unconscious and kidnapped from the realm of the Whiggish Southern Scots into the wild country of the Gaelic 'Other'. The novel is on one level the story of David's protracted and dangerous homecoming, though his experiences with Alan Breck Stewart change him so much that, although he does finally come back to Edinburgh, it is not the same David who returns: 'But as I went on my way to the city, I felt so lost and lonesome, that I could have found it in my heart to sit down by the dyke, and cry and weep like any baby.... and when I passed... into the streets of the capital... there was a cold gnawing in my inside like a remorse for something wrong' (*T6* 223). The Gaelic 'Other' has in some sense become part of himself, and to separate from Alan and his world means a painful self-sundering.[18] The sequel to *Kidnapped, Catriona* (or *David Balfour* in the American edition), is in part about David's attempts to come to terms with the Gaelic 'Other' he can no longer live without. Interestingly, however, it was during the writing of this 'continuation of *Kidnapped*' in early 1892 that Stevenson wrote to J.M. Barrie that he was 'pleased to see how the Anglo-Saxon theory fell into the trap: I gave my Lowlander a Gaelic name, and even commented on the fact in the text;[19] yet almost all critics recognised in David and Alan a Saxon and a Celt.... I deny that there exists such a thing as a pure Saxon, and I think it more questionable if there be such a thing a pure Celt. But what have [we] to do with this?... Let us continue to inscribe our little bits of tales...' (*L7* 238–9) Even if, as Graham Balfour pointed out (*B* 281n.), Stevenson was wrong when he claimed in this letter to Barrie, as well as in *Catriona* (*T7* 143), that Gaelic was spoken in Fife up until the mid-eighteenth century, nevertheless the destabilising of mutually exclusive binary opposites proliferates in *Kidnapped*. The Jacobite Alan Breck had fought on the Hanoverian side at Prestonpans; the dour Uncle Ebenezer, canny to the point of miserliness, had in his romantic youth joined the Jacobite rebellion of 1715; and the minister of the Borders parish of Essendean bears the Highland name of Campbell, a name hated in the Highlands for the Campbells' collaboration with the government from the infamous Massacre of Glencoe to the crushing of the rebellion of 'Forty-Five'. If such contradictions create 'a trap' for the binary oppositions of 'Anglo-Saxon theory' (and perhaps anticipate more modern Continental theory with its notions of 'undecidability'), for Stevenson the self-contradictoriness of the Scottish psyche is an inexplicable fact: 'The fact remains: in spite of the difference of blood and language, the Lowlander feels himself the sentimental countryman of the Highlander. When they meet abroad, they fall upon each other's necks in spirit; even at home there is a kind of clannish intimacy in their talk' (*T29* 11).

Inexplicable as this fact ultimately may be, perhaps the 'little bits of tales' inscribed by Scott above all, but also by Stevenson himself, may have had some share in producing the historical and cultural paradoxes which characterize Scottish identity.

It is the murder of one of the much-hated collaborating Campbells which forms the centre of *Kidnapped*. Stevenson had been planning to write something on the murder of 'Red' Colin Campbell of Glenure on 14 May 1752, at least since early November 1881, when he wrote from Davos to his father asking for records of the trial of James Stewart ('James of the Glens') for the so-called 'Appin Murder'. The rudiments of the famous case were in Scott's Introduction to *Rob Roy*: 'A remarkable Highland story must here be alluded to. Mr. Campbell of Glenure, who had been named factor [steward] for Government on the forfeited estates of Stewart of Ardshiel, was shot dead by an assassin as he passed throught the wood of Lettermore, after crossing the ferry of Ballichulish'.[20] This murder, which David Balfour accidentally witnesses,[21] thus unwittingly becoming the accomplice of the chief suspect, Alan Breck, forms the core of *Kidnapped*. However, Scott was less interested in the murder itself (Stevenson later commented: 'Why Scott let it escape him I do not know' (*L5* 187)) than in the role played by Rob Roy's son, James Mohr (or More) Drummond, in the Campbells' designs to take vengeance not only on the unjustly accused James of the Glens, but also on Alan Breck Stewart, 'supposed to be the actual homicide'. This latter material forms the basis of *Catriona*, though by the time Stevenson finally wrote it up in Samoa in 1892, it was handled rather differently than in the pacy adventure yarn *Kidnapped*. In *Catriona*, the historical material becomes pretext for, and background to, other interests, both romantic and political.

The audience Stevenson had in mind when he originally planned to write up Scott's 'remakable Highland story', or what he himself described in a letter to Gosse in 1881 as 'an odd little historical bypath of a tragedy: very picturesque in its circumstances; a story of an agrarian murder, complicated with fidelity to chiefs, clan hatreds, an unjust trial...' (*L3* 248–9), is not entirely clear. A letter to his father in November 1881 suggests that Stevenson may have seen the projected article as connected with his campaign to secure the chair of History and Constitutional Law at Edinburgh University. This unlikely campaign, which was conducted on his behalf by his father in Edinburgh while Stevenson returned to Davos, depended largely on the Stevensons assembling an impressive array of testimonials (or what Stevenson called with jokey embarrassment 'antimonials) from as many of 'the great and the good', and, on the advice of Fleeming Jenkin, as many of the *English* 'great and good', as possible. 'Now I *only* know' Stevenson wrote to Colvin, practically giving a *Who's Who* of Victorian literati, '[Leslie] Stephen, [John Addington] Symonds, [Andrew] Lang, [Edmund] Gosse and you, and [George] Meredith, to be sure.... The chair is in the gift of the Faculty of Advocates, where I am more wondered at than loved' (*L3* 197; italics added). Although Thomas Stevenson had the collected testimonials printed as a pamphlet (*L3* 242), the Faculty of Advocates was unimpressed, and only nine out of a hundred odd voted for Stevenson. In late 1881 Gosse seemed to offer the possibility of a different home for the proposed article, 'The Murder of Red Colin: a Story of "the Forfeited Estates"', in the *Century Magazine*;[22] and in June 1882 Stevenson wrote to Gosse that, during a trip into the Highlands with his father, he had 'visited my murder place and found *living traditions* not yet in any printed book; most startling' (*L3* 335). Nothing came of the proposed article, however, and it was not until March 1885, in Bournemouth, that the Appin Murder story emerged again, though this time with a very different audience in mind than the Faculty of Advocates at Edinburgh University. Stevenson wrote to Henley: 'I have a great story on hand; boy's story: a crackler; very picturesque I think.... I have proposed to Henderson to print from the sheets and to let the book appear when it is about half way through.' (*L5* 89) Stevenson was hoping to repeat the modest successes of *Treasure Island* and *The Black Arrow*, which had appeared in James Henderson's *Young Folks* in 1881–82 and 1883 respectively. Henderson (a Scot himself) accepted the new story, at fifteen shillings per column, with the proviso that Stevenson should avoid having 'much broad Scotch in it...a little of that goes a long way with our readers' (*S* 104). Although Stevenson would claim, when trying to sell his manuscript to Scribner's for American publication, that 'the Scotch is kept as low as possible' (*L5* 179), he took a rather different tack when writing in February 1886 to seek Charles Baxter's permission to dedicate the book version of *Kidnapped* to him: 'What's mair, Sir, it's Scotch: no strong, for the sake o' they pock-puddens [English], but jist a kitchen [condiment] o't, to leeven the wersh [insipid], sapless, fushionless [useless], stotty [stumbling], stytering [faltering] South-Scotch they think sae muckle o'' (*L5* 206).

In fact there are three languages in *Kidnapped* (four if you count Rankeillor's addiction to Latin tags): Scots, English and Gaelic. David's ignorance of the latter is total; he was unaware, he tells the reader, of his exclusion from the Gaelic song which Alan composed to celebrate 'his' victory in the round-house (*T6* 68). Later, when the fishermen return to Earraid to relieve David of his 'pitiful illusion' that he is a cast-away and that their previous neglect of him was due to their 'wickedness' (rather than to his stupidity in not realizing that Earraid is a tidal island), there is a tragi-comic sequence in which it transpires that not only is David unable to understand Gaelic, he is unable even to understand the attempts of Gaelic-speakers at English:

> Then he stood up in the boat and addressed me a long while, speaking fast and with many wavings of his hand. I told him I had no Gaelic; and at this he became very angry, and I began to suspect that he thought he was talking English. Listening very close, I caught the word "whateffer" several times; but all the rest was Gaelic and might have been Greek and Hebrew for me (*T6* 97).

David's cultural arrogance is only sufferable because of the ironic distance allowed by the retrospective narration. Similarly, in his account of how he felt impelled in Cluny's Cage to 'bear a testimony' against the proposed game of cards, a wiser narrator-David concedes: 'indeed it must be owned that both my scruples and the words in which I declared them, smacked somewhat of the Covenanter, and were little in their place among wild Highland Jacobites' (*T6* 163–4). Cluny's response to David's ignorance of the Gaelic culture and language is pointed: ' "Your name [Balfour] has more sense than yourself, then, for it's good Gaelic." ' (*T6* 166).

During his Highland wanderings David begins to weary for the sound of 'the broad south-country tongue' (*T6* 110), and in Morven is delighted to come across Mr. Henderland, a catechist 'şent out by the Edinburgh Society for Propagating Christian Knowledge, to evangelise the more savage places of the Highlands' (ibid.). Henderland, a character Stevenson probably introduced to please his father (*L5* 182), happens to be using pious works translated into the Gaelic by David's old friend Mr Campbell of Essendean. This detail may be anachronistic, however, because, in a act of cultural exclusion characteristic of eighteenth century Whiggism, the use of Gaelic was officially banned by the Society until 1766.[23] Between Scotch and English, David makes a clear distinction, as, for example, when he says of that 'dreadful sense of illness' he experiences on Earraid that 'we have no name for it either in Scotch or English' (*T6* 96). He is amazed when, uncomfortably close to a Redcoat, he hears for the first time what he calls 'the right English speech', evidently cockney, with its 'clipping tones and the odd sing-song . . . and that strange trick of dropping the letter "h" ' (*T6* 141). With respect to both the English accent and 'the English grammar', David rather defensively claims that he has 'never grown used to it ... as perhaps a very critical eye might here and there spy out even in these memoirs' (*T6* 141–2). Stevenson's mock defensiveness is undermined, however, by an irony of publishing history. According to Barry Menikoff, what Stevenson originally wrote in the holograph of *Kidnapped*, now in the Huntington Library in California, was: 'indeed I have never grown used *with* it' (italics mine),[24] a perfectly acceptable *Scots* expression, but one which the English publishing process eliminated from the text. Menikoff argues that 'from simple misreadings to deliberate revisions, from small changes in vocabulary to the elimination or recasting of sentences, the printed editions [of *Kidnapped*] represent major departures from Stevenson's handwritten text. The changes bore particularly on his deliberate and pervasive use of Scots.'[25] Compositors and proof-readers notwithstanding, Stevenson was able on the whole to make good his claim to Charles Baxter that *Kidnapped* was 'Scotch', though what is perhaps most characteristic of the novel is the flexibility of the language deployed. Like his creator, Alan is a master of words: a poet in his native Gaelic, and presumably fluent in French (if Stevenson does not explicitly tell us this, Scott does[26]), he can modulate his Scotch from the very broad, as when he is coaxing young Alison Hastie in Limekilns to procure a boat, to the anglicised formality of his threateningly quiet rejoinders to David at the height of the quarrel scene (*T6* 176). Like James Durie in *The Master of Ballantrae*, Alan Breck can convincingly appear all things to all people (although, in contrast to Durie, it is always clear where his heart is). David, on the other hand, due partly to youth and partly to his countrified Whiggishness, is inflexible and incapable of appearing other than he is. His all-too-transparent attempt at hedging his bets when he first meets 'the Jacobite' only earns him the nickname 'Mr. Betwixt-and-Between'; and 'that's naething,' comments Alan (*T6* 58).

To many a Highland Scot less reckless than Alan Breck Stewart, the dismissive nickname he gives David does precisely sum up their position. Charles Stewart, the Edinburgh lawyer who is the exiled Appin's agent, replies as follows to David's boast of being 'as big a Whig as grows':

"My case is dooms hard. See, sir, ye tell me ye're a Whig: I wonder what I am. No Whig to be sure; I couldnae be just that. But – laigh in your ear, man – I'm maybe no very keen on the other side. ... For my private part I have no particular desire to harm King George; and as for King James, God bless him! He does very well for me across the water. I'm a lawyer, ye see: fond of my books and my bottle, a good plea, a well-drawn deed, a crack [gossip] in the Parliament House with other lawyer bodies, and perhaps a turn at the golf on a Saturday at e'en. Where do ye come in with your Hieland plaids and claymores?" (*T7* 17–18).

Here in *Catriona* we are in different world from that of *Kidnapped*. The world of Charles Stewart is recognizably modern and, like the hero of a story that has become more of a *Bildungsroman* than an adventure yarn, increasingly grown-up. It is not just that, after 'some five years in the British Linen Company's office' (where *Kidnapped* ends and its sequel begins), David 'seems to have changed his style', as Stevenson wrote to Colvin in early 1892 (*L7* 246, 241). Whereas in *Kidnapped* the politics are there as a context for adventure and what Stevenson called 'romance',[27] in *Catriona* Stevenson is much more concerned with the reality of politics, and with 'romance' in the more modern sense of 'love interest'. It is almost as if, to put it in psychoanalytical terms, the action has moved from the realm of 'the Imaginary', with its archaic and archetypal struggles over ego-identity (it has often been noted that there is something 'mythic' about the action in *Kidnapped* as well as in *Treasure Island* and *Strange Case of Dr Jekyll and Mr Hyde*), into the so-called 'Symbolic Order' where 'subjects' are shuttled around in accordance with 'desire' and 'the Law of the Father' (it is noteworthy how much in *Catriona* depends on the circulation of *letters*[28]). Prestongrange eminently embodies Lacan's *Nom du Père*, with the first (and more substantial) part of *Catriona* being named 'The Lord Advocate' after the figure who dominates it. David's having to accept the necessity of James of the Glens's execution might be seen to symbolize his acceptance of a kind of castration, or power-lessness, which will secure him entry into the world of the Law, in a literal as well as a symbolic sense. Only by compromising with the practically absolute power of Prestongrange, mediated through the sweet offices of Barbara Grant and the murderous offices of Simon Fraser, does David finally attain the object of his desire, Catriona.

Catriona is also authorized by another father-figure, Alan Breck, who tells her at the end of the novel: 'If ever I was to get married, it's the marrow of you I would be seeking for a mother to my sons' (*T7* 287). In one of his intermittent appearances in *Catriona*, Alan feels called upon to initiate David into the skills, already crucially deployed at Limekilns, of charming the ladies. Stevenson mocks (doubtless too gently for modern tastes) Alan's patronisingly patriarchal advice: 'A man should aye give put his best foot forrit with the womankind; he should aye give them a bit of a story to divert them, the poor lambs! It's what ye should learn to attend to, David; ye should get the principles, it's like a trade' (*T7* 104). If Alan's charm again saves the fugitives from real danger, nevertheless this scene, and indeed the novel as a whole, has a comic aspect, as its conclusion makes clear (*T7* 292). This is far removed from the more tragic atmosphere of *The Master of Ballantrae*, and James Durie's sinister boast: 'I never yet failed to charm a person when I wanted' (*T10* 176). In the figure of James More, Catriona's father, the Gaelic charm is certainly dangerous, but not so much sinister as nauseating. David sees through the manipulative 'professional Highlander', and comments: 'I would hearken to this swaggering talk (of arms, and "an old soldier," and "a poor Highland gentleman," and "the strength of my country and my friends") as I might to the babbling of a parrot' (*T7* 247–8). In More's sentimentalizing renditions into English of the 'melancholy airs of my native land', Stevenson parodies the exploitation of 'the Celtic heritage':

"It says here," [More] would say, "that the sun is gone down, and the battle is at an end, and the brave chiefs are defeated. And it tells here how the stars see them fleeing into strange countries or lying dead on the red mountains: and they will never more shout the call of battle or wash their feet in the streams of the valley. But if you had only some of this language, you would weep also because the words of it are beyond all expression, and it is a mere mockery to tell it in English" (*T7* 248).

The death of James More is narrated by David with undisguised impatience (in contrast to Scott's account of the same material in his Introduction to *Rob Roy*, where he solicits the reader's compassion, if not sympathy, for More[29]). By the time Stevenson drew on the same Scottish heritage as Scott, it had already become part of the heritage industry which Scott had a large hand in creating (though even in Scott's first novel *Waverley* it was, so to speak, always already ironised). However, despite his awareness of the dangers of too close a proximity to the Scottish heritage industry, Stevenson does sail pretty close to the wind in his presentation of Catriona's pseudo-Highland English which, as one contemporary reviewer put it, does 'rather irritatingly' remind us of those literary examples of picturesque Highland English that 'have at last become woefully hackneyed'.[30]

   The fate of James of the Glens (or, more accurately, the affect of James's fate on David's conscience and self-esteem), which had dominated the earlier chapters, is allocated only a couple of paragraphs in the chapter entitled 'I continue to move in good society'. Before continuing with his own story, David sententiously observes:

> He had been hanged by fraud and violence, and the world wagged along, and there was not a pennyweight of difference; and the villains of that horrid plot were decent, kind, respectable fathers of families, who went to kirk and took the sacrament (*T7* 188).

As the progress of Master David in this *Bildungsroman* proceeds apace, the 'Gaelic Other' which had acquired such a presence in *Kidnapped* diminishes – though not without a final hopeless fight. In a shift of character which destabilizes any easy stereotyping, the jaundiced lawyer Charles Stewart forgets his customary cynicism when David unexpectedly turns up at James's trial in Inverary. 'Leaping with excitement', Stewart shouts: ' "we'll ding the Campbells yet in their own town".' (*T7* 148) David realizes that 'this, that had the externals of a sober process of law, was in essence a clan battle between savage clans. I thought my friend the Writer [Charles Stewart] none of the least savage. Who, that had only seen him at a counsel's back before the Lord Ordinary, or following a golf ball...on Bruntsfield links, could have recognized for the same person this voluble and violent clansman?' (*T7* 149) Prestongrange himself, like the Duke of Argyle, is a Highlander. As he tells David: 'The Duke and I are Highlanders. But we are Highlanders civilised, and it is not so with great mass of our clans and families. They have still savage virtues and defects. They are still barbarians, like these Stewarts; only the Campbells were barbarians on the right side, and the Stewarts were barbarians on the wrong' (*T7* 37). If David, as the representative Lowland Scot, is in *Kidnapped* all but overwhelmed by the savagery of the Highland people and terrain, the plot of *Catriona* moves towards the reconciliation of the 'most uneven pair' of the Highland girl and the Low Country boy (*T7* 223). This reconciliation is more of an assimilation, however, as Catriona is married into the House of Shaws. Almost the only remaining trace of the Highland 'Other' in this 'good Whig house' is the late night visit of Chevalier (Alan Breck) Stewart, alias 'Mr. Jamieson', to lead the young Balfour named after him into mischief by 'drinking the king's health *across the water*' (*T7* 291).

The issue of the assimilation, or 'civilization', of 'savage' clans, though pertaining to Scottish history, was also highly relevant to Samoa at the time Stevenson was writing *Catriona* there, very much the laird (like David Balfour of Shaws) finally arrived in his own 'policies' (or estates) at Vailima. Indeed the writing of *Catriona* literally overlapped with

Stevenson's writing of *A Footnote to History*, a brief contemporary history of Samoan politics. Fanny, who claimed she had persuaded Louis to write *A Footnote to History* rather than embarking on the 'book, for boys, on Scotch history'(*S* 162) which he preferred to write, claims in her Prefatory Note to *Catriona* that, though it might seem a far cry from Samoa to Scotland, 'in many ways one recalled the other' (*T7* xvi). Reminiscent of Scotland was not just (occasionally) the weather, and the scenery, but also the clan system, especially in time of war; she sums up: 'In times not so remote affairs were so ordered in the Highlands of Scotland' (*T7* xvii). And it was during a time of war, or at least of rumours of war, in Samoa that Stevenson wrote *Catriona*. Emma Letley stresses the relevance of the Samoan context to our understanding of *Catriona*, claiming that even the 'Tale of Tod Lapraik', although it is strongly Scottish both in language and setting, can be connected with Stevenson's observation in *A Footnote to History* that at times of political instability: 'a sudden crop of superstitious stories buzzed about the islands' (*T21* 216).[31] The injustice of James of the Glens's trial and execution is a reflection of the injustice and corruption of the colonial system which Stevenson experienced at first hand in Samoa, Letley argues.[32] But whatever Stevenson's commitment to 'the right side' in the context of Samoan politics, it did not prevent him from 'lairding it' at Vailima. There is more than one irony in the letter he sent to Charles Baxter in September 1892 announcing that the end of *David [Balfour]* (as he always referred to the sequel to *Kidnapped*) 'should come in the next mail'. After his reference to the novel's end, with David idyllically settled in the (presumably much improved) House of Shaws, Stevenson goes on to talk about the 'possible heavy expense' of 'the new wing at Abbotsford'[33] (*L7* 377) – though Stevenson more usually referred to Vailima as 'Subpriorsford', a subprior being two down from an abbot (*L7* 249).

It is perhaps significant that when Stevenson wrote in *Kidnapped* about the unhoused wanderings of the boy David, he himself was in Bournemouth, stuck 'like a weevil in a biscuit' (*L7* 280) in what was not really his own house (Thomas Stevenson having gifted the house to Fanny as a way of keeping some kind of rein on Louis). In contrast, the classically happy ending of *Catriona*, which sees David established as the Laird of Shaws, may reflect Stevenson's own position once he had come into his inheritance and had settled, his wanderings over, in 'Subpriorsford'. These issues of inheritance, and of foiled circuitous wandering as opposed to the settled enjoyment of an estate, lie at the heart of another novel Stevenson set amid the upheaval of post-1745 Scotland.

The Master of Ballantrae was written in the years 1887–89, between *Kidnapped* and *Catriona*. Despite being, as Stevenson put in his dedication to Sir Percy and Lady Shelley, 'a tale which extends over many years and travels into many countries' (from India to the North American wilderness), and a tale written 'among distant and diverse scenes' (from the North American wilderness to Honolulu) (*T10* xxvii), *The Master of Ballantrae* has Scotland at its heart not only in terms of its plot, but also in terms of the themes it explores. While the sprawling structure of *The Master of Ballantrae* derives from Stevenson's re-reading of Marryat's *The Phantom Ship* at Saranac Lake in the Adirondacks in October 1887, the supernatural element in Marryat's novel also resonated with Stevenson's own fascination with the powers of darkness. The Scottish obsession with the Devil or the 'black man', which had manifested itself in Stevenson's projected *Black Man* collection, appears also in *The Master of Ballantrae*. Indeed the latter was originally conceived in the summer of 1881 (when Stevenson wrote 'Thrawn Janet', 'The Merry Men' and 'The Body Snatcher') 'on the moors between Pitlochry and Strathardle, conceived in the Highland rain, in the blend of the smell of heather and bog-plants, and with a mind full of the Athole correspondence and the memories of the Chevalier de Johnstone' (*T10* xxiv). The 'Athole correspondence' concerns the sons of the Duke of Atholl who, like the Durie brothers, took opposite sides at the 1745 rebellion; Chevalier de Johnstone was the aide-de-camp of Lord George Murray, the youngest of the Atholl brothers, and the Young Pretender's leading general in 1745. It was nine years before this material was assimilated to another idea which had been preoccupying Stevenson, 'the singular case of a buried and resuscitated fakir' (*T10* xxiii), as told to him by his uncle Dr John Balfour, who been in Delhi at the time of the Indian Mutiny. The villain of *The Master of Ballantrae*, the Master himself, who is presented in Ephraim Mackellar's narrative as the Devil incarnate, has acquired during his stay in India his own 'black man', Secundra Dass. Although in the remote and superstitious house of Durriseer the Indian is predictably called 'the black man' (*T10* 143), and although his attempt to teach the Master to fake his own death by swallowing his tongue may be rather shocking by Western standards, there is nothing supernatural about him; in that sense he is like the black man in 'The Merry Men'. The 'black man' in the sense of a diabolical or uncanny figure is 'the Master' himself – at least as he appears in Mackellar's narrative, ranging from his sublime entrance to Durrisdeer: 'He had all the gravity and something of the spendour of Satan in the *Paradise Lost*' (*T10* 144), to his youthful practical jokes at the expense of a neighbour: 'A fine employ it was; chapping at the man's door, and crying 'boo' in his lum, and puttin' poother in his fire, and pee-oys [fireworks] in his window; till the man thocht it was Auld Hornie was come seekin' him' (*T10* 16–17).

There has been some critical discussion of exactly how unreliable Mackellar's narrative is in its treatment of James Durie. Douglas Gifford's contention that Mackellar's narrative is an example of the Scottish tradition of dramatic monologue (for example Burns's 'Holy Willie's Prayer' and the 'Sinner's Account' in Hogg's *Confessions of a Justified Sinner*)[34] does not avail itself of Stevenson's own appropriation of the term in his 'Note to *The Master of Ballantrae*'. The uses Stevenson sees in Mackellar's 'dramatic monologue', including the introduction of 'a certain subdued element of comedy',[35] do not include the problematization (which Gifford argues for) of Mackellar's interpretation of James as diabolical. Indeed – to trust the teller – Stevenson himself was apparently quite serious about the devil in the Master when he wrote to Colvin in December 1887: 'the Master is all I know of the devil; I have known hints of him, in the world, but always cowards; he is bold as a lion, but with the same deadly, causeless duplicity...' (*L6* 87) It is the alleged causelessness (questioned by Gifford) of James's duplicity which marks him out from, for example, Alan Breck. Alan appears briefly in *The Master of Ballantrae* in a quarrel scene with the Master, when the latter flees from him, not from any cowardice, Durie later claims in a plausible if typically ambiguous piece of reasoning, but because it is a more effective way of keeping secret the fact that he had survived Culloden (*T10* 29–31). Whereas Alan can skilfully *deploy* a variety of masks, secure in his own identity and in the knowledge that 'Mr. Betwixt-and-Between' is 'naething', Mackellar suspects that the Master *is* only a series of masks, with literally nothing behind 'the veneer of his fine manners':

> Sometimes my gorge rose against him as though he were deformed – and sometimes I would draw away as though from something partly spectral. I had moments when I thought of him as of a man of pasteboard – as though, if one should strike smartly through the buckram of his countenance, there would be found a mere vacuity within. This horror (not merely fanciful, I think), vastly in creased my detestation of his neighbourhood; I began to feel something shiver within me on his drawing near.... (*T10* 162–3)

The horror which with Mackellar recoils from the Master recalls the reaction of the other characters to Mr Hyde in *Strange Case of Dr Jekyll and Mr Hyde*, and to Robert Wringham and Gil-Martin in *Confessions of a Justified Sinner.* This sense of uncanny horror at the presence of the Devil, and the theme of the double (Henry and James are clearly 'doubled' in a way which, with its sense of mutual contamination, parallels Jekyll and Hyde, and Wringham and Gil-Martin), places *The Master of Ballantrae* in a particular tradition of the Uncanny in Scottish literature. Yet it may also stand, Douglas Gifford has argued, in another tradition, that of the 'reversible interpretation' characteristic of Presbyterian and Puritan literature; this tradition would include 'Tam o' Shanter', *The Scarlet Letter, Moby-Dick*, and *The Portrait of a Lady*, and arguably would reach its most characteristic expression, though Gifford does not mention this, in *The Turn of the Screw.*[36] Whether or not *The Master of Ballantrae* is susceptible to mutually exclusive interpretations, Mackellar's version (replete with traditional Scottish horrors and pieties) is perhaps finally less disturbing than another version which finds behind the play of masks – just nothing. Andrew Lang's detection of the 'very modern gloom' at the heart of 'this remarkable, elaborate, melancholy, and almost hopeless book' (*M* 162) does point forward to the possibility of existentialist and perhaps 'postmodernist' readings of the text. Roderick Watson, who quotes Lang's unsigned review, offers a reading of *The Master of Ballantrae* as:

> a subversion of romance, a dark revision of Scott, and a left-handed reappraisal of both the territory and the imaginative resources which had been so successfully deployed in *Treasure Island and Kidnapped.*... Mackellor...suspects the Master of Satanic powers. At least there would be *some* sort of order to the tale if James can be seen as a follower of evil.... But the randomness of the coin is the true symbol of James's condition. As a marker of the ultimate indifference of the universe the spinning coin stands at the heart of this tale of causeless fraternal enmity, and in the end it subverts all romance.... It is not just the family crest which has a blank space at the core of its being.[37]

If there had always been an existentially dark undercurrent to Stevenson's work, it had previously emerged in the form of a kind of dark anarchic farce. Notwithstanding the 'subdued element of comedy' provided by Mackellar, *The Master of Ballantrae* approximates more to the tragic. What in the late 1880s may have caused Stevenson to make this dark subversion of romance is not obvious. Perhaps it was an awareness that the new-found freedom he had acquired with his father's death depended precisely on his father's death. The description of the death of the old lord Durrisdeer is hard to keep separate from our knowledge that Stevenson's father had died in not dissimilar circumstances not long before Louis began writing *The Master of Ballantrae*. However, the death of old lord Durrisdeer – 'to the end he managed to discover something of his former courtesy and kindness, pressing the hand of any that helped him ... and in a thousand ways reminding us of the greatness of that loss which it might almost be said we had already suffered' (*T10* 122–3) – is perhaps more the end Louis Stevenson would have wished for his father than the reality of the sporadically aggressive and ultimately uncomprehending dementia into which Thomas Stevenson sank. Writing in April 1886 from Smedley's Hydropathic, Matlock Bridge, where he had taken his father, Louis, who was far from well himself, complained to his mother of 'a full dose of Hyde' at breakfast (*L5* 245–6). Louis's final encounter with his father, when he and Fanny were summoned to the deathbed in Edinburgh in May 1887, is summed up in the last line of his poem 'The Last Sight': 'And the dread changeling gazed on me in vain' (*T22* 167). Louis was too unwell to attend his father's funeral, and was only able to welcome the mourners at the family home in Heriot Row. He offered his considered reaction to his father's death in a letter of late May 1887 to Colvin:

> About the death, I have long hesitated, I was long before I could tell my mind; and now I know it and can say that I am glad. If we could have had my father, that would have been a different thing. But to keep that changeling – suffering changeling, any longer, could better none and nothing. Now he rests; it is more significant, it is more like himself; he will begin to return to us in the course of time as he was and as we loved him (*L5* 411).

Of Henry's reaction to his father's death, Stevenson/Mackellar writes: 'He was becomingly grave; I could scarce say sorrowful, or only with a pleasant sorrow; talking of the dead with a regretful cheerfulness, relating old examples of his character, smiling at them with a good conscience; and when the day of the funeral came round, doing the honours with exact propiety. I could perceive, besides, that he found a solid gratification in his accession to the title' (*T10* 124). In his account of the genesis of *The Master of Ballantrae* Stevenson identifies himself with the Master, claiming that: 'for the Master I had no original, which is perhaps another way of confessing that the original was no other than myself'; and he distances himself from Henry by saying that: 'I have been at school and college with Mackellar and with Henry'.[38] We might wonder, however, whether, especially given the ultimate identity-in-difference of James and Henry consummated in death, there was perhaps rather more of Louis Stevenson in Henry Durie than he cared to acknowledge.

The problematic relations between sons and fathers (or father-figures), which are especially evident in *The Master of Ballantrae* and *Catriona*, emerge again in what is often claimed as Stevenson's unfinished masterpiece, *Weir of Hermiston*. In fact, at the end of his life Stevenson was working simultaneously on four novels set mainly in Scotland, none of which was completed. In a letter to J.M. Barrie in March 1894 Stevenson reported on the progress to date of each of this 'Scotch' quartet which comprised: *Weir of Hermiston*; *The Young Chevalier*; *Heathercat*; and *St Ives* (*L8* 259). Stevenson himself did not rate *St Ives* highly, referring to it in the same letter to Barrie as: 'a mere story: to tickle gudgeons and make money for a harmless fambly' (ibid.). The Scottish setting of *St Ives* is mainly there to provide local colour for an adventure yarn which, according to Louis in a letter of June 1894 to his cousin Bob, 'is nothing – it is in no style, in particular, a tissue of adventures, the central character not very well done, no philosophic pith under the yarn, and in short, if people will read it that's all I ask – and if they won't, damn them! I like doing it, though; . . . After that I am on *Weir of Hermiston* and *Heathercat*, two Scotch stories, which will either be something different or I shall have failed' (*L8* 306). Despite Stevenson's diffidence, *St Ives* does have its moments. Chapter Ten, entitled 'The Drovers' describes St Ives's escape from the henhouse at Stevenson's beloved Swanston via the Borders to England, in the company of two drovers Candlish and Sim and their dogs, 'beautiful, indefatigable beings' with whom St Ives would rather claim kinship than with their masters (*T15* 90). This chapter is notable for its rendition of the drovers' broad Scots, for example when (sounding just like Charles Baxter's and Stevenson's personae of 'Johnstone and Thompson') Sim comments: 'that for "a rale, auld stench bitch, there was nae the bate of Candlish in braid Scotland" '. (ibid.) It also includes a meeting with 'the Shirra' or Sherriff who, as everybody except St Ives knows, is Sir Walter Scott. In a playful piece of intertextuality, Stevenson recounts how Scott tells St Ives a story relating to a ruin they happen to pass, a story which years later ('after the great man had already succumbed under the load of his honours and misfortunes') St Ives recognizes in one of the Waverley novels (*T15* 86). Of the four Scottish stories Stevenson was working on at the time of his death, *St Ives* came closest to completion, close enough to tempt Stevenson's literary executor Colvin to commission a completion by another hand. After Arthur Conan Doyle had declined the commission, it passed to Arthur Quiller-Couch, whose ending became the accepted version and appeared in many editions of the novel. However, in an edition of *St Ives* published in 1990,[39] Jenni Calder, prompted by the research of R.J. Storey, claimed that Quiller-Couch's ending misrepresents Stevenson's intentions. These included an episode in which St Ives's attempt to escape from Scotland in a balloon comes to grief off the West Coast of Scotland (and not in the English Channel, as Quiller-Couch implausibly has it); and in which St Ives becomes involved in a raid by an American privateer on the town of Bowmore on the isle of Islay. Quiller-Couch appears to have been ignorant of hostile activities by American privateers in the years 1812–14. Stevenson was not, as is indicated by a reference in *Records of a Family of Engineers* (*T19* 188–9); the context of this reference is a voyage made by Robert Stevenson in 1813, the year before his voyage with Walter Scott during which an American cruiser was again sighted, as Scott recorded in the introduction to *The Pirate*.[40] Calder provides an ending to *St Ives* closer to Stevenson's intentions, and which restores a significant Scottish dimension to the novel.

The Young Chevalier was left the least complete of the Scottish novels Stevenson was working on at the time of his death. Based on an idea suggested to him by Andrew Lang, it was to have narrated the adventures of the Young Pretender, starting from Avignon in 1749. It involved the recycling of some old Stevenson favourites such as Alan Breck, returning to Scotland on a quest for buried treasure, and the Master of Ballantrae. The latter has a substantial part in the existing fragment, including a characteristically entertaining and ambiguous aside on the crucial role played by his mole in his sexual conquests: ' "The height of beauty is in the touch that's wrong, that's the modulation in a tune. 'Tis the devil we all love; I owe many a conquest to my mole" ' (*T16* 175). Talking of the devil, Stevenson's predilection for introducing characters from previous stories is apparent also in *Heathercat*, where, thirty years before the events recounted in 'Thrawn Janet', Janet M'Clour is observed by young Francie Traquair, nicknamed 'Heathercat' for his skill in fulfilling secret missions for his Covenanting mother, in the act of 'drinking of the bottle, and daffing and laughing together' with the infamous Episcopalian curate 'Hell' Haddo (*T16* 147–50). Haddo is confronted over his alleged misconduct with Janet by M'Brair, a 'forfeited' Covenanting minister, in the same Balweary manse that was to be the setting for the Reverend Soulis's terrifying experiences. *Heathercat*, wrote Stevenson in June 1894 to his cousin Bob, 'is an attempt at a real historical novel to present a whole field of time; the race – our own race – the west land and Clydesdale blue bonnets... I was going to call it *The Killing Time*, but this man Crockett has forestalled me in that. All my weary reading as boy, which you will remember well enough, will come to bear on it' (*L8* 306). The reference is to S.R. Crockett's Covenanting novel *The Men of the Moss Hags*, whose original title had been *The Killing Time*. Stevenson had written to Crockett in May 1894 trying to warn him off: 'I say, if you're on the Covenanting racket, let the wheels of your chariot move a little slowly for pity's sake! Is it the Cameronians you're after? It is a fine subject but give unto the flying hart, time to breathe how short so ever' (*L8* 286, n.5) This is followed by a mock 'No Trespassing' sign which reads:

This is to give
Notice
that the United Societies
[the Cameronians]
is Reserved Strictly
R.L.S.

In the same letter Stevenson made reference to the run-in he had had with Crockett, whom he told he was 'very angry' over the publicity Crockett had derived (without Stevenson's permission) from the encouraging letter Stevenson had sent him in August 1893 about his book *The Stickit Minister* (1893). This letter had contained, in response to Crockett's dedication of his book to Stevenson, the famous poem beginning:

Blows the wind to-day, and the sun and the rain are flying,
Blows the wind on the moors to-day and now,
Where about the graves of the martyrs the whaups are crying,
My heart remembers now!

Crockett had written in the dedication of *The Stickit Minister*: 'To/Robert Louis Stevenson/of Scotland and Samoa,/I dedicate these stories/of the grey Galloway hills,/where, about the graves of the martyrs,/the whaups are crying – /his heart has not forgotten how' (*L8* 153 n.2). These words, Stevenson told Colvin, 'brought the tears to my eyes every time I looked at them. . . . Singular that I should fulfil the Scots Destiny throughout, and live a voluntary exile, and have my head filled with the blessed, beastly place all the time!'(*L8* 159).

Such an approximation to sentimentality on Stevenson's part raises the question of his relation to the so-called 'Kailyard School' of Barrie,

Crockett and Ian Maclaren.[41] In the letter of August 1893, containing the celebrated lines in response to Crockett's dedication, Stevenson compared himself to both Crockett and Barrie. Two stories in *The Stickit Minister* are, he said, *'drowned* in Scotland, they have refreshed me like a visit home.... I am, by many directions, sib to your volume' (*L8* 153). From Crockett's first page, wrote Stevenson, 'with the Stickit Minister ploughing, I knew I was in Scotland', and 'I knew I was not with Gavin Ogilvy [Barrie]', he added (ibid.). According to Stevenson, Barrie had little talent for 'out-of-doors' and 'scenery and atmosphere'; his skill lay rather in scenes 'within doors'. As Stevenson insisted to Crockett: 'You could die (and I think all the rest of us might be hanged) ere we could write the inimitable tragedy called 'The Glove' in the *Window* [*in Thrums*]. That is great literature' (ibid.). In a letter to Barrie of December 1892, in which he defended himself against Barrie's accusation, made under the pseudonym of Gavin Ogilvy, that Stevenson displayed 'no deep knowledge' of Scotland and Scottish religion,[42] Stevenson again praised Barrie's work in *A Window in Thrums* and *The Little Minister*, and claimed, showing some 'anxiety of influence', that: 'there are two of us now that the Shirra [Sir Walter Scott] might have patted on the head.... I am a capable artist; but it begins to look to me as if you were a man of genius'(*L8* 447). In a long last letter to Barrie in July 1894, Stevenson harked back to the sharp practice of Crockett, whose *Stickit Minister* he continued to admire even while dismissing its author in a bitchy aside: 'He went up like a crocket and came down like a stick' (*L8* 322). Nevertheless he clearly saw himself as belonging, with Barrie and Crockett, to a group of contemporary Scottish writers, for which he sarcastically proposed a handbook entitled: ' "The Professional Etiquette of Scottish Authors; being a handbook of the Courtesy and Chivalry practised by Scottish Authors among themselves: with an Appendix ... on the Art of Advertisement by ---"ay, by whom? [then follows the 'crocket' jibe].' The group of writers for whom Stevenson proposed the handbook would be known in historical retrospect as 'the Kailyard School', though Stevenson himself would not usually be included in their number. Nevertheless Stevenson's supposedly transcendent position in relation to the Kailyard School is open to discussion. On the one hand, the Kailyard School itself is susceptible of a more positive reading than it is often given; even Ian Mclaren shows himself in the archetypal Kailyard novel *Beside the Bonnie Brier Bush* to be more knowing than has often been assumed by those who may not have read as far as the chapter entitled 'The Cunning Speech of Drumtochty'.[43] If Stevenson's superiority to the Kailyard School is partly eroded by the upgrading of the latter, it is further eroded by the revision downwards of the critical estimate of Stevenson's own work, for example when Douglas Gifford denounces 'that unfortunate later tendency of Stevenson towards Crockett and Barrie and the Kailyard which I suggest would have spoiled even *Weir of Hermiston*.'[44]

Weir has also been linked intertextually with George Douglas Brown's *The House with Green Shutters*, famous for 'sticking the Kailyarders like pigs' (though the distance between Brown and especially Barrie's work has been greatly exaggerated[45]). It has been suggested that '*Green Shutters* represents a kind of thematic completion of the novel that Stevenson was unable to achieve in *Weir of Hermiston*'.[46] If one of the main themes in the work of Barrie and Mclaren, as well as in Brown's *Green Shutters*, is an obsessive mother-son relationship which hovers between the sentimental and the pathological, an equally Oedipal theme which links Brown to Stevenson is that of the brutal and terrifying father. In *Green Shutters* John Gourlay, Senior is, with his ruthless bullying, strongly reminiscent of Adam Weir. What Weir and Gourlay Senior have in common is that their bullying is not merely a symptom of inner weakness, but rather has a kind of relentless consistency which borders on grandeur. *Green Shutters* is clearly tragic, with obvious allusions to Greek tragedy (the 'nesty bodies' gathered at the Cross figure as the chorus); Gourlay Junior kills his father and goes to bed with his mother, not for sex but in a regressed quest for protection from his murdered father's pursuing eyes. It seems that Adam Weir was also doomed to die, in shock at having to condemn his own son to death. How exactly Stevenson intended to manage this scenario, which would have been very difficult to reconcile with the procedures of Scots law, is unclear; it is also unclear how, exactly, *Weir* was to end. According to Belle Strong, Stevenson's amenuensis, there was to have been a happy ending in which young Archie Weir was rescued from prison by the Four Black [Elliot] Brothers, and escaped to America with the younger Kirstie. However another, more tragic, ending was later supplied by S.R. Lysaght, who had visited Vailima in 1894.[47] Stevenson himself wrote to Barrie in November 1892 that: 'there is a fine tempting fitness to this [the hanging of Archie Weir]; and I meant he was to hang' (*L8* 414). Nevertheless he ultimately preferred to follow Barrie's example in *The Little Minister*. The latter 'ought to have ended badly', Stevenson wrote to Barrie, but 'we [the readers] are infinitely grateful to you for the grace and good feeling with which you lied about it. . . . If you are going to make a book end badly, it must end badly from the beginning. Now your book began to end well. You let yourself fall in love with, and fondle, and smile at your puppets. Once you had done that your honour was committed – at the cost of truth to life you were bound to save them' (*L8* 413).

The possibility that *Weir* may have begun 'to end well', and that Stevenson may have let himself 'fall in love with, and fondle' his puppets, may perhaps help to explain that tendency towards the Kailyard which Gifford claimed to detect in Stevenson. However, such a tendency is balanced by a much grimmer tendency in Stevenson, which goes back to his *Covenanting Story-Book*, alias *The Black Man*. This other tendency is apparent in the doom-laden Introductory section of *Weir*, and militates against the sunnier version of the novel's conclusion offered by Belle. The opening of *Weir of Hermiston* is located in 'the wild end of a moorland parish' at the gravestone (chiselled by 'Old Mortality' himself) of the Praying Weaver of Balweary, a Cameronian whom 'Bloody' Claverhouse 'shot with his own hand' (*T16* 1). We are back in the Balweary of 'Thrawn Janet' and *Heathercat*, with the same dark themes of brutal religious persecution and supernatural visitation (the traditional name for this haunted spot is the 'Deil's Hags'). This tradition of brutality and demonic possession was to surface again, *mutatis mutandis*, in Brown's *Green Shutters*, which in this sense is the heir to the dark reading of *Weir*. Crockett too, of course, was into 'the Covenanting racket'. Even in *The Stickit Minister* there is reference (in the second story, 'Accepted of the Beasts'[48]) to the last of the martyrs of the Covenant, James Renwick, whose *Life and Death* by Alexander Shields is listed by Stevenson among his recent reading in a letter of December 1893 (other items included the 'Covenanting books' *The Cloud of Witnesses* and Wodrow's *Analecta*, as well as *Rob Roy* 'for the eight hundred and fiftieth time') (*L8* 203). But in contrast to Crockett's stories, there is a darkness lurking in Stevenson's work which connects it with Brown's desperate tale. Colvin was perhaps right to mention in his Editorial Note to *Weir of Hermiston* the suggestion of Henley that there may be in *Weir* an echo of the dark story of Edinburgh's notorious Major Weir, accused of witchcraft, bestiality and incest, and 'burned as a warlock, together with his sister, under circumstances of particular atrocity' in 1670[49] (*T16* 131).

Whether the darkness in Stevenson was caused by some kind of Oedipal conflict with his father is a matter of speculation. Colvin suggested in his Editorial Note that *Weir* derived in some measure from 'the difficulties often attending the relation of father and son in actual life [which] had pressed heavily on Stevenson's mind and conscience from the days of his youth' (*T16* 130). Another ingredient in the potent Oedipal mix of *Weir*, in addition to hatred of the father, excluded from the intense relationship between young Archie and his doting mother, is the obvious sexual feelings of the elder Kirstie for Archie. Such a sexualized mother-figure recalls the role of Fanny Sitwell in Stevenson's own experience, and its reprise by a later occupant of the 'second Mother, first Wife' role, Fanny Stevenson herself, to whom *Weir* is dedicated in a poem all-too-susceptible of a vulgar Freudian reading. Like Louis's feelings about Thomas Stevenson, Archie Weir's feelings about his father, the Lord Justice-Clerk are deeply ambivalent. Such ambivalence is also apparent in Stevenson's sympathetic response, recorded in 'Some Portraits by Raeburn' in *Virginibus Puerisque* (*T25* 101–3), to Raeburn's portrait of Lord Braxfield, the model for Adam Weir. Stevenson's reasons for regarding Braxfield with 'a sneaking kindness', notwithstanding his inhumanity, include, in the first place, his sheer Scottishness: 'He was the last judge on the Scottish bench to employ the pure Scottish idiom. His opinions, thus given in Doric, and conceived in a lively, rugged conversational style, were full of point and authority' (*T25* 102). Stevenson's description of Braxfield reads like a sketch of Adam Weir (as well as foreshadowing John Gourlay Senior), and culminates in the affirmation of what was most admirable in this much-hated man: 'he was also perfectly intrepid. You may look into the queer face of that portrait as long as you will, but you will not see any hole or corner for timidity to enter in' (*T25* 103). In *Weir* we glimpse the figure of the archetypal Scottish 'hard man', who is hardbitten, hard drinking and 'hard but fair'. Whether such an apotheosis of 'hardness' (with its modern incarnations in the work of writers such as William McIlvanney and Ian Rankin) may have to do with Oedipally-tinged fantasy is a matter for discussion. While Thomas Stevenson was not in any real sense a 'hard man', there is evident in Louis an anxiety that, like Archie Weir (and *a fortiori* John Gourlay Junior), he may be letting down his father and the tradition of upright 'manliness' which he embodied. This is nowhere more obvious than in the poem beginning:

> Say not of me that weakly I declined
> The labours of my sires, and fled the sea,
> The towers we founded and the lamps we lit,
> To play at home with paper like a child (*T22* 95).

Such anxiety may have been one of the motives which drove Louis Stevenson to over-work. Certainly there is a fittingness in the fact that he died, as he wished (*L7* 287), 'with his boots on', midway through what stands as the final line both of *Weir*, and of his *oeuvre*. It is tempting for biographers to write that Stevenson's uncompleted masterpiece, and his short life, ended with the dramatically appropriate words: 'It seemed unprovoked, a wilful convulsion of brute nature...' (*T16* 124). While it may be true to say that these words were the last that Stevenson dictated to Belle on the day he was struck down by a cerebral haemorrhage, it is not the case that they are the last words of *Weir*. An earlier manuscript of 1892 also exists, and takes the novel a page or so beyond the version Stevenson was dictating to Belle on the day of his death. In what could be seen as an example of Henry James's observation that Stevenson 'has *superseded*, personally, his books',[50] the need for Stevenson's Literary Life to end in such a dramatically appropriate fashion has encouraged the omission of reference to these alternative final pages – pages which strengthen the view that Stevenson was moving closer to the Kailyard. To end *Weir* with the famous words: 'a wilful convulsion of brute nature...' secures, at one stroke, both the dramatic conclusion to the Life and Work of the tragically doomed artist, and the suppression of an unsettling development of Stevenson's writing towards such sentimental exchanges as the following:

> 'O, aye, far raither,' she said, and she put up her hand and drew it down the lapel of his coat with a slow dragging caress, like an affectionate cat's. It was customary to her, intoxication to him.
>
> His voice broke. 'I am afraid you cannot be serious!' he said, and laughed softly in spite of himself, so sweet was the demonstration to his heart, however much at such a moment his mind might disapprove it.
>
> 'O no, I can be serious too. I *am* serious,'she said, and laid her face timidly against his breast and lifted her eyes in a beatitude.[51]

Whether Stevenson could have held together in *Weir* the contending impulses that were to split apart into the Kailyard School, and its dark other, *The House with Green Shutters*, is something we will never know. It may be that the unfinished masterpiece would have proved unfinishable; or if finished, not, after all, a masterpiece.

4
America

Long before his first trip to America in 1879, Stevenson had already come under the decisive influence of American literature through his discovery of Walt Whitman. In an autobiographical fragment composed in San Francisco early in 1880, Stevenson recalled that what had helped him to move on from his miserable 'days of green-sickness' as a young man in Edinburgh was 'the study of Walt Whitman' (*B* 84–6). As he put it in his essay on Whitman, *Leaves of Grass* was 'a specific for the malady of being seventeen years old. Green-sickness yields to [Whitman's] treatment as to a charm of magic.' (*T27* 65) When the young Stevenson called a friend, whom he was 'wading into' with favourite Whitman passages, 'a poor unbeliever', he was only half-joking (*L1* 322–3). His discovery of Whitman (at the appropriate age of seventeen[1]) had come with the force of a religious revelation. *Leaves of Grass* was, Stevenson later wrote in 'Books Which Have Influenced Me', 'a book which tumbled the world upside down for me, blew into space a thousand cobwebs of genteel and ethical illusion, and, having thus shaken my tabernacle of lies, set me back on a strong foundation of all the original and manly virtues' (*T28* 64). The first published version of Stevenson's essay on Whitman in the *New Quarterly Magazine* in October 1878 was entitled, significantly if by now somewhat ironically, 'The Gospel of Walt Whitman'.

This essay was written over a long period. According to Colvin, Stevenson had an essay on Whitman 'already on hand' when they first met in Suffolk in July 1873 (*T31* 64). There is regular reference in Stevenson's correspondence in the latter part of 1873 to his continual honing of the Whitman essay; at one point he remarks: ' "Walt Whitman" is in the meantime in a pitiable bad way. The style sticks in my throat like badly made toffy' (*L1* 336). Of this early version of the essay Stevenson later wrote in the 'Preface, by Way of Criticism' to *Familiar Studies of Men & Books* (1882): 'I had written another paper full of gratitude for the help that had been given me in my life, full of enthusiasm for the intrinsic merit of the poems, and conceived in the noisiest extreme of youthful eloquence' (*T27* xvii). Stevenson kept redrafting this early version of the essay until it was lost during a cruise round the Scottish islands in the summer of 1874. He did not return to the subject until 1878, when, in an over-reaction to his earlier enthusiasm, 'the big words and emphatic passages were ruthlessly excised [though] along with exaggeration, some of the truth [was] sacrificed; and the result is cold, constrained, and grudging'. 'In short,' continued Stevenson in the 1882 Preface, chastened perhaps by his discussions at Davos with that great advocate of Whitman, J.A. Symonds,[2] 'I might have almost everywhere have spoken more strongly than I did' (*T27* xvii–xviii).

By the time Stevenson's essay was reprinted in *Familiar Studies of Men & Books*, its title had been shorn of the allusion to Whitman's status as an evangelist. The proselytising quality of Whitman's writing is inescapable, however. In contrast, wrote Stevenson, to the self-indulgent, world-weary 'literature of woe, as Whitman calls it, this *Maladie de René*, as we like to call it in Europe' (*T27* 62) – or incipient *fin de siècle* decadence, as we now might say – Whitman preached 'the liveableness of life' (*T27* 63). Whitman's optimistic spiritual athleticism, promoting 'a certain high joy in living, or what [Whitman] calls "a brave delight fit for freedom's athletes"' (ibid.) is, in contrast to any elitist aestheticism, pointedly democratic and aimed at ordinary people in ordinary circumstances. Stevenson quotes approvingly (without bothering to give a reference) from the Preface to the 1855 edition of *Leaves of Grass*:

> The passionate tenacity of hunters, woodmen, early risers, cultivators of gardens and orchards and fields, the love of healthy women for the manly form, seafaring persons, drivers of horses, the passion for light and air, – all this is an old unvaried sign of the unfailing perception of beauty, and of a residence of the poetic in outdoor people (*T27* 63–4).

What seemed to Stevenson to be 'truly original in this choice of trite examples' was the inversion of the expected and obvious (to Stevenson and his world) 'love of healthy men for the female form' (*T27* 64). Whether Whitman's rhetorical inversion, and indeed Stevenson's response to it, may have to do with 'inversion' in Havelock Ellis's sense[3] remains a moot point.

Whatever other motives Stevenson may have had for undertaking in 1879 the gruelling journey from the Clyde to California (and his motivation was no doubt 'overdetermined'), on one level the journey was a development of his by now established practice of travelling in order to make a book. As he wrote to Charles Baxter from California: 'I went over here for literary purposes in order to write up emigracy' (*L3* 12). During his 'Inland Voyage' Stevenson had written to his mother: 'an easy book may be written and sold, with mighty little brains about it, where the journey is of a certain seriousness and can be named' (*L2* 189). Although the journey to California certainly met these criteria, and therefore did not need, as Stevenson had put it, to be 'clever', nevertheless he did boast to Colvin about his latest travel book: 'it seems to me rather a *clever* book, than anything else: the book of a man that is who has paid a great deal of attention to contemporary life, and not through the newspapers' (*L3* 30). For all Stevenson's contempt for Realism in general, and for Zola in particular, *The Amateur Emigrant* comes as close to documentary realism as anything in later nineteenth century literature. It was perhaps this element of reportage[4] that above all disturbed Sidney Colvin, who wrote to Charles Baxter that the work Stevenson had sent him from California was '*not good*', probably not saleable, and even if it were, likely only to do 'harm to his reputation'; Colvin concluded: 'I find it on the whole quite unworthy of him' (*L3* 37–8). Despite their reservations, Colvin and Henley finally managed to sell the manuscript of *The Amateur Emigrant* to Kegan Paul, who had published *An Inland Voyage* and *Travels with a Donkey*. In the event, however, Stevenson deferred to his father's wishes and the manuscript was bought back from Kegan Paul at Thomas Stevenson's expense, with an announcement appearing in the *Athenaeum* in October 1880 to the effect that: 'Mr. R.L. Stevenson has determined to suppress his *Amateur Emigrant*, announced by us some little time ago, and has withdrawn it from his publishers' hands.'

Thomas Stevenson not only disapproved of *The Amateur Emigrant*; he also deeply disapproved of the whole business of Louis chasing a married woman half-way round the world, commenting: 'I lay all this at the door of Herbert Spencer. Unsettling a man's faith is indeed a *very* serious matter' (*L3* 43) Henley viewed the affair less theologically, but in a letter to Charles Baxter expressed his anxiety that Louis would not keep his promise to Colvin and himself that he would only go as far as New York, but would 'be induced to go to Monterey, and there get mixed up once more in the miserable life of alarms and lies and intrigues that he led in Paris. If he don't do that, I've not much fear for him. It will end in a book, I expect...' (*L3* 5). Henley was to be disappointed, however.

Louis did go to Monterey and became even more deeply involved than in Paris, Fanny Osbourne proving reluctant to fulfil Henley's hope that 'she would be brave and generous enough to have given him up; – to have shown herself worthy of him by putting herself out of his way forever' (*L3* 4). And although Stevenson's transatlantic adventure did end in a book, it was not published during his lifetime. His journey to Monterey was not unpremeditated. It had been a year since Fanny had returned to California, supposedly to negotiate a settlement with Sam Osbourne, though this had proved to be a frustratingly inconclusive business. As Louis wrote to Colvin from *S.S. Devonia*, an hour or two out of New York: 'Man, I was sick, sick, sick of this last year' (*L3* 6). What exactly precipitated his departure is uncertain; letters from this turbulent period were lost or suppressed.[5] It seems clear, however, that in late July 1879 Stevenson received an urgent cable (which has not survived) from Fanny Osbourne; whatever its contents, the cable decided him. As he wrote to his cousin Bob, indicating both his concern for Fanny and his need to resolve the intolerable indecision: 'F. seems to very ill; at least I must try to get her to do one of two things' (*L3* 3–4). He secretly purchased a ticket for New York, and excused himself from accompanying his parents on a spa holiday, claiming that he needed to make a business trip to London. In fact he was going for a final confab – and no doubt a trawl for funds – with his friends in London: Henley, Colvin and Gosse. These made a vain effort to dissuade Louis from what Gosse called 'the maddest of enterprises',[6] which he was not expected to survive. Colvin and Henley saw Louis off on the night train to Glasgow, where on 7 August 1879, under the assumed name of Robert Stephenson, he embarked on *S.S. Devonia* bound for New York.

Stevenson did not actually travel steerage because, as he wrote, 'although anxious to see the worst of emigrant life, I had some work to finish on the voyage.' (*T18* 1) The second cabin, where Stevenson was berthed, was 'a modified oasis in the very heart of the steerages. Through the thin partition you can hear the steerage passengers being sick, the rattle of tin dishes as they sit at meals, the varied accents in which they converse, the crying of their children terrified by this new experience, or the clean flat smack of the parental hand in chastisement' (*T18* 2). The chief advantage of the second cabin, apart from the provision of bedding and crockery, was a table, which allowed Stevenson to work. As he wrote to Henley:

Dear lad, I have passed the salt sea with comparative impunity, having only lost a stone and got the itch. I could not eat, and I could not sh-shush! – the whole way; but I worked, [expletives deleted] I worked, and am now despatching a story as long as my arm to the vile [Kegan] Paul, all written in a slantindicular cabin with the table playing bob-cherry with the ink bottle. The voyage was otherwise great fun; passengers singing and spewing lustily (*L3* 6–7).

Stevenson was elsewhere less jolly about the squalor, sickness and stench which pervaded steerage. In a passage he deleted from the version of *The Amateur Emigrant* that he was eventually persuaded, shortly before his death, to publish, Stevenson wrote:

I presume (for I never saw it) that some cleaning process was carried on each morning; but there was never light enough to be particular; and in a place so full of corners... and partitions, dirt might lie for years without disturbance. The pens, stalls, pews – I know not what to call them, were... beyond the reach of bucket and swab.... When the pen was fully occupied, with sixteen live human animals, more or less unwashed, lying immersed together in the same close air all night, and their litter of meats, dirty dishes and rank bedding tumbled all day in foul disorder, the merest possibilities of health or cleanliness were absent.... A writer of the school of M. Zola would find here an inspiration for many pages; but without entering farther into detail, let me mention the name of sea sickness, and leave its added horrors to the imagination of the reader.[7]

Another deletion Stevenson made in deference to his readers' sensibilities is a passage in the chapter entitled 'The Sick Man' in which he praises the sick man's sense of honour in struggling to hand Stevenson a handkerchief after the latter had, in coming to his assistance, kneeled in the man's vomit. Such 'unaffected courtliness' impressed Stevenson: 'It is easier to say a fine thing on the field of honour than in such a scene of physical disgrace.'[8]

The importance of remaining 'a gentleman' in conditions of physical degradation was at the heart of Stevenson's moral and political response to his experience on *S.S. Devonia*, which was, as Noble points out, a microcosm of late Victorian society.[9] In steerage, Stevenson writes, 'there are males and females; in the second cabin ladies and gentlemen. For some time after I came aboard I thought I was only a male; but in the course of a voyage between the decks, I came on a brass plate, and learned that I was still a gentleman. Nobody knew it, of course' (*T18* 3). Stevenson jokes that when out of sorts he could go and refresh himself 'with a look at that brass plate' (*T18* 4); but for the most part he seems delighted by the fact that he had 'fallen in life with absolute success and verisimilitude' (*T18* 55). In *An Inland Voyage* Stevenson had attributed his passing for a peddler in France to the difference of language; here on *S.S. Devonia* he was 'among his own countrymen, somewhat roughly clad to be sure, but with every advantage of speech and manner', yet passing for anything except an educated gentleman' (ibid.). He continued the experiment, begun in London, of approaching members of his own class incognito. In London, women had passed the underdressed Stevenson 'like a dog', and the saloon passengers on *S.S. Devonia* 'gave me a hard dead look, with the flesh about the eye kept unrelaxed' (*T18* 56). In contrast to such merely external markers of class, Stevenson claims to have found the manners of his companions in steerage 'as gentle and becoming as those of any other class that I have had the opportunity of studying'; indeed he so identified with the steerage passengers that he felt himself 'at heart growing hostile to the officers and cabin passengers who looked down on me' (*T18* 58). The visit of some cabin passengers slumming it in steerage 'galled me to the quick', Stevenson wrote, and continued: 'I have little of the radical in social questions, and have always nourished an idea that one person was as good as any other. But I began to be troubled by this episode. It was astonishing what insults these people managed to convey by their presence. They seemed to throw their clothes in our faces' (*T18* 22).

Such feelings of hostility on Stevenson's part did not run to any sympathy with class war, however.[10] He had heard 'enough revolutionary talk among my workman fellow-passengers; but most of it was hot and turgid, and fell discredited from the lips of unsuccessful men' (*T18* 41). What struck him as 'ominous and grave', however, was when a successful working man from Tyneside (the 'gentlemanly' sick man[11]), after having expressed cynicism about 'selfish and obstructive' masters, and 'selfish, silly, and light-headed' men, and having called into question 'the wisdom and even the good faith of the Union delegates' (*T18* 40), nevertheless 'could think of no hope for our country outside of a sudden and complete political subversion'; such principles, he said, 'were growing "like a seed" ' (*T18* 41). In contrast to such revolutionary talk, which would 'rend the old country from end to end, and from top to bottom, and in clamour and civil discord remodel it with the hand of violence' (ibid.), it seemed to Stevenson that 'there is but one question in modern home politics, though it appears in many shapes, and that is the question of money; and but one political remedy, that the people should grow wiser and better' (*T18* 61). On the question of the redistribution of wealth Stevenson was agnostic. What seemed clear to him, however, was that those who preached revolution in the hope 'that they might remain improvident and idle and debauched, and yet enjoy the comfort and respect that should accompany the opposite virtues' were losers (ibid.). 'Let them go where they will, and wreck all the governments under heaven, they will be poor until they die', Stevenson wrote, for 'it is not by a man's purse, but by his character, that he is rich or poor.' (ibid.) Political naïvety, or blindness, from which Stevenson claimed no particular exemption (*T18* 60–1), had led most of the emigrants to create the fantasy of an America where, as one passenger put it: 'you get pies and puddings' (*T18* 64). In reality, wrote Stevenson: 'we were a company of the rejected; the drunken, the incompetent, the weak, the prodigal, all who had been unable to prevail against circumstances in the one land, [and] were now fleeing pitifully to another; and though one or two might succeed, all had already failed' (*T18* 10). For all that Stevenson liked to say that money was 'the *atmosphere* of civilized life' (*L1* 380), success in life was for him ultimately not about wealth or social rank, for 'to be a gentleman is to be one the world over, and in every relation and grade of society. It is a high calling, to which a man must first be born, and then devote himself for life' (*T18* 59). Stevenson rejected the hegemony of the mores of 'a clique' or 'a certain so-called upper grade' of society, and insisted, in a kind of democratic humanism, that: 'manners, like art, should be human and central' (ibid.).

However forcibly Stevenson may have been made aware on *S.S. Devonia* of the class-ridden nature of European, and particularly British, society, his real interest lay with the individual, or 'the character'. He discovered that he shared with a fellow-passenger called Jones a taste for the study of character, and together they set about 'dissecting our neighbours in a spirit that was too purely scientific to be called unkind' (*T18* 7). Much of *The Amateur Emigrant* is a series of character sketches, with a whole chapter devoted to 'Steerage Types'. It is interesting, therefore, to read in 'The Story of a Lie', the piece which Stevenson told Henley he was writing in the 'slantidicular' cabin for 'the vile [Kegan] Paul' (*L3* 6–7), that the hero Dick Naseby was 'a type-hunter among mankind' (*T14* 143). Though 'experimental as to its method', the interest of Dick Naseby in human types, unlike that of Messrs. Stephenson and Jones, is 'an artistic interest'. Stevenson continues in 'The Story of a Lie':

> There is no science in the personal study of human nature. All com-
> prehension is creation; the woman I love is somewhat of my handi-
> work; and the great lover, like the great painter, is he that can so

embellish his subject as to make her more than human, whilst yet by a cunning art he has so based his apotheosis on the nature of the case that the woman can go on being a true woman, and give her character free play, and show littleness or cherish spite, or be greedy of common pleasures, and he continue to worship without a thought of incongruity. To love a character is only the heroic way of understanding it (*T14* 143–4).

It is not difficult to imagine how these observations, which represent an intrusion of the belletristic Stevenson into the narrative, might derive from Stevenson's own reflections on his relationship with Fanny Osbourne in the past and the (at that point uncertain) future. Another connection between 'The Story of a Lie' and Stevenson's personal life is the description in the novella of the tempestuous relationship between Dick and his father. There are passages, such as the following, which seem a direct transcription of Louis's intensely difficult relationship with his own father, a relationship which was, if not a direct cause of Louis's flight to America, then certainly the main reason why he left without informing his parents:

Dick and his father were henceforth on terms of coldness. The upright old gentleman grew more upright when he met his son, buckramed with immortal anger; he asked after Dick's health, and discussed the weather... with an appalling courtesy; his pronunciation was *point-device* [perfectly correct], his voice was distant, distinct, and sometimes almost trembling with suppressed indignation.... [Dick] came out of his theories and clevernesses; his premature man-of-the-worldness... [W]ounded honour, pity, and respect tussled together daily in his heart; and now he was within an ace of throwing himself upon his father's mercy, and now of slipping forth at night and coming back no more... (*T14* 154).

It is revealing that, in one of his first letters from California, Louis wrote to Charles Baxter: 'and how for God's sake is my father? Tell me, please Charles. Since I have gone away I have found out for the first time how much I love that man: he is dearer to me than all except F' (*L3* 14). 'That man' in the fictional form of old Mr Naseby, and 'F.' in the fictional form of the moody Esther, are central to the story Louis was working on as he travelled ever farther from the former, and ever nearer to the latter. 'The Story of a Lie' is about the disastrous consequences of emotional dishonesty, which only a *deus ex machina* in the final chapter can avert. Louis's journey to America might be seen as a dramatic attempt to force certain issues and thereby achieve a degree of clarity, if not resolution, in his tangled relationships with his father and his lover.

There is something in Stevenson's correspondence at this time that prefigures a mood that would later be called 'existentialist'. He wrote to Colvin form Greenock: 'I have never been so much detached from life; I feel as if I cared for nobody, and as for myself I cannot fully believe in my own existence. I seem to have died last night.' (*L3* 2–3) Such feelings of estrangement and depersonalization are also evident in Stevenson's letter to Colvin from the train crossing America: 'I had no idea how easy it was to commit suicide. There seems nothing left of me; I died a while ago; I do not know who it is that is travelling' (*L3* 8). Also in this letter was a poem, which included the lines:

> Of where or how, I nothing know;
>   And why, I do not care;
>   Enough if, even so,
> My travelling eyes, my travelling mind, can go
> By flood and field and hill, by wood and meadow fair,
> Beside the Susquehannah and along the Delaware

By the time he reached California on 30 August, Stevenson was, physically and psychologically, practically *in extremis*, and his wretched condition may have been partly responsible for Fanny's ambivalent reaction to his arrival. In early September he wrote to Colvin: 'all is in the wind; things might turn well, or might not; . . . and frankly, no decided news. I am in good health [but] was supposed to be dying when first I came here' (*L3* 11). More frankly, perhaps, he wrote to Charles Baxter on 9 September: 'This is not a letter, for I am too perturbed. . . . My news is nil. I know nothing, I go out camping . . . ; I shall send you a letter from there with more guts than this and now say good-bye to you, having had the itch and a broken heart' (*L3* 11–12). It was in fact nearly a final good-bye to Baxter, for on his solitary camping trip Stevenson became so ill that it was only because two rancheros found him, took him in and tended him (*L3* 12), that he survived; as Furnas comments, this was the first time that Stevenson 'unquestionably came near to dying'.[12] But even recovering at the angora goat ranch in the Carmel Valley, under the care of the old bear hunter Captain Smith and his partner, Stevenson was working at his notes of the voyage, though the book, he warned Colvin, 'will not be very like a book of mine' (*L3* 13).

The Stevenson who emerged from the 'near death' experiences of his journeys to and in America, represents, if not quite Christopher Isherwood's 'I am a camera with its shutter open, quite passive, recording, not thinking',[13] then, with its reduction of the literary self to 'My travelling eyes, my travelling mind', a similar kind of literary askesis. 'God only knows,' wrote Stevenson to Colvin in April 1880, 'how much suffering and courage is buried in that MS [*The Amateur Emigrant*]. The second part was written in a circle of hell unknown to Dante; that of a penniless and dying author. For dying I was, although now saved.... I think I shall always think of it as my best work' (*L3* 75). The second part of *The Amateur Emigrant*, ultimately entitled 'Across the Plains', was withdrawn along with the rest of the manuscript in 1880, though it was serialised in *Longman's Magazine* in 1883. Unlike the first part, which Stevenson could work on during the voyage, thanks to his 'slantindicular cabin', the second part (originally entitled 'The Emigrant Train') proved much more difficult to write because during the journey he was 'ill the whole time', and therefore had 'scarce a note, only about three pages in pencil in a penny notebook' (*L3* 51). The address of Stevenson's circle of hell was 608 Bush Street, San Francisco, where he rented a cheap room in an Irish boarding house (later to appear, like much of Stevenson's San Francisco experience, in *The Wrecker*). Although Fanny had obtained a divorce from Sam Osbourne on 12 December 1879, it had been agreed that she and Louis would keep their relationship low key for a decent period, and therefore Fanny only came to San Francisco twice a week, leaving Louis to his lonely struggle with *The Amateur Emigrant*. It was 'uphill work', he wrote to Colvin, adding: 'I have never fought with a book yet, always did it from an easy flowing vein. But in spite of the devil it shall be done' (*L3* 51).

If San Francisco contained the circle of hell in which Stevenson wrestled to complete *The Amateur Emigrant*, then purgatory had been the railroad's Ferry Depot in New York (*T18* 83). Jammed into a long shed in the dark, with the wind howling through, was 'a great block of passengers and baggage, hundreds of the one and tons of the other' waiting for the river boat to Jersey City like sheep, with the porters 'charging among us like maddened sheep-dogs' (*T18* 82–3). Whatever system there may have been, it had utterly broken down under the strain of so many passengers (*T18* 81). The latter 'had accepted this purgatory as the conditions of the world', Stevenson records, so utterly daunted were their spirits; he himself had neither hope nor fear, his entire being having been reduced to 'one massive sensation of discomfort' (*T18* 83). The boat to Jersey was in danger of capsizing because, despite the warning shouts of the seamen, the emigrants were huddled on the port side where they had boarded, and, being 'under a spell of stupor', did not stir (ibid.). By now Stevenson and the rest of the 'wet and silent emigrants' had acquired 'a fixed sense of calamity', and the landing at Jersey was done in a stampede, dominated by 'a panic selfishness' in which the screams of a lost child 'verging towards a fit' went unremarked (*T18* 83–4). Stevenson was, he says, 'too crushed to observe his neighbours', having become, like them, 'cold, and wet, and weary, and driven stupidly crazy by the mismanagement to which we had been subjected' (*T18* 84).

The chaos of the following day was due not only to mismanagement, but also to a rail accident during the night; as a consequence, Stevenson was unable to obtain a meal until the train reached Pittsburg on the evening of the second day. This meal was the occasion of his 'first introduction to a coloured gentleman', who 'did me the honour to wait upon me after a fashion' (*T18* 87). Any irony in Stevenson's use of the term 'gentleman' is directed at himself, since, in striking contrast, he says, to the stereotypes of Mrs Beecher Stowe and the Christy Minstrels, every word, look, and gesture of the waiter sent him 'farther into the country of surprise' (ibid.). 'Imagine a gentleman', wrote Stevenson, 'certainly somewhat dark, but of a pleasant warm hue, speaking English with a slight and rather odd foreign accent, every inch a man of the world, and armed with manners so patronisingly superior that I am at a loss to name their parallel in England' (ibid.) The 'certainly', and the 'but', in the previous sentence reveal Stevenson's unconscious immersion in prejudices concerning colour. However, he was ready to acknowledge, and indeed to welcome, the fact that his desire 'to prove in a thousand condescensions that [he] was no sharer in race prejudice' was made to seem ridiculous in face of the waiter who treated him 'much as, with us, a young, free, and not very self-respecting master might behave to a good-looking chambermaid', as Stevenson puts it in an image which, in defamiliarizing racial stereotypes, invokes familiar gender stereotypes (ibid.).

Stevenson's antipathy to racial prejudice is evident also in the passages about the Chinese emigrants. The latter had a carriage to themselves, which, despite the prejudice of the 'very foul and malodorous Caucasians' that it alone stank (*T18* 117), was in fact 'notably the least offensive' (*T18* 112). Indeed, in a passage deleted from the published version, presumably in deference to Victorian sensibilities, Stevenson adds that it was the stink of the women and children's carriage that was 'by a good way the worst. A stroke of nature's satire.'[14] In a chapter entitled 'Despised Races' Stevenson analysed the prejudices of his fellow-Caucasians, of which the ill-feeling 'towards our companions in the Chinese car was the most stupid and the worst' (*T18* 116). The Chinese were declared to be, in a phrase of historical resonance, 'hideous vermin' (ibid.), and 'there was no calumny too idle for the Caucasians to repeat, and even to believe (ibid.). Such race hatred was fuelled, as usual, by shortage of work in an economic depression 'of catastrophic proportions'.[15] In 'that cruel and treacherous battle-field of money' the Chinese were the enemy, since 'they could work better and cheaper in half a hundred industries', and 'their dexterity and frugality [could] enable them to underbid the lazy, luxurious Caucasians'(*T18* 116–17). In San Francisco the Chinese had replaced the Irish as the victims of racism, and it was with 'some bitterness' that Stevenson heard an Irishman[16] 'roaring for arms and butchery' in the streets of San Francisco, and proclaiming, with the distorted logic of the oppression which 'drives a wise man mad' (*T18* 119): ' "At the call of Abraham Lincoln...ye rose in the name of freedom to set free the negroes; can ye not rise and liberate yourselves from a few dhirty Mongolians?" ' (*T18* 117). For himself, wrote Stevenson, he could only look 'with wonder and respect' on the Chinese and their ancient culture (*T18* 117–18). He described those native Americans who appeared at way-stations as 'disgracefully dressed out in the sweepings of civilisation', and felt that their silent stoicism, and the pathetic degradation of their appearance, 'would have touched any thinking creatures', though not his fellow-passengers who 'danced and jested around them with a truly Cockney baseness' (*T18* 118). Stevenson was ashamed of 'the thing we call civilisation', and added: 'We should carry on our consciences so much at least of our forefathers' misconduct as we continue to profit by ourselves' (*T18* 118–19). The eviction of the Cherokees, along with similar outrages, is 'a chapter of injustice and indignity such as a man must be in some ways base if his heart will suffer him to forget or pardon' (*T18* 119).

Injustice and indignity are not always dispensed along racial lines, however. The abuse of power was routine on the emigrant train. As Stevenson noted: 'Equality, though conceived very largely in America, does not extend so low as an emigrant', and the disrespect shown to emigrants was 'both wanton and petty' (*T18* 100). Many conductors, Stevenson discovered, 'will hold no communication with an emigrant' (ibid.). Even a newsboy acquired considerable power in these circumstances. One 'bullying, contemptuous, insolent scoundrel...treated us like dogs' (ibid.), though another turned out, after a bad start, to be one of the guardian angels that Stevenson seemed to attract, and for the rest of the journey Louis was 'petted like a sick child' (*T18* 102). The emigrants were also routinely exploited, having to pay over the odds for a board and some straw cushions to construct a makeshift bed; Stevenson had to pay five times the ultimate going rate for this crude equipment (*T18* 96–8). If the same kind of exploitation and profiteering were in evidence on both the emigrant train and the emigrant ship,[17] the passengers Stevenson encountered on the train were very different from those he had mixed with on *S.S. Devonia*. In contrast to the camaraderie on board ship, Stevenson's fellow-passengers on the emigrant train were: 'mostly lumpish fellows, silent and noisy . . . with an extraordinary poor taste in humour, and little interest in their fellow-creatures beyond that of a cheap and merely external curiosity' (*T18* 112–13). It had taken Stevenson some time to adjust to what he calls 'the uncivil kindness of the American, which is perhaps their most bewildering character to one newly landed' (*T18* 101). The selfishness and callousness of the passengers on the emigrant train astonished him. Not only did the fact that he fell ill while passing through Wyoming 'meet with little but laughter'; one young man amused himself, and his fellow-passengers, by 'incommoding' the ill writer (Stevenson does not say exactly how), and expecting Stevenson to join in the merriment – not from ill-nature, Stevenson added, taking literary revenge, but from a 'mere clod-like incapacity to think' (*T18* 113). In contrast to the ship, all the emigrants on the train were American-born, save one German family and a party of Cornish miners.

The fact that most of the emigrants on the train were American made Stevenson think with despair of his companions on *S.S. Devonia*; they had travelled 3,000 miles from the Clyde to the east coast of America, only to find that the eastern states 'were not places for immigration, but for emigration' (*T18* 114–15). So bad was the economic depression of the late 1870s that the emigrants travelling west were implored to turn back by other emigrants returning east: 'On the plains of Nebraska, in the mountains of Wyoming, it was still the same cry, and dismal to my heart, "Come back!"' (ibid.). The California in which Stevenson arrived on August 1879 was no El Dorado, despite the invigorating splendour of its scenery after the 'desolate and desert scenes' and the miserable, 'broken and unsightly' landscapes he had experienced *en route* (*T18* 115, 122, 107). The Sand-lot of San Francisco was, he wrote, 'crowded with the unemployed' (*T18* 115). Stevenson's journey did not end at San Francisco. Despite the fact that he 'looked like a man at death's door' (*T18* 101), he had to travel a further 130 miles to Monterey to meet Fanny and family. It was in his essay on Monterey that Stevenson's observations on life in California were first published. Originally entitled 'The Old Pacific Capital', the essay appeared in *Fraser's Magazine* in November 1880. Again Stevenson contrasts the richness of the natural environment with the poverty of the exploited population. The latter was predominantly Mexican, though the land was almost wholly owned by Americans (*T18* 136). The town of Monterey itself was, by American standards, primitive, with houses built of unbaked adobe brick, no streetlights, and sidewalks so erratically constructed that they 'only added to the dangers of the night' (*T18* 134–5). 'There was no activity', Stevenson says, 'but in and around the saloons, where people sat almost all day playing cards' (*T18* 135). The locals made even the shortest journey on horseback, in true Vaquero style, 'always at the hand-gallop...round the sharpest corner, urging their horses with cries and gesticulations and cruel rotatory spurs, checking them dead with a touch, or wheeling them right-about-face in a square yard' (*T18* 135). In manners and appearance the inhabitants of Monterey were 'surprisingly un-American' (ibid.). Perhaps recalling his experience on the emigrant train, Stevenson found that 'it was a matter of perpetual surprise to find in that world of absolutely mannerless Americans, a people full of deportment, solemnly courteous, and doing all things with grace and decorum' (ibid.). 'Physically the Americans had triumphed' Stevenson comments; 'but it is not entirely seen how far they have themselves been morally conquered' (*T18* 137). Stevenson foresaw that the States on the Pacific coast would become 'some monstrous hybrid – whether good or evil, who shall forecast? – but certainly original and all their own' (ibid.). In Simoneau's little restaurant at Monterey, with its 'Frenchman, two Portuguese, an Italian, a Mexican, and a Scotsman...a nearly pure-blood Indian woman,...a naturalized Chinese,...a Switzer and a German' (*T18* 137–8), he saw a microcosm of a future society. Old Monterey did not survive for long, however; in the perpetual revolution of capitalism, the developers had already moved in by the time Stevenson had written up his impressions of the little town, and 'the poor, quaint penniless native gentlemen of Monterey must perish...before the millionaire vulgarians of the Big Bonanza' (*T18* 142).

In an essay on San Francisco entitled 'A Modern Cosmopolis', published originally in *The Magazine of Art* in 1883, and posthumously coupled with the Monterey essay to form *The Old and New Pacific Capitals*, Stevenson contrasted the rapid decline of Monterey with the rapidity of San Francisco's growth. He records meeting persons 'not yet old' who had hunted, 'wading with [a] fowling-piece in the sand and scrub', on the site of what was now downtown San Francisco; for him, such an 'evocation of a roaring city, in a few years of a man's life, from the marshes and blowing sand' surpassed any enchantment in the Arabian Nights (*T18* 143–5). The uncanny swiftness of San Francisco's growth was matched only by the strangeness of its racial mix, with a mass of nationalities moving past like 'the slides of a magic-lantern' (*T18* 146–7). The mixture of races and cultures that had delighted Stevenson in Simoneau's restaurant at Monterey had been a foretaste of his experience in San Francisco. Stevenson revelled in the exuberant diversity of race and culture in a 'town which is essentially not Anglo-Saxon; still more essentially not American' (ibid.). This celebration of San Francisco was written up in Davos, two years later. When actually living in San Francisco, Stevenson's mood could be much less celebratory. On 26 December 1879 he wrote to Colvin: 'For four days I have spoken to no one but to my landlady or landlord or to Restaurant waiters. This is not a gay way to pass Christmas, is it? And I must own the guts are a little knocked out of me' (*L3* 39). This was Louis's 'circle of hell' period, when he could meet Fanny, by now living across the Bay in Oakland, only infrequently. He also had the responsibility of supporting Fanny and her family, as well as himself, on his slender literary earnings. His letters are filled with references to the modest amounts he was counting on receiving for the work he struggled to produce despite his poor health. *The Amateur Emigrant* was his major project, though he was also working on *A Vendetta in the West*, a novel set in Monterey, which was more than half written before it was abandoned, for no apparent reason. It has been speculated that Stevenson abandoned the novel because its central figure was based on Fanny's daughter Belle, with whom he seems to have fallen out at this period, perhaps because of her secret marriage to Joe Strong, or perhaps, as Frank McLynn has suggested, because of something more scandalous.[18] A piece of fiction which Stevenson did complete while in California was 'The Pavilion on the Links', a 'blood-and-thunder tale' which the young Conan Doyle was later to praise as 'the high water mark of [Stevenson's] genius',[19] and which was set in an unnamed part of Scotland, either on the Lothian coast, or more probably on the northern coast near Wick.[20]

More in tune with his American context was the essay on Thoreau which Stevenson researched while at Monterey in the autumn of 1979, and wrote up during December and January in San Francisco. 'Henry David Thoreau: His Character and Opinions' appeared in the *Cornhill* in June 1880, and subsequently in *Familiar Studies of Men and Books* in 1882. In the Preface to the latter, Stevenson qualified some of his comments in the original essay on the basis of his discussions at Braemar with Thoreau's biographer A.J. Japp (discussions which incidentally resulted in Japp's being instrumental in the publication of *Treasure Island*). The original impact made on Stevenson by his reading of Thoreau remained profound, however: 'I have scarce written ten sentences since

I was introduced to [Thoreau's work], but his influence might be somewhere detected by a close observer' (*T27* xviii). Thoreau's views on work and money must have seemed particularly (and at times ironically) relevant to Stevenson as he struggled to earn money by his pen to support Fanny and her family as well as himself. The supreme value for Thoreau was quality of life. Stevenson quotes him as saying: ' "The cost of a thing . . . is *the amount of what I will call Life*" ' (*T27* 85). Work is 'in itself and when properly chosen, delightful and profitable to the worker; and when your toil has been a pleasure, you have not, as Thoreau says, "earned money merely" ' (*T27* 90); for ' "to have done anything by which you earned money merely", says Thoreau, "is to be . . . idle and worse" ' (*T27* 89). For Thoreau, work should be an end in itself, and 'we may escape uncongenial toil, only to devote ourselves to that which is congenial' (*T27* 90). In a kind of pragmatist version of *l'art pour l'art*, the highest kind of 'work for the sake of work' is the artist's devotion to his art (ibid.). 'The most profitable work', wrote Stevenson, expounding Thoreau, 'is that which combines into one continued effort the largest proportion of the powers and desires of a man's nature; that into which he will plunge with ardour, and from which he will desist with reluctance; and in which he will know the weariness of fatigue, but not that of satiety; and which will be ever fresh, pleasing, and stimulating to his taste' (ibid.). The tension of this ideal with the reality of Stevenson's experience of work, as he scraped a living by his pen in San Francisco, can be seen when he moaned in a letter to Colvin: 'It bored me hellishly to write the *Emigrant*; well, it's going to bore others to read it; that's only fair' (*L3* 60). Evidently Stevenson could only take so much of Thoreau's nobility of mind.

Stevenson's sojourn in San Francisco marked a transition between a stage of his life when he could live off his father, and for himself and his art; and a new stage, when he became responsible for supporting himself, and Fanny and her family, solely, it seemed, through his earnings as professional writer. This was 'the circle of hell . . . that of the penniless and dying author'. From this hell in San Francisco Louis was rescued, firstly by Fanny who, flinging propriety to the winds, brought him over the Bay to Oakland to nurse him after he succumbed to malaria and his first haemorrhage; and secondly by his father, whose telegraph 'Count on 250 pounds annually' arrived as a *deus ex machina*. 'You may imagine what a blessed business this was', Stevenson wrote to Colvin in the letter of mid-April 1880 that described 'the circle of hell' from which Louis had been providentially saved (*L3* 75). That he had been spared the sole responsibility of supporting himself and his new family is evident in the fact that his first act, on receiving the good news that he had become a remittance man, besides releasing Colvin from the obligation to pay back immediately some money he owed him, was to instruct the latter to recover the sheets of *The Amateur Emigrant*. Being no longer in a position where he '*had* to go on anyway, for dear life (ibid.), he now had the leisure to rewrite it in light of Colvin's criticisms. Breaking the happy news of his remittance to Edmund Gosse in a letter of 16 April, Stevenson joked about gambling with death, or Hades, for six weeks, and admitted, if not to a death-wish, then at least to feeling 'unable to go on further with that rough horseplay of human life; a man must be pretty well to take the business in good part' (*L3* 77). He added that the £250 a year was intended as a 'marriage present (though they do not so name it)' from his parents; and that on the way to the mountains, where he planned to go as soon as the weather cleared, 'I marry myself; then I set up my family altar among the pinewoods, 3000 feet, sir, from the disputatious sea' (*L3* 78).

It was equally *en passant* that Stevenson mentioned his marriage (performed on 19 May 1880 by a Scots Presbyterian minister in San Francisco) in a letter to Colvin written in late May from Calistoga, a small spa-town in the Napa valley at the foot of Mount Saint Helena. Between a lengthy discussion of the *Amateur Emigrant* sheets, and an equally lengthy review of the reading matter Colvin had sent him (including Henry James's *Hawthorne*, which Stevenson found so 'very clever, very well written, . . . snobbish and . . . provincial' that he proposed to take James's scalp), Stevenson slipped in: 'I am certainly recovering fast: a married and convalescent being' (*L3* 83). Stevenson's married life intruded only tangentially into his literary life when he commented: 'I think my new book should be good; it will contain our adventures for the summer, so far as these are worth narrating; and I have already a few pages of diary which should make up bright' (ibid.). Stevenson's hope 'to get a house at Silverado, a deserted mining camp, eight miles up in the mountains' seems to have as much to do with his search for health and copy as with any plans for a romantic honeymoon. His apparent diffidence about his marriage was perhaps to do with the dis-approval with which he knew it was viewed back home, though the decision to get married may have been in fact less romantic than the Stevenson hagiographies have suggested.[21]

Stevenson's journal of the expedition to Calistoga and ultimately Silverado, which he told Colvin 'should make up bright', has survived and was published in full in 1954; a partial version was published as *The Silverado Diary* in the Vailima edition of Stevenson's works in 1922, and subsequently in the Tusitala edition of 1924.[22] The opening words of *The Silverado Squatters* – 'The scene of this little book is on a high mountain' (*T18* 155) – could easily be amended to: 'The scene of *writing* of this little book is on a high mountain', since the journal was rewritten, or 'made up bright', at Davos in the Swiss Alps early in 1882. The scene of writing seems to have influenced the emphasis on mountain scenery, including a reference to Mont Blanc, in the opening of *The Silverado Squatters*. The opening of the *The Silverado Diary* could hardly be more different; it begins at Vallejo junction on 22 May 1880, three days after the Stevensons' wedding, and moves swiftly to the dismal prospect of South Vallejo, with its hostelry shattered by flood or earthquake and surrounded on every side by marshes and stagnant water (*T18* 251). South Vallejo does also appear in *The Silverado Squatters*, but only briefly; like many Californian towns, it is 'a blunder', the site having proved 'untenable' (*T18* 156). The *Diary*, however, lingers on such curiosities as South Vallejo's 'singing cobbler', a former opera singer reminiscent of M. de Vauversin in *An Inland Voyage* and M. Berthelini in 'Providence and the Guitar'. It also reveals more about the everyday life of Louis and Fanny, for example the fact that the latter ate as greedily at supper as the rough men in shirtsleeves, and later blushed 'for such gross indulgence' (*T18* 252).

From Vallejo the newly-weds took the train up 'the long green strath of Napa Valley' to Calistoga (*T18* 156), as Stevenson put it in his native Scots. There is considerable reference to Stevenson's Scottishness in *The Silverado Squatters*, including the chapter entitled 'The Scot Abroad', with its claim that, despite there being 'no special loveliness in that grey country, with its rainy, sea-beat archipelago; its fields of dark mountains; its unsightly places, black with coal ...', nevertheless: 'the happiest lot on earth is to be born a Scotsman.' (*T18* 172) Stevenson recounts various stories about Scots in California, including one concerning a fellow 'about fifty, filthy, ragged, roguish, with a chimney-pot hat and tail coat, and a pursing of the mouth that might have been envied by an elder of the kirk' (*T18* 174), who had trespassed on Stevenson's 'property' at Silverado with clear criminal intent. 'A more impudent rascal I have never seen' says Stevenson in a passage deleted from the published version of *The Silverado Squatters*: 'had he been American, I should have raged. But then – he came from Aberdeen'.[23] A similarly strong sense of race emerges in the chapters grouped under the title 'With the Children of Israel', which focus on the figure whom Stevenson decided to call 'Mr. Kelmar'. Kelmar was the storekeeper in Calistoga, 'a Russian Jew, good-natured, in a very thriving way of business' (*T18* 177); he also had, Stevenson was convinced, 'something of the expression of a Scottish country elder, who, by some peculiarity, should chance to be a Hebrew' (ibid.). Although he so warmed to the Kelmars that 'they almost persuaded me to be a Jew' (*T18* 189), Stevenson skirts uncomfortably close to anti-semitic prejudice when he claims that, despite being not quite like other 'Jew store-keepers of California, [who] profiting at once by the needs and habits of the people, have made themselves in too many cases the tyrants of the rural population', Kelmar nevertheless exerted considerable power over the settlers in a radius of seven or eight miles round Calistoga (*T18* 177–8). He 'is their family friend, the director of their business, and, to a degree elsewhere unknown in modern days, their king' (*T18* 178). It was Kelmar who decided that the very place Stevenson needed was Silverado, an abandoned silver mine up the mountainside from the Toll House Hotel. The hotel was a kind of health resort, housing several consumptives; in a phrase that echoes the scene of writing of *The Silverado Squatters*, Stevenson calls the Toll House 'a kind of small Davos' (*T18* 218). The expedition to view Silverado was made with the Kelmars *en famille*, the latter seeming determined both to make a day of it, and to 'place' a batch of kettles with various friends they visited *en route* (*T18* 189).

In contrast to Stevenson's fantasies of a mountain retreat (complete with 'a trout stream brawling by'), they found that at Silverado 'mountain and house and old tools of industry were all alike rusty and downfalling' (*T18* 187). Nor was the outlook altogether inspiring: 'The view up the canyon was a glimpse of devastation; dry red minerals sliding together, here and there a crag, here and there dwarf thicket clinging in the general *glissade*, and over all a broken outline trenching on the blue of heaven.' (ibid.) But for better or for worse, as Stevenson says of what was in effect his honeymoon retreat, the die was cast (ibid.). Not only did the accommodation (doorless, with poison oak growing through the floor boards, and tiers of bunk-beds), and the weather (constant wind), leave something to be desired; the neighbours, too, were at best unreliable. Stevenson was careful to avoid placing his nearest neighbours, the Hansons, into the category of 'Poor Whites', a group largely unknown to English readers, for whose instruction he offered a thumbnail sketch of such American backwoodsmen. But the Hansons were, as he tactfully puts it: 'in many points not unsimilar to the people so-called' (*T18* 203–4). Mrs Hanson's brother, Irvine Lovelands, provided Stevenson with the material for a memorable sketch of 'the most unmitigated Caliban I ever knew' (*T18* 206). Constantly chewing pine-tree gum and spitting on the floor, Irvine was lazy, vain, rude, very stupid, and 'as beautiful as a statue'; beneath the exterior of a Greek god lurked 'the soul of a fat sheep'. At length Stevenson, who had taken on Irvine as a woodcutter and general handyman, felt that he had to point out to him that he 'could not continue to give him a salary for spitting on the floor'. When this concept had 'at last penetrated his obdurate wits', Irvine replied that: 'if this was the way he was going to be spoke to, he reckoned he would quit. And no one interposing, he departed' (*T18* 206–9). Since there turned out to be no one else in the neighbourhood to employ, Irvine was persuaded to return, morosely, to his job of woodcutting. The rest of the work was shared between Fanny and Louis, the former having to do most of the heavy work because of Louis's convalescent state and general handlessness, while Louis only had to make breakfast and teach some Euclid and Latin grammar to young Sam, as Lloyd was still called at this period.

At first there were four of them: Louis and Fanny, the King and Queen of Silverado; 'Crown Prince' Sam; and the Grand Duke Chuchu, a setter crossed with spaniel (*T18* 194). During their rule at Silverado there was 'a melancholy interregnum', Stevenson archly says, when 'the queen and the crown prince with one accord fell sick'; since Louis was sick to begin with, this rendered their position at Silverado 'no longer tenable', and they had to 'hurry back to Calistoga and a cottage on the green' (*T18* 223). Such a twee understatement, coming more than three quarters of the way through *The Silverado Squatters*, seems starkly at odds with what Stevenson wrote to Fanny Sitwell on 17 June 1880 (the tone of this description of his honeymoon may have been influenced by the fact that this was the first letter he had written, following his marriage to Fanny Osbourne, to the first great love of his life):

My dear, We have had a miserable time. We were six days in Silverado. The first night I had a cramp and was quite worn out after it; the second day Fanny mashed her thumb while carpentering and had a nervous chill; the third day, she had another from sleeplessness; the sixth day, she and Sam both began to have diphtheria. I got them down in an open cart . . . (*L3* 85–6)

Thus the gang of four did not reign for long at Silverado. When the Stevensons returned to Silverado after ten days or so of recuperation, they were accompanied by Belle's husband Joe Strong, and later joined in the cramped quarters by Belle herself and Fanny's sister Nellie. The chapter entitled 'A Starry Drive' describes this return to Silverado at night with Joe Strong, 'the painter',[24] in language so extraordinarily vivid that it seems to anticipate Van Gogh. Along with much of *The Silverado Squatters*, this purple passage represents a return on Stevenson's part to the kind of literary impressionism that characterised his French travel writings, in contrast to the more realistic style which he developed to document his emigrant journey. When Stevenson sums up the time at Silverado in *The Silverado Squatters*, therefore, we sense that, in contrast to the letters and the journal, a process of idealization has been at work. The impression given by *The Silverado Squatters* is that, apart from the inconvenience caused by rattlesnakes, the occasional intruding grizzly, or a deluge of sea fog, life at Silverado passed, if not quite idyllically, then peacefully and in complete privacy: 'hour melted insensibly into hour; the household duties . . . dwindled into mere islets of business in a sea of sunny daytime; and it appears to me, looking back, as though the greater part of our life at Silverado had passed, propped upon an elbow, or seated on a plank, listening to the silence that there is among the hills'(*T18* 237).

About a month after the Stevensons had returned to Silverado with Joe Strong, they left it for good and moved back to San Francisco. From there they travelled by rail to New York, where they embarked on 7 August bound for Liverpool. Presumably they travelled first class, mixing with the set that Louis had come to view with such hostility on his journey over to America as an amateur emigrant. As ever, Louis collected friends, including on this occasion a businessman James Cunningham, who recorded that on board the *City of Chester*: 'to the accompaniment of endless cigarettes, or . . . a perilous cocktail which [Stevenson] compounded with much zest from a San Franciscan recipe, the stream of his romantic and genial talk flowed on'.[25] They were met at Liverpool on 17 August by Sidney Colvin, who had travelled up from London; and by Louis's parents who were anxious to see for themselves Louis's state of health and his new American wife. On both counts his parents seem to have been reassured. Colvin, however, wrote bitchily to Henley: 'whether you or I will ever get reconciled to the little determined brown face and white teeth and . . . grizzling hair, which we are to see beside him in the future – that is another matter' (*L3* 93). The Stevenson clan, enlarged by the addition of Louis's new wife and stepson, departed for a holiday in the Scottish Highlands. Before leaving San Francisco Louis had written to Fanny's brother Jacob Vandegrift to say that, after the journey to Scotland to introduce Fanny to his parents (who, he reassured Jacob, would take care of Fanny in case of Louis's death), he hoped to return to California the following spring, after wintering somewhere warm (*L3* 91). In fact the Stevensons spent the next two winters, on medical advice, at the Swiss resort of Davos. It was to be eight years before they visited California again.

* * *

In some imaginary interstice between California, the Scottish Highlands and Davos, there came to be in 1881 a place that was no place, that existed briefly on a map which was painted with cheap water-colours, and went missing in the post. *Treasure Island* first appeared, Stevenson tells us in his 1893 essay 'My First Book', as a map which he made with his stepson's shilling box of water-colours one wet summer afternoon in 'the late Miss McGregor's cottage' at Braemar (*T2* xxv). As he pored over his map of *Treasure Island*, 'the future characters of the book began to appear there visibly among imaginary woods; and their brown faces and bright weapons peeped out... as they passed to and fro, fighting and hunting treasure, on these few square inches of a flat projection. The next thing I knew, I had some paper before me and was writing out a list of chapters' (ibid.). Stevenson later detected (or introduced) 'the finger of predestination' in the whole affair, for, having begun a boys' story with a boy conveniently 'at hand to be a touchstone' (*T2* xxvi), along came A.J. Japp to discuss Thoreau, and 'charged by my old friend, Mr Henderson, to unearth new writers for *Young Folks*'[26] (*T2* xxviii). The captive audience for the first readings of *Treasure Island* (or *The Sea Cook*, as it was originally entitled) included not only Louis's stepson, and Japp, but also Louis's father, who was possibly more enthusiastic about the tale than anyone else – 'it was *his* kind of picturesque', says Stevenson (*T2* xvii). Thomas Stevenson meticulously invented the contents of Billy Bones's chest, named Flint's old ship the *Walrus*, and 'elaborately *forged* the signature of Captain Flint' on the map of *Treasure Island*, which was redrawn in his office after Louis's original water-colour version was lost (*T2* xvii–xxx). He also contributed his own experience of eavesdropping from a ship's apple barrel, later recounted by Stevenson in *Records of a Family of Engineers* (*T19* 194). At first Stevenson was able to dash off a chapter a day of *The Sea Cook*. Not only was there a hungry audience at the late Miss McGregor's cottage, there were also (metaphorically speaking) hungry mouths to feed. As Stevenson put it later in 'My First Book': 'I was thirty-one; I was head of a family; I had lost my health; I had never yet paid my way, had never yet made two hundred pounds a year.' (*T2* xxviii–xxix) Japp told a delighted Stevenson that he hoped get to 100 for *The Sea Cook*, though in the event James Henderson offered only twelve shillings and sixpence per column, which

Stevenson worked out at about £30 overall. This was the going rate, even for well-known writers of boys' stories. After the first 19 chapters (rather than the 15 he recalled in 'My First Book' (*L3* 231 n.12)), Stevenson got writer's block. He had lung problems, and was put on a respirator – 'a pig's snout', he told Henley (ibid.) – and ordered south from the 'absolutely and consistently vile' Braemar weather (*L3* 228). Stopping off at London *en route* for Davos, he received the proofs for the early chapters of *The Sea Cook*, which at this point changed its title, at Henderson's instigation, to *Treasure Island*. The author was named as Captain George North.[27] Stevenson completed *Treasure Island* in Davos.

If we can locate geographically the scenes of writing of *Treasure Island*, there is considerable uncertainty as to the geographical location of the fictional island itself. Treasure Island is often assumed to lie somewhere in the Caribbean, due to the association of pirates with the Spanish Main. However, as John Seelye has pointed out, some of the flora and fauna of Treasure Island are out of place in the Caribbean, and instead seem to belong somewhere on the Pacific side of the American continent.[28] Treasure Island is covered with live-oaks and rattlesnakes, indigenous to America, and it is dominated by what can only be redwoods, native to California. The Californian connection of *Treasure Island* had been spotted even in Stevenson's own day, Seeleye records, and proceeds to argue that the landscape depicted in *Treasure Island* is not only that of Silverado but also of the Monterey Peninsula, whose outline, Seelye claims, resembles that of Treasure Island in the map drawn by Stevenson.[29] If *Treasure Island* was literally shaped by the American landscape, in another sense it received some of its most distinctive features from the American literary landscape. The book is dedicated to 'S[amuel] L[loyd] O[sbourne], An American Gentleman', and figuring prominently among the literary debts acknowledged (or perhaps touted) in the epigraph 'To the Hesitating Purchaser', is 'Cooper of the wood and wave'. James Fenimore Cooper, though best know for his Leatherstocking tales including *The Last of the Mohicans* (1826), also wrote tales of the sea such as *The Sea Lions*, from which, according to Seelye,[30] Stevenson made significant, if unacknowledged, borrowings. In 'My First Book' Stevenson did acknowledge literary debts to Defoe, Kingsley (whose *At Last* provided the Dead Man's Chest), and to two American authors: Poe, whose tale about buried treasure, 'The Gold-Bug', suggested the pointing skeleton; and Washington Irving, whose *Tales of a Traveller* featured an old sea dog tyrannizing an inn, unmistakably the ancestor of Billy Bones. Another American literary connection suggested by Seelye is Mark Twain's *The Adventures of Tom Sawyer* (1876), whose piracy, treasure-hunting and opportune eavesdropping may have had an influence on *Treasure Island*, which in its turn impressed the author of *Huckleberry Finn*.[31] Stevenson read the latter on its appearance in 1884, just at the time the American John Singer Sargent was painting his famous portraits of Stevenson at Skerryvore (*L5* 41 n.1). As Stevenson later wrote to Mark Twain, he had insisted that *Huckleberry Finn* be read aloud during the sittings, much to the disappointment of Singer, who would have preferred Baudelaire (*L6* 161–2). Stevenson was writing to arrange a meeting with Twain, which took place, Stevenson recalled in a later letter to Twain, on a 'very pleasant afternoon we spent together in Washington Square among the nursemaids like a couple of characters out of a story by Henry James' (*L8* 57). In this letter Stevenson mentioned his 'boy on the premises [Fanny's grandson, Austin Strong] who would consent to read nothing at all except *Tom Sawyer, Huck Finn* and (from family partiality) *Treasure Island*.' (ibid.) On leaving to go to school, Austin had had to pack away all his books, with the sole exception of *Tom Sawyer*, with which 'bracing volume in his hand' he 'faced the universe' (*L8* 58). 'If I were a jealous man,' Stevenson wrote to Twain, 'this would be wounding; it is my consolation that I was packed in the hold in company with Defoe. Try and bear your triumph meekly' (ibid.). Such literary banter aside, the real reason for Stevenson writing to Twain was to sound him out about the possibility of placing *David Balfour* with Twain's publishing firm, though in the event, Stevenson resolved his differences with Scribner's, and Twain's publisher failed disastrously the following year (*L8* 54 n.13, 145).

* * *

It was in early June 1887, a month after the death of his father, that a second trip by Stevenson to America emerged as serious possibility. Louis wrote to Henley that he had been advised by his doctors that 'a year in Colorado would do me good' (*L5* 420), Colorado being preferable to an Indian hill-station[32] because of its proximity to Fanny's family. Louis's mother, who was partly funding the trip out of money she had received from the family business, accompanied Louis, Fanny, Lloyd and the maid Valentine Roch, when they embarked on the *Ludgate Hill* at London docks on 22 August 1887, bound for New York. Preferring 'air and space' to luxury, they had gone for 'one of the less frequented lines' when booking their passage on the *Ludgate Hill* (*L6* 1). Unfortunately, the latter turned out to be a cattle-boat which picked up from Le Havre over a hundred horses plus a consignment of apes for American zoos, and consequently it stank like a menagerie. It had a tendency to roll even on a calm sea, which was not often the case on what was an exceptionally rough crossing; and the Stevensons' berths were not of the best. But Louis himself was never happier, he wrote to his cousin Bob, than on this transatlantic voyage (*L6* 17). Being on a tramp-ship meant that 'we could cut about with the men and officers, stay in the wheel house, discuss all manner of things, and really be a little at sea' (ibid.). And the case of champagne presented by Henry James as a parting gift no doubt helped.

When the Stevenson party arrived at at New York on 7 September, it was met by a figure from the past, Will H. Low, the American artist whom Louis and Fanny had known in France; and by two figures who were indicative of the future: Edward L. Burlingame, editor of *Scribner's Magazine*; and a reporter from the *New York Herald*. Unlike Stevenson's previous landing in New York as an anonymous face in 'a great block of passengers' (*T18* 82), he arrived this time as a celebrity, the famous author the best-selling *Dr Jekyll and Mr Hyde*. He was whisked away immediately to a luxury suite in the Victoria Hotel as a guest of the millionaire Charles Fairchild, and on the following day travelled to the latter's house in Newport, Rhode Island. Fairfield's wife Elizabeth was an admirer of Stevenson, and it was for her that Fairfield had commissioned the famous portraits of Stevenson by Sargent. Fairfield had invited the Stevensons to Newport when he had visited them at Bournemouth (*L5* 428–9). At the Victoria Hotel Stevenson gave interviews to journalists, whom on the whole he liked, writing to Colvin that they 'were too good for their trade; avoided anything I asked them to avoid; and were no more vulgar in their reports than they could help' (*L6* 5–6) He claimed to dislike his experience of literary superstardom, anticipating a later superstar in New York, John Lennon, when he wrote: 'My reception here was idiotic to the last degree; if Jesus Christ came, they would make less fuss' (ibid.). He told Walter Simpson: 'Fame is nothing to a yacht; *experto credite* [believe me, I know]. There are nice bits of course; for you meet very pleasant and interesting people; but the thing itself is a bore and a fraud' (*L6* 18).

Fame had its advantages, however. As Stevenson continued to Simpson: 'One thing is they do not stick for money to the Famed One.' (ibid.) Joseph Pulitzer of the *New York World* commissioned S.S. McClure to offer what Stevenson considered the enormous sum of $10,000 a year for a weekly article (*L6* 26), but Stevenson declined, telling Colvin that 'they would drive even an honest man into being a mere lucre-hunter in three weeks' (*L6* 10). Instead Stevenson accepted the offer of $3,500 a year for twelve articles in *Scribner's Magazine*. The first of these articles was 'A Chapter on Dreams', which contained an account of the genesis of *Dr Jekyll and Mr Hyde*, the work that had made Stevenson famous in the States. It was completed during the first month that the Stevensons spent at Saranac Lake in the Adirondacks in upper New York State, where a sanatorium for consumptives had recently been established by Dr E.L. Trudeau. The Stevensons decided to winter here rather than in Colorado, which for several reasons had turned out to be unsuitable; and the Adirondacks reminded Louis of the Scottish Highlands, notwithstanding the lack of heather (*L6* 16). In a letter to John Addington Symonds, Stevenson described the country surrounding Saranac Lake as: 'a kind of insane mixture of Scotland, with a touch of Switzerland and a dash of America'; the climate 'although not charming like that of Davos, [is] essentially bracing and briskening' (*L6* 64). The air at Saranac Lake was 'harsh but pure and antiseptic', Louis wrote in a puff in the New York *Evening Post* for his neighbour Dr Trudeau's 'Adirondack Cottages for the Treatment of Pulmonary Disease'; it gave a chance to those 'not wealthy enough to flee to Florida or Colorado, to the Riviera or Davos' (*L6* 122–3). If the climate agreed with Louis, it disagreed with just about everyone else in the party, and especially with Fanny, who took herself off temporarily to New York, and for a more extended period on a cross-country trip ending in California. Saranac was a kind of 'Arctic St Andrews', Louis wrote to 'Coggie' Ferrier, 'and the miseries of forty degrees below zero [Fahrenheit] with a high wind have to be felt to be appreciated' (*L6* 137). The severe climate was turned into a literary joke. To 'see what Gosse says' meant to check the thermometer given by Mrs Edmund Gosse, which hung in the sitting room, and which often indicated freezing and below. The thermometer hanging on the veranda, which often registered minus 40 degrees, was nicknamed 'the *Quarterly Reviewer*', though to write this to Gosse was to tread on thin ice, given that the latter had recently been savaged in the *Quarterly Review* (*L6* 141, n.2).

The twelve articles Stevenson produced at Saranac Lake were published monthly in *Scribner's Magazine* from January 1888. There was some discussion with Scribner about publishing them together in a single volume; this proved difficult, however, because of their heterogeneity, and the idea was eventually dropped, though nine did appear in the 1892 collection, edited by Colvin, entitled *Across the Plains*. The articles are indeed a mixed bag. Two of the most significant, 'A Chapter on Dreams' and 'The Lantern-Bearers' manage to combine a vivid evocation of incidents from Stevenson's past with important observations about the role of the unconscious and the imagination in literary creation. Others are closer to lay sermons, including an actual 'Christmas Sermon' that is far from orthodox, and also what Stevenson called 'a Darwinian sermon' entitled 'Pulvis et Umbra' (from Horaces's 'pulvis et umbra sumus' [we are dust and shadow][33]). Despite some hesitation on Stevenson's part over the latter (*S* 164), both sermons appeared in *Across the Plains*, and ultimately appeared in volume 26 of the Tusitala edition under the title *Lay Morals and Other Ethical Papers*. This collection of essays was organised round an unfinished fragment entitled *Lay Morals*, which had been begun in 1879, probably based on papers Stevenson had written for the Speculative Society, and further developed in October 1883. Writing that month to his father, Stevenson discussed the progress of *Lay Morals* and gave him a lecture in a kind of Calvinistic Stoicism: 'To fret and fume is undignified, suicidally foolish and theologically unpardonable; we are here not to make, but to tread predestined pathways; we are the foam of a wave, and to preserve a proper equanimity, is not merely the first part of submission to God, but the chief of possible kindnesses to those about us' (*L4* 183). In the same letter he mentioned James Walter Ferrier, whose recent death from drink had much affected him: 'I have learned more, in some ways, from that ex-sot, ex-sponge, and ex-buffoon, than from any other soul I ever met; and he, strange to think, was the best gentleman, in all kinder senses, that I ever knew' (ibid.). The question of what constitutes a gentleman had preoccupied Stevenson especially during his emigrant journey, and it is significant that in an article entitled 'Gentlemen', written at Saranac Lake for *Scribner's Magazine*, and ultimately located in the *Lay Morals* collection, he returned to material already used in *The Amateur Emigrant*. Like morality, the essence of being a gentleman was for Stevenson only on a superficial level relative to context, and especially the context of class. As he had intimated in *The Amateur Emigrant*, true decency transcends culture, class and circumstance; or, as he puts it in 'Pulvis et Umbra':

> if I could show you these men and women, all the world over, in every stage of history, under every abuse of error, under every circumstance of failure, without hope, without help, without thanks, still obscurely fighting the lost fight of virtue, still clinging, in the brothel or on the scaffold, to some rag of honour, the poor jewel of their souls! They may seek to escape, and yet they cannot; it is not alone their privilege and glory, but their doom; they are condemned to some nobility, the desire of good is at their heels, the implacable hunter (*T26* 64–5).

Though not without its share of Victorian rhetoric, Stevenson's idea of being condemned to seek the good in a world where all foundations and supports have disappeared, or are fast disappearing, has a distinctively modern ring to it. There is a hint of Iris Murdoch's existentialist Platonism here, and also when he writes in 'Gentlemen': 'And yet for all this ambiguity, for all these imperfect examples, we know clearly what we mean by the word [gentleman]' (*T26* 96). This knowledge cannot, however, be defined; in place of a definition Stevenson offers to tell a story: 'History instead of Definition' (*T26* 100). His article on 'Gentlemen' in the May edition of *Scribner's Magazine* was thus followed in the June edition by 'Some Gentlemen in Fiction', where Stevenson made the bold claim that it is above all in the novels of Thackeray, and in specifically in the character of Colonel Newcome in *The Newcomes*, that we can find the clearest delineation of a 'gentleman': 'If the art of being a gentleman were forgotten, like the art of staining glass, it might be learned anew from that one character' (*T26* 112).

From such a lofty view of the role of literature Stevenson switched in his next *Scribner's* article to the opposite end of the literary spectrum when he wrote on 'Popular Authors'. By putting all the popular authors' names in capital letters 'since most of them have not much hope of durable renown' (*T28* 20), Stevenson sought at once to valorise popular culture and to recognise the pleasure he had derived from the 'penny press'. But while celebrating this pleasure, and deflating the 'genteel illusion' of the literary author 'addressing a mere parlour coterie and quite unknown to the great world outside the villa windows' (*T28* 29), Stevenson did not disguise the fact that popular fiction was simply not about generating the moral insight that could be derived from reading fiction: 'The tales were not true to what men see; they were true to what the readers dreamed. . . . They can thus supply to the shop-girl and shoe-black vesture cut to the pattern of their naked fancies, and furnish them with welcome scenery and properties for autobiographical romancing' (*T28* 30–1). This kind of reading as a 'migration' in which the reader 'escapes from the narrow prison of the individual career, and sates his avidity for other lives' (*T28* 32) is morally dubious.

The hollowness of mimesis as imitation or mimicry, and its use in the manipulation of fantasy, were also central themes of the major piece of fiction Stevenson was writing at Saranac Lake, *The Master of Ballantrae*, also destined for publication in *Scribner's Magazine*. Ephraim Mackellar's memorable expression of his horror at the Master's hollowness – 'if one should strike smartly through the buckram of his countenance, there would be found a mere vacuity within' (*T10* 163) – arises out of a description of Ballantrae reading aloud to Mackellar on board the *Nonesuch* bound for America. Ballantrae read beautifully, says Mackellar, as well as any elocutionist, first from *Clarissa*, and then from Mackellar's Bible; however, in Ballantrae's reading they become 'a source of entertainment only, like the scraping of a fiddle in a change-house' (*T10* 162). Ultimately Ballantrae read, not out of any love or respect for what these books might communicate, but merely out of love for the sound of his own voice: 'he loved the note of his own tongue, as, indeed he entirely loved all the parts and properties of himself; a kind of imbecility which almost necessarily attends wickedness' (*T10* 163). So writes the Puritan Mackellar; and though Stevenson claimed to find the Master of Ballantrae in himself,[34] there was also in Stevenson, in a duality typical of him and perhaps of Scottish culture generally, a deal of 'the good Ephraim'.

The climate and terrain of the Adirondacks is reflected in the concluding sections of *The Master of Ballantrae* set in the Wilderness beyond Albany. A moral climate of anguish caused by treachery and double-dealing is also common to the novel and to the Stevenson household at Saranac Lake. In a later draft preface to *The Master of Ballantrae*, Stevenson sketched the Master thus:

> Abjectly fond of admiration, he is careless, how or for what he is admired in error; whether for a fact or a lie, or ... for incongruous pretensions. An avaricious vanity, monstrous in its exactions, and unusual, although far from unparalleled, in its unveracity. Of such are the persons (one of whom was known to me) who pass themselves off as authors of other people's books.[35]

It is difficult to resist relating the above passage, with its reference to the diabolical crime of plagiarism, to the storm which was unleashed by a letter which arrived at Saranac Lake in March 1888 concerning a case of alleged plagiarism. The letter, marked 'private and confidential', was from Henley, and amid a stream of self-pitying and typically bitchy 'babble' (Henley's own term), it raised the issue of the authorship of a short story called 'The Nixie', published in the March edition of *Scribner's Magazine* (alongside Stevenson's essay 'Beggars') under the name Fanny Vandegrift Stevenson. 'It's Katharine's; surely it's Katharine's?' wrote Henley, who failed to understand, he said, 'why there wasn't a double signature' (*L6* 130). The facts of the case, as far as they can be detached from the intensely emotional constructions put on them by those involved in the furore, are roughly as follows. Sometime before the Stevensons left England, Katharine de Mattos, Louis's cousin and the dedicatee of *Dr Jekyll and Mr Hyde*, had discussed with Fanny, in the presence of Henley whose protégée Katharine had become, an idea for a story in which one of the two characters who meet on a train is a girl recently escaped from a lunatic asylum. Fanny had liked Katharine's story and had suggested that the girl should be a Nixie, or water sprite. Katharine rejected Fanny's suggestion, but conceded a reluctant undertaking that if her version of the story could not be sold, then she would inform Fanny so that the latter could try her luck with her version of the story (though since Fanny was the wife of the celebrated 'RLS', currently published on a monthly basis by Scribner's, luck, and indeed merit, may have had precious little to do with it). Since Katharine's version was 'everywhere refused', she wrote to give her permission to Fanny to proceed with her version. After the quarrel had blown up, however, Katharine wrote to Louis to say that 'she was totally unprepared to see "The Nixie" appear'; this looked to Stevenson like 'real treachery', as he wrote to Charles Baxter from Saranac Lake on 5 April (*L6* 146–7). Increasingly Louis began to see Henley as 'only a handgun for Katharine' (ibid.). In a letter to Charles Baxter later that April he admitted that he could see why Katharine had been so annoyed, given that she had only given Fanny her consent unwillingly, a fact acknowledged by Louis when he had asked Fanny not to proceed with the story (*L6* 172). Henley, who, as everyone knew, doted on Katharine, had as 'poor Knight Errant put lance in rest, and charged – at me', wrote Louis, clearly feeling himself, like everyone else in the affair, to be the innocent victim (ibid.).

Whatever the rights and wrongs of the affair, Stevenson took it very hard. He wrote to Baxter that he was 'utterly miserable', and that he felt this business 'with a keenness that I cannot describe' (*L6* 146–7); it was giving him palpitations, he said, and at night 'sleep is quite out of the question', so that he had to take opiates (ibid.). In his first letter to Baxter on the subject he said that he felt, not so much anger, as despair and even agony (*L6* 133). 'God knows I would rather have died than have this happen', he wrote on 5 April (*L6* 172), a wish he was to repeat in later letters to Baxter in the more specific form of wishing he had died at Hyères (*L6* 160, 161, 193). What caused this overwhelming, and seemingly hysterical, reaction on Stevenson's part is a matter of some speculation. Even if we have reservations about McLynn's psychoanalytic theory that 'in attacking Katharine Louis was really by transference expressing his anger at the one person he could not consciously condemn: Fanny',[36] there must have a some such dynamic at work in order to explain Louis's furiously defensive outbursts when he knew that Fanny had in fact gone against his judgement in publishing her version of Katharine's story. Another factor may have been his sheer isolation at Saranac Lake. Fanny had left on a long trip ending in California, and his mother and Lloyd were periodically absent, leaving him to a lonely wrestle with a punishing work schedule in bleak surroundings and in bitter (even if for him supposedly beneficial) cold. It must have almost insupportable to think that back in England his former friends, including not only Henley and Katharine, but also Bob in the background, were ganging up on him despite that fact that Louis was helping to support all of them financially with his hard literary labour. And it was by the withdrawal of financial support that Stevenson did seek to take a form of revenge on Katharine. Her refusal to confess her 'stubborn pride in wrong-doing' (*L6* 189–90) led him to ask Charles Baxter about adding a codicil to his will which would ensure that the expense of a deferred annuity for Katharine's child (which Fanny had opposed in a separate letter to Baxter from San Francisco (*L6* 187)) would come out of Katharine's legacy, and the resulting reduction in Katharine's share would be added to Lloyd's – if that, Stevenson asked Baxter, did not seem mean? (*L6* 193) It seems appropriate that in this same letter steeped in familial conflict and bitterness, and fraught with issues of inheritance, Stevenson should mention the progress of *The Master of Ballantrae*. Ironically, Katharine's penultimate word to Louis on the overheated topic was: 'I am afraid to speak or breathe. There is devilry in the air' (*L6* 189). Her final word was . her reply to Stevenson's overbearing and sanctimonious rejoinder (for which he himself subsequently felt 'the most hideous revulsion', and for which could not forgive himself for three days, as he wrote to Baxter (*L6* 194)): 'I know this can *never* get better', wrote Katharine, 'but perhaps nothing can make it worse. . . . I was maddened with despair when I read your letter which taxed me with a preconceived plot. I can only myself know how impossible it would have been to me to do such a thing. How deeply sorry I am it is useless to try to say and impossible not to remember all your past kindness which has now turned into life long distrust of me' (*L6* 204). Katharine was right; five years later, again in the context of a letter to Baxter about legacies to Bob and Katharine in his will, Stevenson wrote: 'really R. and K. are the most indifferent and unfriendly people in the world' (*L7* 110).

Of all the attacks and counter-attacks following the furore provoked by the letter Henley sent to Saranac Lake in March 1888, the ultimate act of revenge came after Stevenson's death, in Henley's notoriously acerbic review of Balfour's *Life* in the *Pall Mall Magazine* in December 1901. The real agenda of the whole 'Nixie' affair was the intense mutual dislike of Henley and Fanny Stevenson. Henley's attack may have been partly motivated by his feelings for Katharine, but underneath was a smouldering resentment against Fanny who had increasingly sought to curtail Henley's boisterous visits to Bournemouth, and who ultimately had in some sense taken away from Henley the Lewis (as Henley insisted on spelling Stevenson's forename) of his youth. As Henley put in the review: 'For me there were two Stevensons: the Stevenson who went to America in '87; and the Stevenson who never came back. The first I knew, and loved; the other I lost touch with, and, though I admired him, did not greatly esteem. My relation to him was that of a man with a grievance . . .'.[37] The creation of the Stevenson who never came back from America, 'this Seraph in chocolate, this barley-sugar effigy of a real man'[38] was not so much laid at the door of Balfour, who in Henley's eyes was merely a creature of the Osbournes, as at the door of Fanny herself, who controlled the official biography. Whatever general ill feeling may have existed between Henley and Fanny Stevenson, there was a very specific issue which seems to reveal a continuing animus against Henley on the part of Fanny. When the 'Nixie' affair first blew up, Stevenson took care to see that Henley's legacy in his will was secured, since the Osbournes could obviously not be trusted in that matter. When in July 1894, six years later, and not long before Stevenson's death, Henley sent a conciliatory letter which Louis thought 'in very good taste and rather touching', Fanny, 'with that appalling instinct of the injured female to see mischief, thought it was a letter preparatory to the asking of money' (*L8* 332). Persuaded by Fanny that the letter could be read in this way, Stevenson decided to pre-empt any request for financial help by arranging for Henley to be paid 5 pounds per month (when necessary), adding: 'He can't starve at that; it's enough – more than he had when I first knew him; and if I gave him more, it would only lead to his starting a gig and a Pomeranian dog' (ibid.). This remark, stripped of the explicit reference to Henley, appeared in Balfour's *Life* (*B* 397); Henley's strong over-reaction in the *Pall Mall* review (he mentions Pomeranian dogs five times) suggests that he recognised the reference to himself – as it was Fanny's intention that he should, so several commentators including Baxter himself have suspected (*L8* 332, n.4).

For Henley the second trip to America marked the eclipse of the 'first Stevenson', and the ascendancy of what Henley had called 'the Shorter-Catechist'. Henley's interest in Stevenson was personal: ' "RLS" . . . the successful man of letters does not greatly interest me . . . I remember, rather, the unmarried and irresponsible Lewis: the friend, the comrade, the *charmeur*.'[39] It was 'lay morals' delivered in private, particularly to Katharine and himself, that Henley found insupportable; as he wrote to Baxter: 'Lewis's letter [from Saranac Lake] has exasperated me; I confess it's hard to endure. The immense superiority;...the directions as to conduct and action – all these things have set me wild' (*L6* 168). Henley lost the moral high ground, however, when he could not resist getting personal in a revealing if ambiguous conclusion to this letter: 'Lewis has known me longer than his spouse, and has never known me lie or truckle or do anything else that is base. He can't have slept with Fanny for all these years, and not have caught her in the act of lying' (ibid.).

However seriously Stevenson may have taken himself as 'the Shorter-Catechist', there was a new development at Saranac Lake which revealed that he was able to take himself much less seriously as a writer. In his first surviving letter from Saranac Lake, Stevenson mentions to Henry James that: 'from the next room the bell of Lloyd's type-writer makes an agreeable music, as it patters off (at a rate which astonishes the experienced novelist) the early chapters of a humorous romance.' (*L6* 15). This was Lloyd's first draft of a story initially called *The Finsbury Tontine*, influenced possibly by a popular Victorian detective novel called *The Great Tontine* (1881)[40] and certainly by Stevenson's *New Arabian Nights*; it was subsequently to become *A Game of Bluff*, and finally *The Wrong Box*. In his letters from Saranac Lake Stevenson periodically mentioned Lloyd 'tinkling at his romance', though at first he seemed more taken by the mode of production (the newfangled typewriter) than by the story itself, some of which was 'incredibly bad' (*L6* 38). It was not until early March 1888 that he announced in a letter to Henley that he had agreed to collaborate with Lloyd on the work, a 'merest farce, an Arabian Night on the scale of a novel', and was halfway through his own version (*L6* 125). This was Stevenson's last latter to Henley before the outbreak of the 'Nixie' quarrel, and although it would probably have crossed Henley's bombshell on the Atlantic, its announcement that Louis, having previously collaborated with Fanny on *The Dynamiter*, was now actually collaborating with the nineteen year old Lloyd Osbourne, would have only further irritated Henley, still smarting from what he perceived as Louis's desertion, under the influence of Fanny, from their collaboration on works for the stage.

Thus March 1888 marked both the bitter end of the ultimately unsuccessful collaboration of Stevenson with the literary lion Henley, and the beginning of his considerably more successful collaboration with the literary tiro Lloyd Osbourne. The latter partnership was to produce not only *The Wrong Box*, whose epigraph says of the authors that: 'one of them is old enough to be ashamed of himself, and the other young enough to learn better'; but also the much more significant novella *The*

Ebb-Tide, and the flawed but fascinating novel *The Wrecker*. *The Wrong Box* was begun in Saranac and completed in the South Seas. On 2 June 1888 the Stevenson party (comprising Louis, his mother, Lloyd and Valentine Roch) left New York, and, after meeting up with Fanny at Sacramento, reached San Francisco on 7 June. Here they completed the formalities relating to the charter of the *Casco*, a ninety-four foot, two-masted schooner yacht, for an initial period of seven months, under the captaincy of A.H. Otis (later to figure as Captian Nares in *The Wrecker*). Although Maggie Stevenson saw the sights of San Francisco, and Valentine, according to Fanny, fell in love with very Chinaman she saw (*L6* 203), Louis was very tired and spent much of his time on board the *Casco*, still brooding on the 'Nixie' affair. The last words which he instructed Baxter to send to Henley in the event of his death were: 'Auld Lang Syne'. To Katharine the message was: 'It is never too late to repent and make amends' (*L6* 201). He was 'pretty sick' and could not get over 'this affair', he wrote to Baxter; he just longed to get to sea, he said, and had 'no great mind' ever to return (*L6* 200). On 28 June the *Casco* was towed through the Golden Gate out into the Pacific, and Stevenson saw America for the last time.

5

In the South Seas

That wide field of ocean, called loosely the South Seas, extends from tropic to tropic, and from perhaps 120 degrees W. to 150 degrees E., a parallelogram of one hundred degrees by forty-seven, where degrees are the most spacious.[1]

Away in the islands

In his late poem 'Ship of Death', D.H. Lawrence, who strongly identified with Stevenson in his desperate travels in search of heath,[2] wrote:

> Oh build your ship of death, your little ark
> and furnish it with food, with little cakes, and wine
> for the dark flight down oblivion.

The *Casco* was in a sense Stevenson's 'ship of death'. As he put it at the beginning of *In the South Seas*: 'For nearly ten years my health had been declining; and for some while before I set forth on my voyage, I believed I was come to the afterpiece of life, and had only the nurse and undertaker to expect. It was suggested that I try the South Seas; and I was not unwilling to visit like a ghost, and be carried like a bale, among scenes that had attracted me in youth and health (*T20* 3). In what seems a case of the pathetic fallacy, the dying narrator of *In the South Seas* describes a Polynesian world in terminal decline, arguably a projection of Stevenson's own anxieties about personal and cultural disintegration and entropy.[3] Yet there is also in the book a strong sense of miraculous new beginnings, as when Stevenson describes his first experience of a South Sea island:

The first experience can never be repeated. The first love, the first sunrise, the first South Sea island, are memories apart, and touched with a virginity of sense. On the 28th of July 1888, the moon was an hour down by four in the morning. In the east a radiating centre of brightness told of the day; and beneath, on the skyline, the morning bank was already building, black as ink.... [I]t was half-past five before we could distinguish our expected islands from the clouds on the horizon.... The interval was passed on deck in the silence of expectation, the accustomed thrill of landfall heightened by the strangeness of the shores that we were then approaching. Slowly they took shape in the attenuating darkness. Ua-huna, piling up to a truncated summit, appeared the first upon the starboard bow; almost abeam arose our destination, Nuka-hiva, whelmed in cloud; and betwixt and to the southward, the first rays of the sun displayed the needles of Ua-pu. These pricked about the line of the horizon; like the pinnacles of some ornate and monstrous church, they stood there, in the sparkling brightness of the morning, the fit sign-board of a world of wonders (*T20* 4).

This description, laced as it is with erotic and religious imagery, is echoed in Stevenson's fiction of this period, for example, the landfall evoked at the beginning of the first chapter of 'The Beach of Falesá', entitled 'A South Sea Bridal' (*T13* 1). The landfall described at the beginning of *In the South Seas* took place at Anaho Bay in Nuka-Hiva, the largest of the Marquesas Islands, where the *Casco* arrived on 20 July[4] 1888, twenty-two days after leaving San Francisco.

From the time it was first discussed with S.S. McClure at Saranac Lake in January 1888, the project of the Pacific yacht cruise had involved the assumption that it would be largely paid for out of the money Stevenson would earn from 'letters descriptive of [his] experiences and observations', as McClure put it in a formal letter in March 1888 undertaking to sell such letters 'to syndicates of newspapers...in all countries where such sales can be effected' (*L6* 137, n.2). These '*Casco* letters' were expected to earn Stevenson $300 apiece (*L6* 192, n.9). They were also intended to serve as the basis for another travel book, 'the book of the cruise', as Stevenson called it in a letter to Colvin (*L6* 241). Writing from the *Casco, en route* from the Marquesas to the Pautomu (or Tuamotu) Islands, Stevenson assured Baxter: 'I shall have a fine book of travels, I feel sure; and will tell you more of the South Seas after very few months than any other writer has done – except Herman Melville, who is a howling cheese' (*L6* 207). Melville's novel *Typee* (1846), his best-known work in the nineteenth century,[5] was set in Nuka-Hiva, the island Stevenson had just left. The projected transmutation of the letters into a travel book was far from smooth, however. Stevenson was unhappy with the letters he churned out in order to fulfil his contract with McClure and pay for the cruise. He wrote to his mother that 'the grisly Letters have begun' in January 1891, when they appeared in newspapers in Sydney and Auckland; in the following February they appeared in the *Sun* in New York and *Black and White* in London (*L7* 68, n.5). In May 1891 he responded irritably to Colvin's report that Stevenson's friends had been disappointed by the 'impersonal and even tedious character of some portions of the South Seas Letters', insisting that: '*These Letters were never meant, and are not now meant, to be other than a quarry of materials from which the book may be drawn*' (*L7* 115, n.8). Stevenson's irritation that Colvin could be so 'impenetrably stupid' on this point may be explained by the fact that he had written to him the previous month: 'No one seems to understand my attitude about that [South Seas] book; the stuff was never meant for other than a first state, I never meant it to appear as a book: knowing well that I have never had one hour of inspiration since it was begun, and have only beaten out my metal by brute force and patient repetition: I hoped some day to get a 'spate of style' and burnish it ... I am now so sick that I intend, when the Letters are done ... simply to make a book of it by the pruning knife' (*L7* 101–2).

Stevenson's publishers as well as his critics seem to have felt they were being fobbed off with substandard material. McClure was annoyed because, firstly, the 'Letters' he had commissioned were not in the first instance sent to him; and secondly, they were not letters. What he received was a copy of a book entitled *The South Seas: A Record of Three Cruises* published in London on 12 November 1890 by Cassell, to secure copyright; only two copies of this edition were actually sold, the rest being distributed to friends. The New York *Sun* would only accept this material at a much reduced rate, arguing rather legalistically that: 'the letters did not come as letters are supposed to come. They were not a correspondence from the South Seas, they were not dated and ... in no way ... fulfil the definition of the word "letter" as used in newspaper correspondence' (*S* 142). The London journal *Black and White* was probably more honest when it tried to renege on its agreement on the grounds, as Colvin reported to Stevenson, that the Letters were 'too monotonous' (*L7* 157, n.14). Stevenson's rather unreasonable defence was that he had expected Colvin and McClure to edit the material he sent them. McClure later recorded that Stevenson had asked him why he 'was not cutting the stuff down more' (*S* 137). Colvin was instructed as follows:

'it is your business (and please understand this) to take these Letters as they appear, and whenever a paragraph seems to you reasonably good, leave it; and whenever it does not, delete it; and in this state, with as civil comments as your precision will suffer you to make, despatch them to the toiler, registered, to be ready when I come to try the book' (*L6* 116). However, the problem was not only that the material Stevenson sent was in need of editing; Colvin also felt it that was unstructured and difficult to follow. To Colvin's request that he 'set right the places where you leave us puzzled as to the course, order and geography of your voyages', Stevenson replied tetchily:

The Tahiti part has never turned up, because it has never been written. As for telling you where I went or when, or anything about Honolulu, I would rather die;...How can anybody care when or how I left Honolulu? This is (excuse me) childish. A man of upwards of forty cannot waste his time in communicating matter of that degree of indifference. The Letters, it appears, are tedious; by God, they would be more tedious still if I wasted my time upon such infantile and sucking-bottle details. If ever I put in such detail, it is because it leads into something or serves as a transition. To tell it for its own sake, never! The mistake is all through that I have told too much; I had not sufficient confidence in the reader, and have overfed him' (*L7* 157).

All the information the reader required could be 'given to one glance of an eye by a map with a dotted line on it', Stevenson thought (ibid.). Such a map, showing Stevenson's three Pacific voyages, was included in the posthumously published editions of *In the South Seas*, starting with Colvin's Edinburgh Edition in 1896.

The Tusitala edition of *In the South Seas* substantially reduced the Editorial Note from Scribner's edition of 1898, itself derived from the Edinburgh Edition. The older, fuller version of the Editorial Note offers a frank and helpful account of the genesis of the book. It describes how Stevenson's original plan involving a contract to give an account of his Pacific travels in the form of letters for serial publication 'by and by changed in his mind into that of a book partly of travel and partly of research, which should combine the results of much careful observation and inquiry upon matters of island history, custom, belief, and tradition, with some account of his own experiences and those of his travelling companions'.[6] But before the serial publication had gone very far, it continues, '[Stevenson] realized that the personal and the impersonal elements were not very successfully combined, nor in proportions that contented his readers'.[7] And particularly not his first reader, Fanny Stevenson, who strongly disliked the historical and anthropological turn Louis's work was taking. In a letter to Colvin in May 1889 she expressed her anxiety that: 'Louis has the most enchanting material that anyone ever had in the whole world for his book, and I am afraid he is going to spoil it. He has taken it into his Scotch Stevensonian head, that a stern duty lies before him, and that this book must be a sort of scientific and historical impersonal thing, comparing the different languages (of which he knows nothing, really) and the different peoples... and the whole thing to be impersonal...' (*L6* 303–4) It is as if, continued the outraged Fanny, 'Herman Melville had given us his theories as to the Polynesian language and the probable good or evil results of the missionary influence instead of *Omoo* and *Typee*' (*L6* 304). Working herself into a climax of righteous indignation, she concluded: 'Louis will spend a great deal of time in Sydney actually *reading up* other people's books on the Islands. What a thing it is to have a "man of genius" to deal with. It is like managing an overbred horse. Why with my own feeble hand I could write a book that the whole world would jump at' (ibid.).

Stevenson's attraction to historiography led him to interrupt the writing of *In the South Seas*, in order to develop the section on Samoa into a 'separate opuscule on the Samoan Trouble', he told Baxter in December 1889 (*L6* 345); this opuscule later appeared as *A Footnote to History*. What he called, in the same letter, 'the big South Sea Book' was always going to be a mixed bag; or as he put it to Colvin: 'never was so generous a farrago' (*L6* 312). In December 1889 he wrote to Colvin to distinguish his new book from other kinds of book: '[It] is now practically modelled: if I can execute what is designed, there are few better books now extant on this globe; bar the epics, and the big tragedies, and histories, and the choice lyric poetics, and a novel or so – none' (*L6* 335). Stevenson's readiness to eschew any false modesty is partly explained by his sense of having a unique opportunity: 'nobody has had such stuff; such wild stories, such beautiful scenes, such singular intimacies, such manners and traditions, so incredible a mixture of the beautiful and the horrible, the savage and civilised' (ibid.). The original intention of making a travel book is still evident in the opening chapter where Stevenson writes: 'No part of the world exerts the same attractive power upon the visitor, and the task before me is to communicate to fireside travellers some sense of its seduction, and to describe the life, at sea and ashore, of many hundred thousand persons... as remote in thought and habit as Rob Roy or Barbarossa, the Apostles or Caesar' (*T20* 4). The culture of Polynesia was in fact even more alien than the examples Stevenson gives, because, as he puts it a few pages later: 'I was now escaped out of the shadow of the Roman empire, under whose toppling monuments we were all cradled, whose laws and letters are on every hand of us, constraining and preventing' (*T20* 8). For all that we might now want to claim that Stevenson's experience of the Pacific 'other' was always already textualized,[8] it seemed to Stevenson that he was moving beyond language and text: 'I had journeyed forth out of that comfortable zone of kindred [European] languages, where the curse of Babel is so easy to be remedied; and my new fellow-creatures sat before me dumb like images. Methought, in all my travels, all human relation was to be excluded; and when I returned home...I should have but dipped into a picture-book without a text' (ibid.). The lack of communication on his first encounter with the Marquesan islanders, who sat silently in his cabin watching him as he wrote his journal, disturbed him: 'A kind of despair came over me, to sit there helpless under all those staring orbs, and be thus blocked in a corner of my cabin by this speechless crowd: and a kind of rage to think they were beyond the reach of articulate communication, like furred animals, or folk born deaf, or the dwellers of some alien planet' (ibid.).

Stevenson recorded his mixed responses to these Marquesan islanders, some of whom may still have been practising cannibals. One sticks in his memory, he says, 'as something bestial, squatting on his hams in a canoe, sucking an orange and spitting out it out again to alternate sides with an ape-like vivacity' (*T20* 7) – though better an orange than the human foot at which an islander nibbled provocatively in another incident recorded by Stevenson (*T20* 92). Fear and disgust were replaced on other occasions by amusement, as when he saw 'one lady strip up her dress, and, with cries of wonder and delight, rub herself bare-breeched upon the velvet cushions [of the *Casco*]' (*T20* 11). Culture shock works both ways, however, and the 'alien faces [and] barbaric dresses...[which were] now beheld and fingered...with innocent excitement and surprise' were those in the sober gallery of the Stevenson family album (ibid.). The novelty value of the *Casco* was one of the factors which Stevenson felt enabled him to establish a relationship with the islanders: 'The flying city of Laputa moored for a fortnight in St James's Park affords but a pale comparison of the *Casco* anchored before Anaho' (*T20* 16). Another factor was the similarity he was convinced lay between the culture and people of the Scottish Highlands and Islands and those of the Pacific. 'In both cases', he wrote, 'an alien authority enforced, the clans disarmed, the chiefs deposed, new customs introduced, and chiefly that fashion of regarding money as the means and object of existence. The commercial age, in each, succeeding at a bound to an age of war abroad and patriarchal communism at home' (*T20* 12). Stevenson tried to draw other analogies between Highland and Pacific culture, for example between the proscription of the kilt and of cattle-stealing on one hand, and of tattooing and hunting 'long-pig' [human flesh] on the other. These analogies seem to be as strained, however, as his attempt to make something of the fact that both Polynesians and Scots are prone to what he calls the 'catch' and we would call the glottal stop (ibid.). Of more practical value was Stevenson's insight that the narration of old Scottish tales with barbaric elements could elicit from the islanders stories of equal savagery and superstition (*T20* 13). The traveller must rouse and share a sense of kinship with the natives, Stevenson believed (ibid.). Any idea of the pre-eminence of one race is most insecure and merely 'a matter of the day and hour' (ibid.), he insisted, taking apparent satisfaction in pointing out to the ignorant 'Cockney titterer' that while the polite Englishman is amazed to find the Marquesans tattooed, 'polite Italians came not so long ago to England and found our fathers stained with woad' (ibid.). Stevenson here prefigures Marlow's monologue at the beginning of Conrad's *Heart of Darkness*, just as his later reference in *In the South Seas* to old ship captains 'who would man their guns, and open fire in passing, on a cannibal island' (*T20* 87) seems to point forwards the French steamer in *Heart of Darkness* incomprehensibly, insanely, 'firing into a continent'.[9]

The mutual observation of the Stevensons and the islanders often aroused feelings of fascination and pleasure, but it could also cause fear and loathing. The pleasure of looking could be quickly overtaken by the fear of being looked at, as in one uncanny incident Stevenson recorded. Supposing themselves to be alone on the beach in a world of 'prehistoric emptiness', with a sense of isolation that was 'profound and refreshing', the Stevensons suddenly had revealed to them by a gust of wind the fact that in the tops of two palm trees sat a native 'motionless as an idol and watching us...without a wink' (*T20* 20). This raised the paranoid suspicion in the visitors that they were under constant surveillance without realizing it, though in fact, as Stevenson later discovered, the natives suddenly revealed in the palm trees were actually engaged in the forbidden practice of drawing palm-tree wine, and were probably more troubled at being seen than were the visitors (*T20* 21). Stevenson does not say whether the law forbidding the drawing of palm-tree wine is a form of tapu (as he insists the word should be spelt, in contrast to 'the vulgarly spelt "taboo"' (*T20* 42). In any case, for the Polynesians the distinction between law and tapu is a blurred one, for they 'have not been trained in the bracing, practical thought of ancient Rome;

with them the idea of law has not been disengaged from that of morals or propriety; so that tapu has to cover the whole field and implies indifferently that an act is criminal, immoral, against sound public policy, unbecoming or (as we say) "not in good form" ' (*T20* 43). Or 'not environmentally friendly', as we might nowadays say, for although though Stevenson did not know the phrase, his grasp of the idea can be seen when he approves the use of the tapu to preserve trees in a time of drought (*T20* 45). While Stevenson criticized the misunderstanding of tapu as 'a meaningless or wanton prohibition' (*T20* 43), and defended its value as an 'instrument of wise and needful restrictions' (*T20* 44), nevertheless he was highly critical of its role in the oppression of women in Polynesian society. Without the excuse of the need to protect female 'virtue', on which premise many of the restrictions on women in western society were based, in Polynesia the prejudice against women is undisguised: 'Regard for female chastity is the usual excuse for these disabilities that men delight to lay upon their wives and mothers. Here the regard is absent; and behold the women still bound hand and foot with meaningless proprieties! The women themselves, who are the survivors of the old regimen, admit that in those days life was not worth living' (ibid.). As evidence Stevenson cites the fact that, after the building of roads and bridges, women continue to plunge through the bush and wade through the river: 'roads and bridges were the work of men's hands, and tapu for the foot of women' (ibid.).

On the subject of cannibalism, for which the Marquesan Islands were notorious, Stevenson tried to avoid being judgemental. For all the disgust that the cannibal evokes in westerners, we ourselves, insofar as we are meat eaters, are in the same position *vis-à-vis* the Buddhist and the vegetarian, Stevenson argued, for 'we consume the carcases of creatures of like appetites, passions, and organs with ourselves; we feed on babes, though not our own; and the slaughter-house resounds daily with screams of pain and fear'(*T20* 79). The distinction between those creatures we consider it appropriate to eat, and those we do not, is notoriously variable and relative. And rationally considered, 'to cut a man's flesh after he is dead is far less hateful than to oppress him whilst he lives' (*T20* 80). Cannibalism could be traced from end to end of the Pacific, Stevenson claimed, from the Marquesas to New Guinea, from New Zealand to Hawaii, sometimes 'by scanty but significant survivals', and sometimes 'in the lively haunt of its exercise' (*T20* 81). At this point Stevenson's text moves far beyond his experience in the Marquesas, as he introduces material gleaned both from later visits to other Pacific islands, and from other people's books which, to Fanny's chagrin, he had read up. While he was far from making an apology for 'this worse than bestial vice', Stevenson wanted to understand the complex social meaning of cannibalism. Although it had been long abandoned and almost forgotten among the 'higher' Polynesian races, even before the arrival of the western explorers Cook and Bougainville, nevertheless it still lingered 'in some low islands where life was difficult to maintain, and among inveterate savages like the New Zealanders or the Marquesans' (*T20* 82). Stevenson was acute enough to realize that: 'The Marquesans intertwined man-eating with the whole texture of their lives; long-pig was in sense their currency and sacrament; it formed the hire of the artist, illustrated public events, and was the occasion and attraction of a feast' (ibid.). The Marquesans were now paying the price of 'this bloody commixture' of cannibalism and culture, Stevenson believed, as their whole way of life was found to be 'tainted with a cannibal element' (ibid.). Even their system of justice involved cannibalism: 'Death alone could not satisfy Marquesan vengeance; the flesh must be eaten' (ibid.). In a recent incident some locals had defied the French interdict against the ritual consumption of an executed criminal by each taking body parts home 'in a Swedish match-box' (*T20* 83).

Stevenson's work as a keen and perceptive amateur anthropologist makes for fascinating reading, but it is hardly the kind of material McClure had expected when he commissioned the letters from the South Seas. One can almost feel Stevenson deliberately turning away from his anthropological observations in order to create something more 'exotic' for his readers, when he makes a highly coloured imaginative reconstruction of a cannibal feast based on his experience of the ruins of the cannibal high place near Hatiheu in the Marquesas. It is easy to forget, when reading a passage like the following, that this not an eye-witness account:

> The drums, perhaps twenty strong, and some of them twelve feet high – continuously throbbed in time. In time the singers kept up their long-drawn, lugubrious, ululating song; in time, too, the dancers, tricked out in singular finery, stepped, leaped, swayed, and gesticulated, their plumed fingers fluttering in the air like butterflies.... [W]ild must have been the scene to any European who could have beheld them there, in the strong sun and in the strong shadow of the banyan, rubbed with saffron to throw in a more high relief the arabesque of the tattoo; the women bleached by days of confinement to a complexion almost European; the chiefs crowned with silver plumes of old men's beards and girt with kirtles of the hair of dead women. All manner of island food was meanwhile spread for the women and the

commons; and, for those who were privileged to eat of it, there were carried up to the dead-house the baskets of long-pig. It is told that the feasts were long kept up; the people came from them brutishly exhausted with debauchery, and the chiefs heavy with their beastly food (*T20* 86–7).

This is local colour with a vengeance; Stevenson's compulsion to teach in *In the South Seas* has been overcome by his need to provide some literary delights. But what is perhaps his most memorable and uncomfortably personal reference to cannibalism is saved for the very end of the section entitled 'The Marquesas'. He gives a sketch of the charismatic Marquesan chieftain Moipu, one of whose followers had provocatively nibbled at a human foot for the benefit of a visiting white, and who had filled Stevenson with repugnance and nausea at his 'part boastful, part bashful' attitude to man-eating as a kind of 'dashing peccadillo' (*T20* 118). We are left with an eerie, if grimly funny, final glimpse of the 'incurable cannibal grandee . . . [whose] favourite morsel was the human hand', taking leave of Mrs Stevenson and 'holding her hand, viewing her with tearful eyes, and chanting his farewell improvisation in the falsetto of Marquesan high society (*T20* 119).

On 4 September 1888 the *Casco* left the Marquesas Islands bound for Fakarava in the Paumotu (or Tuamotu) Archipelago, also known as the Dangerous or Low Archipelago. In 'that wide field of ocean, called loosely the South Seas', much of it vacant, much of it closely sown with isles, there is no distinction more significant, says Stevenson, than that between 'low' and 'high' islands (*T20* 123). Volcanic 'high' islands usually come in groups of up to a dozen, and are seldom less than 4000 feet; they are covered in forest, often cloud-capped, and remarkably picturesque and solemn (*T20* 124). 'Low' islands are atolls, ring-shaped coral reefs enclosing a lagoon; often they rise at their highest point to less than the stature of a man, and man, the rat and the land crab are the chief inhabitants (ibid.). Nowhere are the atolls more thickly congregated, and nowhere is navigation more perilous, than in the appropriately named Dangerous Archipelago; the weather is unpredictable, the currents complicated, and the charts are not to be trusted (ibid.). The reputation of the area was so infamous that insurance companies excluded it from their field; only 'the private taste for adventure' of the *Casco*'s captain, Mr Otis, led him to be persuaded by Stevenson to venture into this baffling Archipelago (ibid.). The voyage did turn out to be baffling. They first made landfall at Tikei, one of the so-called Pernicious Islands, thirty miles off course. On the final leg of the journey they got lost at night among reefs, to Captain Otis's despair, and Louis's delight – 'simply the most entertaining night of my life', he wrote to Colvin (*L6* 209). It is worth recalling that Stevenson was accompanied not only by his wife, who hated travelling by sea, but also by his mother. This brief, but highly dangerous, passage from the Marquesas into the Low Archipelago was a voyage to 'a new province of creation' (*T20* 123). Stevenson's numinous first encounter with a South Sea island when he reached the Marquesas was, strictly speaking, his first experience of a *high* South sea island; his first experience of the *low* island of Fakarava was in its own way just as numinous. Here the fascination lay not in picturesque and solemn mountain scenery, but in the 'exquisite hue and transparency of submarine day' in the lagoon where 'the coral branched and blossomed, and the fish . . . cruised visibly below us, stained and striped, and even beaked like parrots' (*T20* 131). Stevenson was later to recycle this description of the arrival at Fakarava in his narrative of the *Farallone*'s arrival at Attwater's island in *The Ebb-Tide* (*T14* 70–3).

The sole distinction of Fakarava was that it had a superb natural harbour. Otherwise it was poor, even for a low island. The low atoll was but a 'thread of residency' between sky and sea and more sea; it evoked in Stevenson the recurring image of a 'narrow causeway . . . lying coiled like a serpent, tail to mouth, in the outrageous ocean (*T20* 133). Like many another low island, Fakarava had been more than once overwhelmed by the ill-named Pacific. The variety of flora and fauna on such an island is strictly limited; so too is the cuisine, which led Stevenson to repeat an old joke of the archipelago (anticipating the Monty Python 'spam' joke): 'cocoa-nut green, cocoa-nut ripe, cocoa-nut germinated; cocoa-nut to eat and cocoa-nut to drink; cocoa-nut raw and cooked, cocoa-nut hot and cold – such is the bill of fare' (*T20* 135). The people of the Paumotos, for all their relative proximity to the Marquesans, could hardly have been more different from the latter. While the Marquesan, according to Stevenson, was beautiful, open-handed, insensible to religion and childishly self-indulgent, the Paumotuan was by contrast 'greedy, hardy, enterprising, a religious disputant, . . . with a trace of the ascetic' – and not even handsome, added Stevenson (*T20* 147). Such ascription of differences in character to whole races seems at best speculative, though presumably there must have been some cultural factor at work in the statistics which showed Stevenson that the Paumotuan population was gradually rising, whereas depopulation was proceeding at an alarming rate in the Marquesas (*T20* 149). The earlier chapter on the topic of 'Depopulation' was perhaps necessarily inconclusive, though clear enough in its insistence that, whatever other factors may have been involved, cultural change was, in itself, a major contributing cause of depopulation (*T20* 37). The most haunting image of depopulation, and indeed of racial extinction, is of a young Marquesan mother holding her baby out to Stevenson with the words: ' "*Tenez* – a little baby like this; then dead. All the Kanaques die. Then no more" ' (*T20* 24). The manifestation of 'so tranquil a despair' is typical of the Marquesan, who, even more than other Polynesian peoples, 'falls easily into despondency' and a sadness that 'detaches him from life' (*T20* 36). In contrast to what Stevenson calls the 'Lotus islands', where 'a livelihood can be had for the stooping', in atolls like the Paumotos 'a man must bestir himself with some vigour for his daily bread, [and] public health and the population are maintained' (ibid.). There is more than a suggestion of the Protestant work ethic here, and what Stevenson described as the Paumotuan national character, particularly its taste for religious disputation, led him to see the Paumotos as a kind of 'Scotland of the South' (*T20* 151). Here Stevenson is extending his characteristic strategy for understanding the peoples of South Seas: if the Marquesans (and Samoans) are like the folk of the Scottish Highlands and Islands, then the Paumotuans are like the canny, lowland Scots (at its most reductive, we seem to be dealing with a Pacific version of 'Highlanders and Covenanters').

Analogies with Scottish culture are also brought into play in 'Graveyard Stories', perhaps the most interesting chapter in the Paumotos section. Here Stevenson describes how he elicited superstitious tales from the islanders by telling stories of his own, presumably of the 'Thrawn Janet' variety, which he had at one time planned to collect under the title of *The Black Man*. While superstition was rife throughout all the South Seas, there was a particular quality of horror in Paumotuan superstitions, Stevenson says, which made him address the matter in this section of his book. He was also fortunate enough to hear the Paumotuan tales told in thrilling fashion by a man with a genius for such narrations (*T20* 164). The Pacific tales Stevenson which recorded in this chapter would send 'a cauld grue' (or shudder) along anyone's bones, just as 'Thrawn Janet' had done back in Pitlochry.[10] In one tale the protagonist was in the margin of the woods when:

he was aware of something drawing swiftly near among the tree-tops. It swung by its heels downward, like an ape, so that its hands were free for murder; it depended safely by the slightest of twigs; the speed of its coming was incredible; and soon Rua recognised it for a corpse, horrible with age, its bowels hanging as it came (*T20* 165).

There was a dark logic in a culture so recently cannibal: 'When the living ate the dead, horrified nocturnal imagination drew the shocking inference that the dead might eat the living.' (*T20* 166) Several of the stories involve metamorphoses, particularly into the form of birds, which anticipates Stevenson's own ghostly tale of 'Tod Lapraik' in *Catriona*. It was upon such folk material that Stevenson was partially to draw when he wrote 'The Isle of Voices' and 'The Bottle Imp' (though the latter derived ultimately from a German folk tale). These were as far as Stevenson got with a planned volume of *Märchen* (folk or fairy tales) which he cited to Colvin as the reason he was unhappy to allow 'The Bottle Imp' to appear together with a realistic narrative like 'The Beach at Falesá' (*L7* 461).

'The Bottle Imp' seems to have been begun in Honolulu (*S* 144) in the Hawaiian Islands, which are the subject of the next section of *In the South Seas*, although it was only with Andrew Lang's 1912 Swanston Edition that the five chapters on 'The Eight Islands' were included as a new section in the book (*S* 138). However, not only is Honolulu not directly mentioned in the 'Eight Islands' section, which focuses on the Kona coast of the island of Hawaii; Stevenson also omitted all mention of his three-month stay in Tahiti (Stevenson's response to Colvin's puzzlement at these omissions is quoted above). Apart from a ballad, and the beginning of *The Ebb-Tide*, set in Papeete, the only explicit literary traces of Stevenson's stay in Tahiti are in his letters. One of these, dated 11 November 1888, to John Addington Symonds, was intended by Stevenson to appear at the beginning of *In the South Seas*, dedicating the volume to Symonds; however, by the time the volume was published posthumously in 1896, Symonds had died and the dedication was not used. The letter was written in the village of Tautira on the peninsula of Tahiti, where, after a month at Papeete, the increasingly ailing Stevenson had been moved with considerable difficulty. In the letter Stevenson urged Symonds 'to conceive us, therefore, in strange circumstances, and very pleasing; in a strange land and climate, the most beautiful on earth; surrounded by a foreign race that all travellers have agreed to be the most engaging' (*L6* 223). 'We are', Stevenson concluded, '*in Heaven here*' (*L6* 224), repeating the claim made in a letter to Baxter written a couple of days previously that Tautira was 'mere Heaven' (*L6* 221). In the letter to Baxter, Stevenson mentions 'Oli', the village sub-chief into whose house the Stevensons had moved, and whom Stevenson had sought to entertain with an impersonation of Henley, funny walk and all (ibid.). By the time he wrote to Symonds, Stevenson had managed to get Ori a Ori's name right. Ori a Ori, also called Teriitera, was a 'a man of great influence' and 'our good angel', Stevenson wrote to Captain Otis in his reply to

Otis's news that both the *Casco*'s masts were rotten, and that therefore their stay in Tahiti would be for longer than planned (*L6* 225). So close did Stevenson and Ori a Ori become that they exchanged names. The latter became *Rui*, and Louis, 'blushing like a schoolgirl', became Teriitera, which, according to Fanny's letter to Colvin, was his 'Christian name', Ori a Ori being his clan name (*L6* 229). Stevenson seems to have delighted in signing himself 'Teriitera (previously known as Robert Louis Stevenson)'. Whatever Fanny's reservations, Louis enjoyed the enforced delay at Tautira, which was 'the most beautiful spot, and its people the most amiable, I have ever found' (*L6* 239). Besides which, as he wrote to Colvin after their departure from Tahiti: 'the climate suited me to the ground; I actually went sea bathing almost every day' (ibid.). In addition, he got material for his book, and collected songs and legends on the spot (ibid.). A Tahitian section of *In the South Seas* never materialized, though Stevenson did publish a ballad entitled 'The Song of Rahéro: A Legend of Tahiti', based on a legend of his own (adopted) clan, with a dedication to Ori a Ori signed by 'Teriitera'.

After a series of delays the *Casco* finally left Tautira on Christmas Day 1888. The parting with Ori was 'heartrending', Louis told Anne Jenkin; 'you never saw such a day of weeping' (*L6* 262). The voyage to Honlulu was difficult, and at times dangerous. Louis wrote to his cousin Bob: 'Our voyage up here was most disastrous, calms, squalls, head sea, waterspouts of rain, hurricane weather all about, and we in the midst of the hurricane season, when even the hopeful builder and owner of the yacht had pronounced these seas unfit for her. We ran out of food, and were quite given up for lost in Honolulu' (*L6* 255–6). The whole venture, he admitted to Bob, was 'extremely foolhardy'; he used the same phrase when confessing to Baxter: 'But man, there have been days when I felt guilty, and thought I was in no position for the head of a house' (*L6* 248). Fanny was frequently seasick and found the whole experience so distressing that she swore never to go to sea again (*L6* 256 n.4). From Louis's point of view, however, 'the perils of the deep were part of the programme', and the cruise was a wonderful success; 'I never knew the world was so amusing', he added (*L6* 256). He made use of the terrifying experience of running before the storm for a memorable scene in *The Wrecker* (*T12* 188–193).

When the Stevensons reached Honolulu on 24 January 1889, two weeks later than expected due to the bad weather, Fanny's daughter Belle greeted them with relief bordering on hysteria (*L6* 242). At first they stayed with Belle, who had lived in Honolulu with her husband Joe Strong, and their son Austin (by now eight), since 1882. The Stevensons soon moved to Waikiki, then a country district three miles from Honolulu, but linked to it by telephone and tramway. Stevenson detested Honolulu, amid whose bustle and electric lights he felt 'oppressed by civilisation', as he wrote to Adelaide Boodle back in Bournemouth (*L6* 279). He gave Miss Boodle a detailed description of the Stevenson quarters at Waikiki, which consisted of three groups of buildings, or 'crazy dirty cottages', as he put it to Colvin (*L6* 265). The third of these, 'a grim little wooden shanty' fenced off from the others, served as a bedroom for Louis and Fanny, and as a study for Louis. Its bare walls were pasted over with pages from American magazines; the floor was covered with filthy matting; and it was infested with spiders, mice, cockroaches, scorpions, and mosquitoes (*L6* 280). On the (condemned) door was pinned a list of items needed for the next trip, including: a duck-hammock for each person; a patent organ like the commandant's at Tai-o-hae; cheap and bad cigars for presents; revolvers; liniment for the head and sulphur. Such a list is 'simply life in the South Seas foreshortened', commented Stevenson (*L6* 281). After Tahiti, Stevenson found the cooler Hawaiian climate 'beastly', and in 'vile' Honolulu, he told Baxter, he was 'always out of sorts, amid heat and cold and cesspools and beastly *haoles* [Hawaiian for 'whites']' (*L6* 295).

Naturally the Stevensons fraternized with the local aristocracy. In this case it was the 'Royal set' surrounding Kalakaua, the last King of Hawaii, and his sister Liliuokalani, who was briefly to succeed him before the annexation of Hawaii by the United States at the end of the century. Two days after their arrival in Honolulu, Stevenson was formally received by the King, and on 1 February Kalakaua visited the *Casco* to receive champagne, sherry and cake, and some improvised entertainment. Two days later a feast was held at which the King was presented with a golden pearl by Fanny, and a poem by Louis (*L6* 243). The poem, entitled 'To Kalakaua, With the present of a pearl', was subsequently published in *Songs of Travel*, and includes two references to 'the Silver Ship', the name which the *Casco* had been given in Fakarava in the Paumotos; Stevenson had at one time thought of giving *In the South Seas* the title *The Cruise of the Silver Ship* (*L6* 217). Entertaining and being entertained by Kalakaua could be a dangerous affair, Stevenson wrote to Baxter, since the King's appetite for champagne was formidable: 'We calculated five bottles of champagne in three hours and a half (afternoon) and the sovereign quite presentable, although perceptibly more dignified, at the end' (*L6* 249). Kalakaua tried to persuade Stevenson to settle in Hawaii, but although the Silver Ship was sent with Captain Otis back to San Francisco, Stevenson's travels in the South Seas were far from over.

Even while staying in Waikiki, Stevenson was keen to get away from his 'large, costly, and no' just preceesely forrit-gaun [less than dynamic] family', as he told Charles Baxter, lapsing into the broad Scots which he loved to adopt in his correspondence with Baxter (*L6* 295). On 26 April 1889 he took the steamer to Hookena on the island of Hawaii, where he was able to escape 'vile' Honolulu and its *haoles* for a blessed week among Polynesians (ibid.). Honolulu only appears in *In the South Seas* as the 'humming city, with shops and palaces and busy wharves, plying cabs and tramcars, telephones in operation and a railway in the building', from which Stevenson escaped to 'a village uninhabited by any white' in the district of Kona (*T20* 179). Here Captain Cook had been killed in 1779, and here also had been the power base of the great Hawaiian king Kamehameha, whose bones and treasures were reputedly hidden in one of the many caverns in the lava. On the leeward side of the volcanic island of Hawaii, which Stevenson had first glimpsed during the final stages of the *Casco*'s voyage from Tahiti, 'all seemed black and barren, and to slope sheer into the sea' (ibid.). Unlike the tourists on the steamer to Hookena, Stevenson had not come to Hawaii to view its volcanoes such as Mauna Loa. Being one of those 'so constituted as to find a man or a society more curious than the highest mountain', he preferred 'a week in an unheard-of hamlet, rather than a visit to one of the marvels of the world' (*T20* 181). Partly Stevenson needed the space in order to get on with some writing he was behind with, specifically the concluding chapters *The Master of Ballantrae*, which had been running in *Scribner's Magazine* since November 1888. He was staying in the home of an ex-judge called Nahino, and, adopting precisely the stern 'Scotch Stevensonian' attitude Fanny deplored, he immersed himself in the day-to-day running of the Hawaiian legal system rather than writing up the spectacular scenery nearby. Stevenson was amazed by the modern life-style of a people who, he says, had one hundred and ten years ago called Cook and his seamen gods and volcanoes, had taken their clothes for a loose skin, and had confounded their hats and their heads. By the time of Stevenson's visit, however, it would seem that nothing, not even the most attractive visiting author, could divert them from discussing the newspapers and 'the novel of the day', which happened to be Miss Porter's *Scottish Chiefs* (*T20* 183).

Stevenson did take time off to take a romantic ride in the forest of the Kona coast. During this ride lasting five and a half hours, as Stevenson boasted to Baxter (*L6* 295), they visited the village of Honaunau and the ruins of Hale Keawe, an ancient temple and city of refuge, where lay the bones of Keawe and other Hawaiian monarchs (*T20* 196). Stevenson gave the central character of 'The Bottle Imp' the name 'Keawe', and his place of birth as not far from Honaunau; Stevenson's host Nahino and the village of Hookena also make a brief appearance in this tale which mixes the fantastic with accurate realistic details. *In the South Seas* records some of the romantic legends surrounding Hale Keawe, which had given refuge to criminals, refugees in time of war, sacrificial victims fleeing their fate, and on one occasion to Kaahumanu, the most beautiful of the great king Kamehameha's wives. Though notoriously unfaithful herself, she had been overcome by jealousy at the king's attentions to another of his wives, and had fled to the temple precincts where she lay hidden, naked and refusing food, till Kamehameha discovered her and fetched her home (*T20* 202–3). But it was another, less romantic, kind of fugitive that really interested Stevenson at Kona. Near Hookena he came across a mother and young girl who had been living rough in the forest, but had been captured, and were being detained until they could be transported. They had been fugitives not because of any criminal offence, but because the girl had leprosy. They were now awaiting transportation to the notorious leper colony at Molokai. Although the lepers were treated relatively well at Molokai, the enforced separation distressed the tightly knit Polynesian families. In the particular case that Stevenson came across at Kona, the mother was going with her daughter to Molokai in the hope that she might be taken on as a Kokua, or 'clean' assistant (*T20* 210). Watching this sad departure for Molokai, Stevenson decided that he must visit the lazaretto himself. Soon after his return to Honolulu, he applied for permission to visit the Leper Settlement, and on 21 May 1889 landed at the remote and inaccessible eastern end of the island of Molokai, where the settlement had been founded 1865.

The 'Letters' about Molokai, which were published in the New York *Sun* in 1890–91, did not appear in the posthumous volume *In the South Seas*, though they were included in the Tusitala edition under the title *Vailima Papers*. Stevenson also gave accounts of his visit in his correspondence. In a letter to Fanny he described the landing at Kalaupapa on 'the leper promontory' along with about a dozen lepers, including 'one poor child very horrid', and two American Sisters, without whose presence, he admitted, 'I do not know how it would have been with me' (*L6* 306). Stevenson's susceptibility to a 'horror of the horrible' was blotted out, he wrote to Fanny, by the 'moral loveliness' of the Franciscan Sisters' devotion to the leper girls in the Home at Kalaupapa (ibid.). This contrast between being, on the one hand, 'hag-ridden by horrid sights' but, on the other, 'really inspired with the sight of so much goodness in the helpers and so much courage...in the sick', as he put it to his mother (*L6* 313), runs through much of what Stevenson wrote about the settlement at Mokoloi. The obvious self-sacrifice and commitment of the volunteer helpers, must have made him uncomfortably aware of his own less than selfless motivation, as he set off across the promontory with his camera. His conscience did prompt him, however, to take what seemed the less offensive precaution of avoiding touching the lepers, rather than wearing protective gloves (*L6* 306). On most of the seven days he stayed at the settlement, Stevenson visited the Home for leper girls and played croquet with them. To Mother Maryanne, head of the Franciscan Sisters, he addressed a poem, later included as number XXXII in *Songs of Travel*; it may not be great poetry, but it does in many ways sum up Stevenson's experience at Molokai:

> To see the infinite pity of this place,
> The mangled limb, the devastated face,
> The innocent sufferer smiling at the rod -
> A fool were tempted to deny his God.
> He sees, he shrinks. But if he gaze again,
> Lo, beauty springing from the breast of pain!
> He marks the sisters on the mournful shores;
> And even a fool is silent and adores.

Stevenson was not naïve about the self-serving element in religious, and (in his view) especially Catholic, devotion. With a staunchly Presbyterian background, he was alert to the dangers of 'works righteousness'. He wrote to Colvin: 'The pass-book kept with heaven stirs me to anger and laughter. One of these Sisters calls the place "The ticket office to heaven". Well, what is the odds? They do their darg [day's work, in Scots], and do it with kindness and efficiency incredible; and we must take folk's virtues as we find them, and love the better part' (*L6* 311). He then went on to talk of Father Damien, the famous Belgian missionary who had gone to the leper settlement in Molokai in 1873, had contracted the disease, and finally died in 1889, six weeks before Stevenson's arrival:

Of old Damien, whose weaknesses and worse perhaps I heard fully, I think only the more. It was a European peasant: dirty, bigoted, untruthful, unwise, tricky, but superb with generosity, residual candour and fundamental good humour: convince him he had done wrong (it might take hours of insult) and he would undo what he had done and like his corrector the better. A man, with all the grime and paltriness of mankind; but a saint and hero all the more for that (ibid.).

In this letter to Colvin in June 1889 Stevenson argued substantially the same case for Damien that he would later make in his pamphlet, *Father Damien*, published in March 1890. The pamphlet, subtitled *An Open Letter to the Reverend Dr Hyde of Honolulu*, was Stevenson's immediate response to a letter by the uncannily named Dr Hyde, reprinted in the Sydney paper *The Presbyterian*, on 26 October 1889, but apparently not read by Stevenson until 25 February 1890. Hyde's letter, in which he called Damien 'a coarse, dirty man, headstrong and bigoted', concluded: 'He was not a pure man in his relations with women, and the leprosy of which he died should be attributed to his vices and carelessness. Others have done much for the lepers, our own ministers, the government, physicians, and so forth, but never with the Catholic idea of meriting eternal life' (*T21* 28). Originally a private letter in reply to a fellow minister back in San Francisco, who had consulted Hyde in light of the controversy in the religious press following Damien's death, Hyde's letter was soon widely published in a variety of Protestant papers. According to Fanny, Louis responded to Hyde's letter immediately he read it on 25 February, in a fury of righteous indignation (*S* 149–50). In retrospect he regretted, if not his defence of Damien, then his very personal attack on Hyde, which he described to Henry James as 'brutal and cruel' (*L6* 402), to Colvin as 'abominable' (*L6* 404), and to Elizabeth Fairchild as 'barbarously harsh' (*L6* 420). In a curious reversal, the language Stevenson used about his attack on Dr Hyde is reminiscent of Mr Hyde's attack on Sir Danvers Carew.

The vitriol of Stevenson's *ad hominem* argument against Hyde is partly to be explained by the fact that Hyde and Stevenson shared essentially the same background, that is, evangelical Protestant; as Stevenson put it: 'You belong, sir, to a sect – I believe my sect, and that in which my ancestors laboured...' (*T21* 29). Stevenson's basic accusation was that Hyde's resentment against Damien was motivated by envy. In contrast to Damien's 'intrusive and decisive heroism', Hyde and his Church showed only inertia in face of the situation in Hawaii (*T21* 30). Instead of accepting this failure with humility, or at least in silence, Hyde chose to make a personal attack on Damien. The accusation that Damien was 'a coarse, dirty man' was all the more offensive on account of the relative opulence of Hyde's residence in Honolulu, argued Stevenson, not hesitating to quote a Honolulu cabby on 'the size, the taste, and the comfort of your home' (*T21* 29). Having positioned Hyde as a hypocrite and a Pharisee, Stevenson then proceeded to demolish his argument against Damien point by point with a zeal reminiscent of the Protestant Reformers (whose successor Hyde claimed to be):

Damien was *coarse.*
It is very possible. You make us sorry for the lepers who had only a coarse old peasant for their friend and father. But you, who were so refined, why were you not there, to cheer them with the lights of culture? Or may I remind you that we have some reason to doubt if John the Baptist were genteel...
Damien was *dirty*
He was. Think of the poor lepers annoyed with this dirty comrade! But the clean Dr. Hyde was at his food in a fine house....
Damien *was not sent to Molokai, but went there without orders.*
Is this a misreading? Or do you really mean the words for blame? I have heard Christ, in the pulpits of our Church, held up for imitation on the ground that His sacrifice was voluntary. Does Dr. Hyde think otherwise? (*T21* 37–8).

Stevenson continued his version of *J'accuse...* for several pages in an ecstasy of invective. So convinced was he that he would be sued for libel, and consequently ruined, that he summoned a family gathering before he published the letter; the unanimous verdict was for publication (*S* 150; *L6* 420). He sent a copy to Baxter, with the note: 'Enclosed please find a libel', asking his advice about offering the piece to Henley for the *Scots Observer*; the latter chose to publish the letter in May 1890 (*L6* 377–8, n.2). In the event, however, Dr Hyde held fire, choosing to dismiss the letter as the work of an attention-seeking 'Bohemian Crank', an epithet Stevenson seemed to enjoy using to sign his letter to Elizabeth Fairchild in September 1890 (*L6* 420).

If Damien was a very earthy saint, then he was well suited to Molokai, which was by no means filled with saints and martyrs. Stevenson chronicled some of the trouble and strife of the settlement's brief history; he was also frank about the degree of sexual activity there. In a community where leprosy is the norm, the shame of deformity disappears, and the young girl whose head Stevenson had seen bent with shame on Hawaii would, he was glad to anticipate, 'walk with face erect among her fellows, and perhaps be attended as a beauty' (*T21* 332). For surely, he continued, 'the most disgraced of that unhappy crew may expect the consolations of love; love laughs at leprosy; and marriage is in use to the last stage of decay and the last gasp of life' (ibid.). But then, as another 'saint' on the island observed: ' "There are Molokais everywhere" ' (*L6* 317). Stevenson was quoting 'Brother Joseph' Dutton, an American who, after serving in the Civil War, converted to Roman Catholicism, and in 1886 went to serve in Molokai until his death in 1931 (ibid. n.2). Years later, Dutton wrote some notes about Stevenson for a friend, in which he suggests that during his visit to the leper settlement Stevenson was actually exploring the possibility of himself spending his declining years as a worker at Molokai, although his family commitments obviously precluded this.[11] In reality, however, Stevenson became desperate to quit the leper settlement; by the day of his departure, he wrote, 'in truth...my heart panted for deliverance' (*T21* 336). His desire to escape the lazaretto was brought home to him when he experienced some problems when trying to board the steamer to leave. Whilst he had secured permission to visit the settlement, he had neglected to secure permission to leave it, and the captain of the steamer at first refused to allow Stevenson aboard. He subsequently relented, and Stevenson was taken to explore the other part of the island of Molokai, from one of whose peaks he looked back at the details of the leper settlement, tiny and safely unreal in the distance, 'all distinct and bright like toys' (*T21* 336–41; cf. *L6* 313–14).

By 1 June 1889 Stevenson was back in Honolulu. Later that month he was to set off again, bound for Samoa via the Gilbert Islands, in the schooner *Equator*, which he had chartered at the beginning of April from Wightman Brothers of San Francisco (*L6* 279 n.2). The terms of the charter were unusual, and allowed Stevenson, at a fixed daily extra charge, to demand a landing on any of the islands on the schooner's trading route; and, at no extra charge, a three day stay at any of the islands where it had stopped for its own business (*L6* 325). Stevenson had at one time applied to sail in the missionary ship *Morning Star*, and his application had been sent, ironically, to the Revd Dr Hyde, whose attitude to Stevenson was patronizing and censorious even before the Damien affair. Stevenson's only redeeming feature, Hyde wrote, was his mother, 'a godly woman... the daughter of a Scotch minister' (*L6* 270 n.1); however plans had already been made for Maggie Stevenson to return to Scotland in May. Lloyd Osbourne recalled how none of the Stevenson party much relished the prospect of: 'no smoking, not a drink,...nightly prayer-meetings, and an enforced intimacy with the most uncongenial of people' (ibid.). When the opportunity of chartering the *Equator* arose, 'giving us more time and a thousandfold more liberty...we determined to cut off the missionaries with a shilling', Stevenson wrote to Adelaide Boodle (*L6* 279). Besides Captain Dennis Reid and his crew, the party in the *Equator* included Louis, Fanny, Lloyd, Joe Strong and Ah Fu, their Chinese cook; they were waved off from the wharf at Honolulu on 24 June, their departure marked by garlands, champagne and musicians provided by King Kalakaua.

On 13 July the Stevenson party reached Butaritari in the Gilbert islands, which straddle the equator, and 'enjoy a superb ocean climate, days of blinding sun and bracing wind, nights of a heavenly brightness', as Stevenson put it in the first of the two sections of *In the South Seas* devoted to the Gilberts (*T20* 213). If the climate was superb, the atoll scenery was not; the interminable flatness of the land- and seascape, uninterrupted by anything so high as an ordinary cottage, was rivalled only by the monotony of a diet of tinned or pickled food, occasionally relieved by shark steak (ibid.). The Stevensons stayed in the house of Robert Maka, an Hawaiian missionary, which lay in the Wightman Brothers' compound in Butaritari, between the trading store and the bar (*T20* 227). The manager of the store was a Prussian named Adolf Rick; he and Mrs Rick, an American, also ran the *Sans Souci*, the bar, 'or rather the casino of the island', says Stevenson, who regularly passed his evenings there (*T20* 230–1; cf. *L6* 326 n.1). While the *Sans Souci* was the preserve of captains and traders visiting Butaritari, the crews tended to frequent the rival establishment, *The Land We Live In*, run by a black American called Williams, of whom Stevenson commented: 'I never knew a man who had more words in his command or less truth to communicate' (*T20* 218). This harsh judgement derived from Stevenson's subsequent dealings with Williams during the events narrated under the title 'A Tale of a Tapu'. This tale tells of a crisis ocasioned by the reluctance of King Tebureimoa to restore the tapu on selling spirits to the natives that he had lifted to celebrate the 4th of July. The natives were liable to drunken violence and therefore the white community was at some risk (though Stevenson does add: 'yet to be just to barbarous islanders we must not forget the slums and dens of our cities: I must not forget that I have passed through Soho, and seen that which cured me of my dinner' (*T20* 243)). When the Ricks reinstated the ban on spirits at the *Sans Souci*, the rival establishment, partly through greed for profit, and partly through fear, continued to supply spirits to the natives. By 23 July the situation was beginning to become dangerous because more savage, and possibly hostile, clans from neighbouring islands were starting to arrive on Butaritari for a great festival in honour of the birthday of the princess. Stevenson drew the predictable analogy when he wrote of the visitors: 'it seemed to us they swaggered into the town, like plaided Highlanders upon the streets of Inverness, conscious of barbaric virtues'(*T20* 254). After witnessing some ugly scenes of mob violence, and having had several missiles thrown into their house, Stevenson decided he had to act. In an atmosphere resembling the 'English garrisons before the Sepoy mutiny' (*T20* 239–40), Stevenson decided to confront the king, whom he informed of his own status as an intimate personal friend of Queen Victoria (as the audience proceeded, he became her son) (*T20* 245). As a result of this interview, a tapu was placed on the house the Stevensons were staying in, which afforded them some protection (ibid.). However the wider situation was still dangerous, so Stevenson decided to confront Mr Muller, the manager of Wightman's rival company on the island, and also of Williams and *The Land We Live In*. In the account of this confrontation, Stevenson is clearly the hero of his own narrative. When describing the preparation of revolvers for action on the following day, Stevenson quotes Sir Walter Scott on the pleasurable anticipation of fighting. The Stevensons intended either to help Muller defend his bar against the natives (if he took the right decision not to serve them); or (if he took the wrong decision) to occupy *The Land We Live In* and deal with the dastardly Williams themselves (*T20* 251–2).

To Louis's disappointment, the situation was defused when the tapu on the sale of spirits was restored the following day. This was not a day too soon, comments Stevenson, since 'the boats began to arrive thickly, and the town was filled with the big rowdy vassals of Karaiti' (*T20* 252). The neighbouring chief Karaiti was, in accordance Stevenson's by now familiar strategy for cross-cultural interpretation, quickly assimilated to 'the Black Douglas', a legendary figure from Scottish history (his rival Kuma becoming 'the Red Douglas') (*T20* 258). The Stevensons came to be on familiar terms with Karaiti during the five-day birthday party, which went ahead peacefully, apart from Karaiti's peremptory demand for a second showing of the Stevensons' 'phantoms', the magic lantern show which for the natives was the highlight of the festival. Stevenson, who had let it be known that he was Queen Victoria's son, felt obliged to insist on the respect his status demanded; and between his indignant looks, and the sharp tongue of Mrs Rick (who could speak the lingo), the upstart chief was reminded of his place (*T20* 260–1). The only other disruption to the festival was the rivalry between the dancing teams of the different islands, which got so out of hand that they kept interrupting each others' performances, with the result that the visitors from Makin walked off, as did the audience, leaving the home team playing to an empty house. The latter was soon refilled for a second showing of the 'phantoms', and a splendid time was had by all, with even the solemn missionary Maka joining in the merriment at the 'ludicrously silly' Scripture slides (*T20* 260–5).

Not all monarchs in the Gilbert Islands were as ineffectual as King Tebureimoa of Butaritari, who seemed in a perpetual haze of drink and/or drugs. King Tembinok' of Apemama was at the time of the Stevensons' stay: 'the last tyrant, the last erect vestige of a dead society' (*T20* 275). 'Everywhere else', according to to Stevenson, 'the white man is building his houses, drinking his gin, getting in and out of trouble with the weak native governments. There is only one white on Apemama, and he on sufferance, living far from court, and hearkening and watching his conduct like a mouse in a cat's ear' (ibid.). The imperial ambition of this 'Napoleon of the Gilberts' had been checked by the arrival of a British warship, which forced him to sink his expensive armoury in the lagoon; nevertheless, 'periodical fear of him still shakes the islands' (ibid.). Naturally Stevenson wanted to visit Apemama, the one island the tourists avoided. His chance came when, *en route* from Mariki to Tapituea, the wind suddenly set fair for Apemama, and the course of the *Equator* was at once changed. Anchored in the lagoon of Apemama, the passengers and crew of the *Equator*, which had been specially scrubbed and prettified for the occasion, awaited the arrival of the absolute monarch. His corpulent, somewhat elephantine appearance was nevertheless impressive:

> a beaked profile like Dante's in the mask, a mane of long black hair, the eye brilliant, imperious, and inquiring. . . . His voice matched it well, being shrill, powerful and uncanny, with a note like a sea-bird's. Where there are no fashions, none to set them, . . . and none to criticise, he dresses . . . 'to his own heart'. Now he wears a woman's frock, now a naval uniform; now (and more usually) figures in a masquerade costume of his own design: trousers and a singular jacket with shirt tails . . . sometimes green velvet, sometimes cardinal red silk. This masquerade becomes him admirably. In the woman's frock he looks ominous and weird beyond belief. I see him now come pacing towards me in the cruel sun, solitary, a figure out of Hoffmann (*T20* 278).

Tembinok' had a random and eclectic greed, and his palace was stuffed with all the items that had fleetingly taken his fancy, from musical boxes to sewing machines. He was thus a target for unscrupulous traders who would tempt him with some novelty. The Stevensons ran into a problem when the king started to eye Fanny's battered dressing-bag. He would not accept their explanations that it had been a gift from a friend, but kept laying English gold sovereigns on the table. It was only when the Stevensons offered it to him as a gift that Tembinok' shamefacedly recognized his mistake – the only time in their experience that the king acknowledged himself to be in the wrong (*T20* 280–1).

Tembinok' was slow to accept, and quick to deport, white traders, or missionaries doubling as traders. The Stevensons' request to stay on

Apemama had come within an ace of refusal. Tembinok' subjected each of the Stevensons to a series of lengthy, undisguised stares of appraisal, over a period of two days. Then the king delivered his verdict: ' "I look your eye. You good man. You no lie," said the king'- 'a doubtful compliment', commented Stevenson, 'to a writer of romance' (*T20* 285–6). The king's terms were that the Stevensons should choose a site, where he would build them a town; his people would work for them, but would only take orders from Tembinok'. One of his cooks would come daily in order to help the Stevensons' cook, and learn from him. Tembinok' was to come to dinner when so inclined; otherwise a dish from the Stevensons' table was to be sent to him. This arrangement, combined with the attitude-problem of the royal cook, had some some unpleasant and (for the cook) potentially lethal consequences, given the immediate and violent manner in which the king dispensed justice. Thus Equator Town – named after the schooner – was founded. The construction of the 'town' (four buildings in all) was supposed to begin on the day after the site had been agreed with the king. When Lloyd went to inspect the building work, and found that nothing had been done, he went straight to Tembinok', who fired two shots from his Winchester into the air from the royal palisade. These warning shots did the trick, his majesty remarking that it would make his labourers 'mo' bright'. The king himself subsequently turned up to superintend the work, sitting on a mat, 'in cardinal red, a pith helmet on his head, a meerschaum pipe in his mouth, a wife stretched at his back with custody of the matches and tobacco' (*T20* 286–7). Stevenson obviously relished the opportunity of writing travel scenes whose exoticism bordered on the surreal.

Although the Stevensons were only to live for two months in Equator Town, which subsequently vanished as quickly as it had appeared, their stay seemed more permanent than that; Fanny even planted a garden of salad and shallots. The Stevenson party occupied themselves in a variety of ways: they read aloud Gibbon and Carlyle; made music with guitars and flageolets; took photographs; hunted (in Louis's case ineffectually); and while some of the party were were away sketching, Louis and Lloyd 'hammered away at a novel' (*T20* 289). The novel in question was *The Wrecker*. The germ of the plot of *The Wrecker* was a tale told by the captain of a crew who had been shipwrecked on Midway Island in the North Pacific, and been rescued in return for all the money they possessed. These castaways had arrived at Honolulu just as the Stevensons were preparing for their departure on the *Equator*. The story told by Captain Walker of the *Wandering Minstrel* had stuck in Stevenson's mind, and while he and Lloyd Osbourne were cruising on the *Equator*, they discussed writing a novel based on it. It was only in Equator Town on Apemama that they began seriously to write up the complex story. According to Fanny's Prefatory Note to *The Wrecker*, the novel had originally been intended to raise the capital required to buy a schooner, to be called the *Northern Light*, and commanded by Captain Reid; it was to be half-yacht, half-trader, and provide a semi-permanent home for the Stevensons (*T12* xviii). Fanny claimed that it was Louis's observation of the South Sea traders' shady dealings, which he realized he would have had to adopt in order to make a going concern of the *Northern Light*, that put him off the project (*T12* xx–xxi). *The Wrecker* was a going concern, however, and it continued to be hammered out by Louis and Lloyd (and increasingly just by Louis) on Apemama, and later in Samoa.

The Stevensons' stay at Apemama turned out to be longer than expected. While Louis and Lloyd were working on *The Wrecker*, Captain Reid and the *Equator* had gone off in search of copra, the basic commodity in the South Seas. However, the schooner's return was so long delayed that it was feared lost. The Stevensons' supplies began to run very low; further supplies were provided by Tembinok', and by Captain Sachs of the *H.L. Tiernan* which had turned up at Apemama. Stevenson was tempted to take passage on the *Tiernan* for Samoa, since hope for the *Equator* had been all but given up. But the price which Sachs asked for the passage to Samoa seemed exorbitant; and besides, as Fanny put it: 'the *Equator* might still be afloat, and we could not consider with equanimity Captain Reid's disappointment should he return and find us gone' (*T12* xxii). In the event, the *Equator* did return after six weeks; and, as fate would have it, the *Tiernan* went down shortly after leaving Apemama. After yet another tearful departure from a South Sea island, the *Equator* left Apemama on 25 October, and after a detour back to Butaritari, headed for Samoa. They were followed by a succession of storms, and lost a fore-topmast and stay-sail in a squall; the *Equator* was only kept afloat, according to Fanny, by the ballast of its fifty ton cargo of copra (*T12* xxiii). On 7 December 1889 they finally reached Apia on Upolu, one of the group of islands sometimes called the Navigator Islands, but better known as Samoa.

At home in Samoa

The arrival at Apia marked the conclusion of the voyage charted in *In the South Seas*. A further cruise was to be made by Louis, Fanny and Lloyd from Sydney in the steamer *Janet Nicoll* during 1890. This cruise, which first went to the Marshall Islands, and then eastwards through the

Gilberts as far as Penrhyn Island, is mentioned at the beginning of *In the South Seas*, and may have provided for the book some general material on the Pacific islands.

However the main contribution of the *Lively Jane* (as the *Janet Nicoll* was nicknamed) to *In the South Seas* was arguably to provide a setting in which Stevenson could write up his South Sea notes – an overheated and highly unstable setting, for, as he put it in a letter to Burlingame accompanying the 'Tembinoka' chapters posted off from Auckland: 'This *Janet Nicoll* is rolling past belief... you never saw such a bitch to roll' (*L6* 387). Among the projects Stevenson worked on when the *Janet* was not too lively was the history of the 'Samoan business', which he had begun to see as 'a separate opuscule' during his first month in Apia (*L6* 345). Even when a section on Samoa had been planned to appear in *In the South Seas*, Stevenson told Colvin that he thought 'it will be all history, and I shall work in observations on Samoan manners under the similar heads in other Polynesian islands' (*L6* 337). Indeed, ten months before he first arrived at Samoa, Stevenson had already written on its recent history. On 10 February 1889, from the yacht *Casco* in the Hawaiian Islands, he had written a letter to *The Times* in order to 'recapitulate a little of the past' before proceeding to 'illustrate the present extraordinary state of affairs in the Samoan Islands' (*L6* 251). In this, the first of the eight letters he would write to *The Times* on the subject of Samoan politics, the last appearing only months before his death, Stevenson offered to the readers of *The Times* a brief version of what appeared in more detail in *A Footnote to History*. One of Stevenson's sources for this letter to *The Times* from Honolulu was his son-in-law, Joe Strong, who had been present as 'government artist' in an ill-fated diplomatic mission to Samoa, sent by King Kalakaua of Hawaii in December 1886 (*L6* 252 n.1).

A Footnote to History also offers a recapitulation of the past before moving on to describe 'the present extraordinary state of affairs in the Samoan Islands'; indeed, ten of its eleven chapters deal with the period before the Stevensons' arrival in Samoa. Technically the Samoan Islands were independent, although in practice they were subject to joint British, German and American control; the Germans, however, held the whip hand. It was true, Stevenson admitted in his letter to *Times* in February 1889, that the Samoan islands had been largely opened up by German enterprise, and that the main port of Apia was the creation of the Hamburg firm of Godeffroys and its successor, the *Deutsche Handels-und-Plantagen-Gesellschaft für Südsee-Inseln zu Hamburg* (a.k.a. the D.H.P.G., or 'the Old Firm', or 'the Long Handle Firm') (*L6* 251; 346 n.4). However, the extraordinary state of affairs in Samoa, which had prompted Stevenson to write to *The Times* from Honolulu, was the 'reign of terror' under the German Consul Dr Knappe, who had pretensions to be 'the Bismarck of a Polynesian island' (*L6* 251–2). Apia had been governed until lately by a tripartite Municipality which consisted of the American, English and German Consuls, plus one other representative of each of the so-called Three Powers. But the German party had sought to appropriate absolute power for itself by a series of political machinations. In August 1887 Malietoa Laupepa ('Malietoa' was the supreme Samoan title), the rightful Samoan King, had been deposed and sent into exile, with a display of German power including five warships in Apia Bay. In his place a puppet king, Tamese, was installed, and the tripartite Municipality dissolved, with the German Consul seated autocratically in its place (ibid.). Samoan opposition to the German puppet Tamase, an opposition backed by British and American interests, centred on the rival Malietoa Mataafa, who was crowned King in September 1888. War broke out between the rival claimants to the Samoan throne, and in December a German naval landing party, which had gone ashore to try to protect German plantations at Fangalii, was massacred by followers of Mataafa. Eighteen Germans were killed, and thirty-six wounded; some ritual beheading took place, but not extensively, since, as a Samoan chief put it: 'We ought not to cut off their heads when they do not cut off ours' (*T21* 183). In the wake of this reverse, in which the supposedly invincible Germans had been routed by Samoan braves under Mataafa (*T21* 185), Knappe declared a state of war and imposed martial law on all residents in Samoa, including Europeans. The British Consul protested and issued a proclamation to the effect that martial law did not apply to British subjects. Knappe replied: 'Since, on the ground of received instructions, martial law has been declared in Samoa, British subjects as well as others fall under its application. I warn you therefore to abstain from such a proclamation as you announce in your letter. It will be such a piece of business as shall make yourself answerable under martial law. Besides, your proclamation will be disregarded' (*T21* 194). Knappe was not, however, acting 'on the ground of received instructions'. On 12 February 1889, two days after Stevenson had written his letter to *The Times*, and a month before its publication on 11 March, Knappe received a despatch from Bismarck himself, which later appeared in *A Footnote to History*: 'You had no right to take foreigners from the jurisdiction of their consuls. The protest of your English colleague is grounded. In disputes which may arise from this cause you will find yourself in the wrong. The demand formulated by you, as to the assumption of the government of Samoa by Germany, lay outside of your instructions and of our design. Take it immediately back' (*T21* 198). Shortly afterwards Berlin issued the recall of the 'insane' Knappe, as Stevenson had called him in his first letter from Samoa to Baxter (*L6* 346). Before leaving Samoa, however, Knappe had to confront a disaster even greater than the massacre at Fangalii, and the wrath of Bismarck. On 16 March 1889 Samoa was struck by a hurricane which destroyed all but one of the seven warships in the harbour at Apia. The only survivor was the British ship *Calliope*, and considerable loss of life was sustained, particularly by the German navy. The hurricane was of epoch-making proportions, Stevenson claimed in *A Footnote to History*. First, it defused the tension that had been building since the Fangalii massacre and Knappe's imposition of martial law, and precipitated the convention of a Conference on Samoan Affairs in Berlin from April to June 1889. Secondly, Stevenson wrote, 'indirectly, and by a process still continuing, it founded the modern navy of the States. Coming years and *other historians* will declare the influence of that' (*T21* 211; italics added). Stevenson clearly had ambitions as a historian, even if his immediate motive in supplementing his letters to *The Times* with a book about 'the Samoan trouble' was the practical one of helping the islanders. He wrote to Burlingame that, if necessary, he was willing to have what he called 'the war volume' published at his own expense. If the book were to prove saleable, it was his first thought that all the proceeds should go to the Samoans, though on second thoughts he felt it only fair that half the profits should come to him (*L7* 196). Stevenson's primary motive was that his '*Historia Samoae*' should be 'useful to the islands', but he was equally clear that there was to be something in it for R.L.S. (*L7* 182). He had long harboured the ambition of being a historian. Although there had been an element of farce about his application in 1881 for the chair of History and Constitutional Law at Edinburgh University, with its list of testimonials that even Balfour saw as 'a tribute to the ingenuity of the human intellect' (*B* 190), nevertheless Stevenson's project of writing a three volume *Historical Description of the Highlands from 1700 to the Present Day* predated his fruitless foray into academe. Eleven years after he had written to his parents from Davos that he seemed to be 'gingerly embarking on a *History of Modern Scotland*' (*L3* 145), Stevenson returned to the idea of writing a book of 'Scotch history', but this time for children. This projected history for children grew out of Louis's experience of trying to give history lessons to young Austin Strong at Vailima; no history book for children was any good, he claimed (*L7* 182). A book of Scottish history was the obvious option for Stevenson, since 'Scotch is the only history I know; [and] it is the only history reasonably represented in my library' (*L7* 183).

But he felt, in a case of Bloom's 'anxiety of influence', that Scott's *Tales of a Grandfather* stood in his way. In his lessons with Austin, Stevenson was using Scott's history of Scotland, with 'all Scott's damned defects, and all Scott's hopeless merit. I cannot compete with that; and yet, so far as regards teaching History, how he has missed his chance! I think I'll try; I really have some historic sense, I feel that in my bones' (ibid.). In the event, Stevenson did not compete with Scott in the Scottish history stakes. Fanny later took the credit for persuading Louis to give priority to the book on Samoan history, despite his preference for writing 'a book, for boys, of Scotch history', which would have brought in much more money (*S* 162).

In writing *A Footnote to History* Stevenson was consciously leaving the realm of the literary. He wrote to Colvin: 'I do not go in for literature; address myself to sensible people rather than to sensitive. And indeed it is a kind of journalism' (*L7* 201). The style he intended was to run 'slackly and easily, as if half in conversation' (*L7* 182). Partly this was dictated by the demands of the situation; as he wrote to Colvin: 'I have no right to dally; if it is to help it must come soon' (ibid.). In addition to the constraints of time, the conditions in which Stevenson was hammering out the Samoan material were not always conducive to fine writing. From the rolling '*Lively Jane*' he wrote: 'All the same this history is a godsend for a voyage; I can put in time getting events coordinated and the narrative distributed, when my much-heaving numskull would be incapable of finish or fine style' (*L6* 389). Yet if Stevenson was putting his literary ambition on the back-boiler, his ambition to cut a figure as a historian is striking: 'Here for the first time,' he wrote to Burlingame, 'is a tale of Greeks – Homeric Greeks – mingled with moderns, and all true; Odysseus alongside of Rajah Brooke....Here is for the first time since the Greeks (that I remember) the history of a handful of men, where all know each other in the eyes and live close in a few acres, narrated at length and with the seriousness of history. Talk of the modern novel; here is modern history' (*L7* 196). Stevenson playfully compared his role to that of the Greek poets without whom, according to Horace,[12] the Greek heroes would have gone unmourned and unknown into a long night, 'because they lacked a sacred poet [*carent quia vate sacro*]' – though the sacredness was not essential, he joked: '*sacer* is another point' (*L7* 196, and n.5).

Much of the material for *A Footnote to History* came from H.J. Moors, an American trader who had risen, from modest beginnings, to become the owner of the second most important planting and trading enterprise in Samoa (*L6* 342 n.2). The introduction to Moors had been set up by

Joe Strong, who had been up till now Stevenson's principal source for information about Samoan affairs, and who had met Moors on an earlier visit to Samoa. After first staying with Moors, the Stevensons rented a little cottage close by, 'in the bush', as Louis put it (*L6* 345). Louis himself lived with Moors in Apia, 'for history's sake', he told Baxter (ibid.). Moors remembered it rather differently, however: 'although he no longer actually lived with me, Stevenson still spent a large part of his time at my house; and, to tell the truth, he never seemed to know where he was going to have his dinner, whether at his own place or mine.'[13] The question of Stevenson's residence was to be settled in an unexpectedly dramatic fashion when, in the month following his arrival in Samoa, he decided to buy some land and build a house of his own. After inspecting several properties, he chose an estate called Vailima (meaning 'five waters') as being the most attractive, and asked Moors to negotiate the purchase.[14] On 20 January 1890 Stevenson wrote to Lady Taylor: 'I am now the owner of an estate on Upolu, some two or three miles behind and above Apia; three streams, two waterfalls, a great cliff, an ancient native fort, a view of the sea and lowlands...are now mine....Besides all this, there is a great deal more forest than I have any need for; or to be plain, the whole estate is one impassable jungle, which must be cut down and through at considerable expense. Then the house has to be built; and then (as a climax) we may have to stand a siege in it in the next native war (*L6* 351).

A month after the purchase of the Vailima estate on 10 January 1890, Louis and Fanny were on board the steamer *Lübeck* bound for Sydney, where Joe, who was thought to be seriously ill, had been sent almost immediately to join Belle and Austin; Lloyd had followed his brother-in-law Joe in early January. One of the main reasons for Stevenson choosing to settle on Samoa was the existence of the regular and reliable mail services that were indispensable for his communication with publishers and printers. Besides the *Lübeck* which ran regularly between Apia and Sydney, there was a service between Apia and Auckland, as well as the monthly steamers, on which Stevenson came to rely, between Sydney and San Francisco, this latter route proving the quickest and safest (*L7* 3, *B* 305). Once at Sydney Louis became unwell almost immediately, and 'made himself a prisoner' in the Union Club (an 'excellent civilised, antipodal club', he wrote to Henry James), where Fanny was allowed to visit him (*L6* 370; 374). His poor health did not prevent him from writing his famous 'Open Letter' to Dr Hyde, but his condition deteriorated as he started haemorrhaging. A voyage to Europe, already booked on the *S.S. Austral*, had to be cancelled. In a desperate attempt to get Louis into a warmer climate, Fanny managed, in spite of a dock strike in Sydney, to extort through sheer importunity the unwilling consent of the owners of the *Janet Nicoll* to accept herself, Lloyd and Louis as passengers on a trading cruise to the Islands (*L6* 383 n.1; *B* 306). The *Janet Nicoll* left Sydney on 11 April, and on 30 April made a brief stop at Apia, when the Stevensons took the opportunity of going ashore to inspect the progress at Vailima. They did not return there until September when they arrived on the *Lübeck* from Sydney, where the *Janet Nicoll* had deposited them after its long and 'very devious' course through the Islands (*T20* vii).

While they had been away, Moors had arranged for an area of Vailima to be cleared, and a small cottage had been constructed for them to inhabit until a larger house was built. Here the Stevensons lived in primitive conditions during the first months after their return to Vailima. A vivid picture of their life at this stage is provided in a notoriously snobbish description given by the American historian Henry Adams, whose grandfather and great-grandfather had been American presidents, and who, following his wife's suicide, was travelling in the Pacific Islands with his companion, the artist John La Farge. Describing an unexpected visit they had made to Vailima in October 1890, Adams wrote in a letter:

At last we came out in a clearing dotted with burned stumps exactly like a clearing in our backwoods. In the middle stood a two-story Irish shanty with steps outside to the upper floor, and a galvanised iron roof. A pervasive atmosphere of dirt seemed to hang around it, and the squalor like a railroad navvy's board hut. As we reached the steps a figure came out that I cannot do justice to. Imagine a man so thin and emaciated that he looked like a bundle of sticks in a bag, with a head and eyes morbidly intelligent and restless. He was costumed in very dirty striped cotton pyjamas, the baggy legs tucked into the coarse knit woollen stockings, one of which was bright brown in colour, the other a purplish dark tone. With him was a woman who…wore the usual missionary nightgown which was no cleaner than her husband's shirt and drawers, but she omitted the stockings. Her complexion and eyes were dark and strong, like a half-breed Mexican.[15]

The bitchiness of Adams, who elsewhere described Louis as 'looking like an insane stork', and Fanny as 'stalwart as any other Apache squaw', may partly derive, Frank McLynn suggests, from the fact that Adams was one of the first Americans to advocate that the United States should compete with the British empire for global hegemony; in a passage leading up to the one just quoted, Adams had introduced Stevenson as: 'Our European rival...'.[16] Whatever imperial axe Adams may have had to grind, his descriptions are nevertheless 'wickedly amusing', admits Ernest Mehew, who supplements the 'insane stork' image with Adams's observation that on another occasion Stevenson was: 'astonishingly agreeable, dancing about, brandishing his long arms above his head, and looking so attenuated in the thin flannel shirt which is his constant wear, that I expected to see him break in sections' (*L7* 43 n.7).

The occasion in question was a dinner that Adams and La Farge had given for the Stevensons. Stevenson commented in a letter to Colvin that it had been 'a good dinner on the whole', over which he had been able to talk about art and 'the lovely dreams of art students' with La Farge, whom he had immediately taken to (whereas he had difficulty at first in remembering Adams's name) (*L7* 33, 43). This letter to Colvin was the second of what came to be known as the *Vailima Letters*, published in 1895 with the subtitle: *Correspondence addressed by Robert Louis Stevenson to Sidney Colvin, November 1890–October 1894*. Colvin took his justification for publishing these letters, in expurgated form, from a remark Stevenson made in a letter in June 1892: 'It came over me the other day suddenly that this diary of mine to you would make good pickings after I am dead, and a man could make some kind of a book out of it without much trouble. So for God's sake, don't lose them and they will prove a piece of provision for my "poor old family"' (*L7* 310) Stevenson was doubtless being disingenuous in telling Colvin that the possibility of publishing his 'diary letter' in some form came over him 'suddenly'; from the beginning, the idea of a letter doubling as a journal seemed to offer the possibility of killing several birds with one stone. Not the least of these economies in Stevenson's writing practice was the fact that his latest 'Vailima letter' could be passed around his friends and family. He asked Colvin, for example, to pass on to his mother the letter he began on 25 November 1890; and in a letter of 29 December he told Henry James that he was sending a long letter to Colvin every month, which Colvin would share with him, 'if it is ever of the least interest' (*L7* 66). Although these letters are at times delightfully written, they also provided Stevenson with a kind of safety-valve where he could, as he put in the first 'Vailima letter', 'sit down every day and pour out an equable stream of twaddle' (*L7* 24).

From the first, the *Vailima Letters* were literally a 'literary life' of Stevenson, as they recorded on a daily basis the advances and setbacks, both great and small, of his writing practice. In the first letter, for example, Stevenson described how he worked all Tuesday morning at the

South Seas, 'and finished the chapter I had stuck upon on Saturday' (ibid.). Fanny, who was 'hove-to with rheumatics and injuries received...chasing pigs', sat on the veranda barking orders in pidgin at the 'boys', her cries chequering Louis's work. After a luncheon of beef, soda scones, fried bananas, pineapple in claret, and coffee: 'Try to write a poem; no go. Play the flageolet. Then sneakingly off to farmering and pioneering' (*L7* 24–5).

The latter was to prove a great temptation to Stevenson: 'I went crazy over outdoor work, and had at last to confine myself to the house, or literature must have gone by the board. *Nothing* is so interesting as weeding, clearing and path-making; the oversight of labourers becomes a disease: it is quite an effort not to drop into the farmer; and it does make you feel so well' – not a feeling Stevenson was used to (*L7* 20). His solitary path-clearing expeditions into the jungle, struggling with 'the unconcealed vitality of these vegetables' and particularly with the *tuitui* or sensitive-plant which seemed semi-conscious,[17] had a strange effect on him, Louis claimed. He described one uncanny experience: 'A strange business it was, and infinitely solitary: away above, the sun was in the high tree tops; the lianas noosed and sought to hang me; the saplings struggled, and came up with that sob of death that one gets to know so well.... Soon, toiling down in that pit of verdure, I heard blows on the far side, and then laughter. I confess a chill settled on my heart. Being so dead alone, in a place by rights none should be beyond me...and only the other day I was lamenting my insensibility to superstition!' (*L7* 25). This kind of experience led to his poem 'The Woodman', and also to a new story, which 'just shot through me like a bullet in one of my moments of awe, alone in that tragic jungle' (*L7* 27). This story, entitled 'The High Woods of Ulufanua', was: 'very strange, very extravagant, I daresay; but it's varied, and picturesque, and has a pretty love affair, and ends wells' (ibid.).

Stevenson blew hot and cold over 'The High Woods of Ulufanua', which was eventually retitled 'The Beach of Falesá'. In the second 'Vailima Letter', dated 25 November 1890, he told Colvin he had given up 'The High Woods' as 'a deception of the devil's', and in early December dismissed it to McClure as 'a temporary insanity, perfectly unsound, perfectly silly, perfectly cheap', although he still intended to 'hammer it square inside a week' (*L7* 39, 49). Though he still thought what he called 'the fable' of 'The High Woods' too fantastic and far-fetched when he re-read it the following April, nevertheless he told Colvin that he 'fell in love with' the first chapter, and for better or worse had to finish it (*L7* 112). Stevenson's ambivalence towards 'The High Woods' is evident in the tenth 'Vailima Letter', begun in early September 1891, where he described the chapter he had just re-read as: 'really very fetching; but . . . the story is so wilful, so steep, so silly – it's a hallucination I have out-lived, and yet I never did a better piece of work, horrid, and pleasing, and extraordinarily *true*: it's sixteen pages of the South seas: their essence' (*L7* 155). By the end of this 'Vailima Letter', which was written, like the others, over a period of several days, Stevenson announced that he had changed the title of his troublesome piece, and signed himself: 'Author of 'The Beach of Falesá' (*L7* 159). The following 'Vailima Letter' begins:

> My dear Colvin, Since I last laid down my pen I have written and re-written 'The Beach of Falesá': something like sixty thousand words of sterling domestic fiction . . . I was all yesterday revising and found a lot of slacknesses and (what is worse in this kind of thing) some literaryisms. . . . There is a great deal of fact in the story, and some pretty good comedy. It is the first realistic South Sea story: I mean the real South Sea character and details of life; everybody else who has tried, that I have seen, got carried away by the romance and ended in a kind of sugar candy sham epic, and the whole effect was lost. . . . Now I have got the smell and look of the thing a good deal. You will know more about the South Seas after you have read my little tale, than if you had read a library (*L7* 161).

'The Beach of Falesá' represents a fine balance between realism and romance. From the beginning, it was conceived as 'a pretty love affair', and, unusually for Stevenson, it had a pretty heroine (*Catriona* at this stage being hardly a twinkle in his eye) (*L7* 27, 113). The reason that Stevenson gave for not usually having women in his fiction (as opposed to the speculations of more recent 'Queer' readings of his work[18]) was that any realism in the depiction of relationships between men and women was unacceptable to mainstream publishers in the English-speaking world, and especially to publishers of family magazines. It was unthink-able, he wrote to Colvin, 'to do love in the same spirit as I did (for example) D. Balfour's fatigue in the heather' (*L7* 284). Ten years after 'The Treasure of Franchard' had been turned down by the *Cornhill* as 'not suitable to British proprieties' (*L4* 39 n.1), Stevenson's experience of censorship was to be repeated in the case of 'The Beach of Falesá'. The story hinges on the recognition by the narrator, the trader Wiltshire, that his feelings for Uma, his Kanaka woman, have developed from a merely exploitative lust into genuine love: 'for there's no use mincing things – Kanaka and all, I was in love with her, or just as good' (*T13* 29).

The fact that the tale is narrated in the jaundiced tones of the cynical trader heightens the sense of genuine affection between Wiltshire and Uma. The point of the story is the emergence of real love, and a genuine marriage, out of an initial sham marriage which was blatantly exploitative. However, for this deeply moral tale to work, the original sham marriage has to be seen clearly for what it was; yet it was precisely Stevenson's frank presentation of the original 'marriage' that was considered morally offensive by his publishers. In Stevenson's manuscript the bogus marriage contract ran as follows:[19]

> This is to certify that <u>Uma</u> daughter of <u>Faavao</u> of Falesá island of -----, is illegally married to <u>Mr John Wiltshire</u> for one night, and Mr John Wiltshire is at liberty to send her to hell next morning
>
> John Blackamoor
Chaplain to the Hulks.
>
> Extracted from the register
> by William T. Randall
> Master Mariner

When 'The Beach of Falesá' was first published in the *Illustrated London News* in July 1892, the marriage contract was omitted altogether, without Stevenson's permission. The book version was to be published by Cassell, who were also unhappy with the bogus marriage contract. Stevenson rightly felt that the point of his story depended on the sham marriage contract, but he was willing to compromise on the details of it; the 'for one night' could be extended to 'for one week', and Wiltshire was at liberty to send Uma to hell 'when he pleases', rather than 'next morning'. Stevenson tried to see the funny side of such moral pettiness: 'Well, well, if the dears prefer a week, why I'll give them ten days, but the real document, from which I have scarcely varied, ran for one night' (*L7* 281). Ironically the 'real document', which Stevenson refers to, had already appeared in the newspaper serialization of *In the South Seas* in exactly the form which the publishers objected to in the context of 'The Beach of Falesá' (*T20* 267). Indeed the 'real document' was even more offensive in the context of the newspaper version of Stevenson's 'South Sea Letter', because there the holders of such bogus marriage certificates were called 'children' (in the later book version of *In the South Seas* they are referred to as 'women'[20]).

Barry Menikoff has argued that Furnas and Calder have exaggerated the importance of their editions of 'The Beach of Falesá' in which the

original marriage certificate has been restored.[21] Their claims that
Stevenson's text was now 'unexpurgated' and 'exactly as R.L.S. wrote it'
are at best naïve, Menikoff suggests: 'That Furnas and Calder are not
textual scholars is no sin. But they contribute to the easy, uncritical
acceptance of a mutilated text. Had . . . he marriage certificate remained
intact, Stevenson's art would have been no less abused.'[22] Menikoff's
argument in *Robert Louis Stevenson and 'The Beach of Falesá': A Study in
Victorian Publishing* was that Stevenson's manuscript of 'The Beach of
Falesá' had been 'abused', 'mutilated' and even 'eviscerated' by the late
Victorian publishing industry, not only by substantial changes such as
the omission or bowdlerization of the marriage certificate, but also by
a host of tiny changes at the level of punctuation, capitalization, spelling,
paragraphing etc.: 'We must recognize that from start to finish there was
nothing in *Falesá* that could truly please the people who were responsible for the production of Stevenson's books and for the promotion of
his reputation. They could not do anything explicit about his chosen
story, his *donnée*, but they could, and they did, eviscerate it.'[23] In a *tour
de force* of close reading, which occasionally may reveal more about his
own textual ingenuity than about the bad faith of the Victorian publishing world, Menikoff sought to show how Stevenson's text had all
but died the death of a thousand cuts. 'The Beach of Falesá' dealt
head-on with the main taboo subjects of late Victorian culture: sex, religion, and the politics of colonial exploitation; consciously and unconsciously, Stevenson's text was systematically 'mutilated and corrupted',
Menikoff claims.[24] Powerful as Menikoff's case (and his rhetoric) may
be, it does depend on an assumption about the absolute priority of the
manuscript over any subsequent printed versions. This assumption has
been challenged by Roslyn Jolly in her 1996 edition of Stevenson's
South Sea Tales, where she argues that, while the manuscript of 'The
Beach of Falesá' represents the text Stevenson originally wrote, it does not
represent the text he finally passed for publication: 'To rate the authority of the manuscript above the authority of the final text corrected by
the author is to assume that none of the changes introduced by the
text's various editors has any authority, even though they were
accepted by the author; this seems to me an untenable assumption. . . .'[25]
Menikoff adopts a 'conspiracy theory' approach to Stevenson's editors,
printers and publishers, and assumes ultimately a kind of collusion on
Stevenson's part, accusing him of the abuse of his own art 'in sanction-
ing the publication of a corrupt text'.[26] Despite Stevenson's stature and
authority, Menikoff claims, '[he] was daunted by distance, by domestic
responsibilities, by the evasive and hesitant practices of publishers, by

the squeamishness of periodical editors, and above all by his trusting relationship with Sidney Colvin' (ibid.). Menikoff's book is not so much a study as an exposé of Victorian publishing; in particular, it is a savaging of Sidney Colvin, who is accused of 'arrogant disdain', of calculation and manipulation, and of being 'essentially a belletrist [who] clearly lacked the hard-headed realism of the businessman'.[27] If Menikoff's edition, with Colvin figuring as the chief villain, has something the excitement of a Victorian melodrama or mystery (the 'masters of suspicion'[28] were, after all, Victorians), Jolly's edition has the advantage of using the final text as corrected by Stevenson, with reference in the notes to significant variants between this text and the manuscript.

Menikoff's claim that it is naïve to believe that restoring the original marriage certificate somehow gives us the authentic text of 'The Beach of Falesá', itself depends on the claim that a myriad of small cuts and alterations have mutilated Stevenson's manuscript more effectively than any major omission.[29] This concentration on minutiae leads Menikoff to play down a largish omission that was actually made in the edition produced by Cassell: this omission was of a piece of advice, and a yarn, offered by Case, which Wiltshire recounts in order to show how initially susceptible he was to Case's patter: 'There was no smarter trader, and none dodgier, in the islands' (*T13* 4). Case's advice (to fire 'any christian money' up to Sidney to the bank) was backed up by a yarn which told how Case had engineered the ruin of a rival on an island in the Ellices – a yarn which ought to have alerted Wiltshire, the latter says, to 'the danger of that man [Case] for a neighbour'.[30] This yarn, Stevenson told Colvin, was: 'the preparatory note to Case, and the whole tale: the reader must be shown how far men go, and Case has gone, to get copra' (*L7* 364). It does not depict Case doing anything actually illegal to bring about the ruin of his rival, but 'merely' organizing a campaign to undercut him, in a piece of naked capitalist aggression. Perhaps such explicit financial predatoriness was considered to be as unedifying as the explicit sexual predatoriness which led to the excision of the marriage certificate; or perhaps the details of South Sea financial intrigue seemed too remote. It is interesting to note, however, that the trader ruined by Case in his yarn had provoked the hostility of his fellow traders by buying a schooner wrecked in the lagoon 'for an old song' – 'the way these things are usually managed', Case adds. It was precisely this practice of buying wrecks as a financial speculation that lay at the heart of the novel was intermittently working on during this period – *The Wrecker*.

Although 'The Beach of Falesá' was finished by October 1891, a month before an exhausted Stevenson finally managed to complete *The Wrecker*

(*L7* 188–9), it took longer than the latter to get into print. Its run in the *Illustrated London News* began in July 1892, the month in which *The Wrecker* concluded its run in *Scribner's Magazine*. 'The Beach of Falesá' took even longer to appear in book form. This delay was partly due to problems posed by the novella's awkward length. While Stevenson admitted to Baxter that, unlike the 'very big' *Wrecker*, 'The Beach of Falesá' was 'a very small book', it was even shorter than 50,000 words he claimed in a letter to Burlingame (*L7* 229, 224). The latter replied that at his count there were only 30,000 words, and advised against the separate publication of such 'an exceedingly small book' (*L7* 256 n.2). Colvin decided unilaterally to solve the problem by lumping together 'The Beach of Falesá' with 'The Bottle Imp' in one volume. Stevenson was furious when he heard that this proposal had got as far as being advertised in *The Scotsman*, and wrote to Baxter in August 1892: '*Apropos* of 'The Beach of Falesá' I reply to you, although I believe it's through Colvin I have received the proposal. You will kindly communicate to him my answer. The B. of F. is *simply not* to appear along with 'The Bottle Imp', a story of a totally different scope and intention, to which I have already made one fellow, and which I design for a substantive volume.' (*L7* 350) Cassell's had already set up a proof-volume of 'The Beach of Falesá' and 'The Bottle Imp', which they sent to Stevenson (the so-called 'Trial Issue'), with the reassurance that they would respect his wishes (though not to the extent of publishing 'The Beach of Falesá' as a separate volume). 'When I heard you and Cassell's had decided to print 'The Bottle Imp' along with 'Falesá', I was much too disappointed to answer (*L7* 436), Stevenson explained to Colvin in early December 1892, after a 'cooling off' period, and added later that month: 'What annoyed me about the use of 'The Bottle Imp', was that I had always meant it for the centre piece of a volume of *Märchen* which I was slowly to elaborate' (*L7* 461). If 'The Beach of Falesá' had to appear in a collection of stories, then Stevenson proposed to entitle the collection: *Island Nights' Entertainments*. Other stories were mooted, but the only other tale finally to be included, besides 'The Beach of Falesá' and 'The Bottle Imp', was 'The Isle of Voices'. Although 'The Beach of Falesá' was 'the child of a quite different inspiration', said Stevenson, all the stories shared 'a queer realism, even the most extravagant, even 'The Isle of Voices': the manners are exact' (ibid.). In the same letter Stevenson addressed the thorny issue of the responsibilities devolving, in Stevenson's absence, on Colvin and Baxter. During the negotiations over 'The Beach of Falesá' (conducted via a very slow and unreliable mail service), it had seemed at times as if the right hand had not known what the left hand was doing. This had resulted in mixed messages and confusion, though Menikoff's reading of Colvin's role in the proceedings inclines more to a conspiracy theory.[31] Stevenson's solution ran as follows, as he tiptoed round Colvin's vanity: 'I had just last mail placed all my business in C.B.'s hands, and determined to be quite done with negotiations. Your very welcome proposal (it seems to me) ought therefore to go to him; I do not like to give one month and take away the next; so all I have done, or care to do, is to write to him announcing your willingness to help in what is much a strange business to him; and if you please, I would have you two arrange grounds and responsibilities between the twae o' ye, and without my intervention. . . . I have written him that in any case, the financial aspect should be his' (L7 461–2). To Baxter, Stevenson was able to write more bluntly:

> It is understood that Colvin has nothing to do with the Business.
> "   "   "   "   Baxter   "   "   "   "   "   "   Proofs.
> *Est-ce clair?*   (L8 52)

The 'queer realism', with 'the manners exact', that Stevenson attributed to all the stories in *Island Nights' Entertainments*, applied particularly to 'The Beach of Falesá', which he had earlier described to Colvin as: 'a piece of realism *à outrance* nothing extenuated or adorned' (L7 282). *The Wrecker*, too, evinces a kind of realism, as Stevenson wrote to Baxter: 'I believe *The Wrecker* is a good yarn of its poor sort, and it is certainly well nourished with facts; no realist can touch me there' (L7 192). Stevenson was increasingly willing to characterize his work as in some sense 'realist', despite his earlier fulminations against realism in general, and Zola in particular, in his defence of Rodin (L5 311–12).[32] He wrote to Henry James, who had sent him a copy of Zola's latest, *La Bête Humaine*, that he had already read the novel, but had found it 'not very interesting' (L6 402). To Edmund Gosse he later declared *La Bête Humaine* 'perhaps the most excruciatingly silly book that I ever read to an end', though he admitted to a kind of pornographic pleasure on reading it 'because the animal was interested in lewdness. Not seriously, of course; my mind refusing to partake in it; but the flesh was slightly pleased. And when it was done, I cast it from me with a peal of laughter and forgot it' (L8 104). *La Bête Humaine* was presumably another example of what Stevenson had meant some years earlier when he called Zola's work: 'realistic in the evil sense, meaning that it is dead to the ideal, and speaks only to the senses' (L5 312). In contrast to such realism in the 'evil' or 'privative' sense, Stevenson had defended Rodin's art as 'real in the sense that it is studied from the life, and itself lives' (ibid.). It was in this latter, more positive sense of realism, that Stevenson and Lloyd Osbourne claimed in the Epilogue to *The Wrecker* that they had sought to impart to the 'very modern form of the police novel or mystery story' that 'impression of reality or life' whose conspicuous absence seemed to them to be the 'inevitable drawback' of the genre (*T12* 404–5). Their mystery story might be made to 'seem to inhere more in life' if it were infused with 'the tone of its age, its movement, the mingling of races and classes in the dollar hunt, the fiery and not quite unromantic struggle for existence...' (*T12* 405). In the dedication of *The Wrecker* to Will H. Low, a complex metafictional game was being played out. Low, who was '*devilish recognizable*' (*L6* 376) in the character of Loudon Dodd, the failed artist who is the main narrator of the novel, was in some respects identified with the kind of idealism in art which was fundamentally opposed to realism. It was Low who had publicly taken issue with Stevenson over the latter's notorious comparison of 'the career of art' with the oldest profession, that of the 'Daughter of Joy' (to use the 'romantic evasion' of the French) (*T28* 8).[33] There is considerable irony, therefore, when the Epilogue to *The Wrecker* addresses Low:

> If you were not born in Arcadia, you linger in fancy on its margin; your thoughts are busy with the flutes of antiquity, with daffodils, and the classic poplar, and the footsteps of the nymphs, and the elegant and moving aridity of ancient art. Why dedicate to you a tale of a caste so modern; – full of the details of our barbaric manners and unstable morals; – full of the need and the lust of money, so that there is scarce a page in which the dollars do not jingle; – full of the unrest and movement of our century, so that the reader is hurried from place to place and sea to sea, and the book is less a romance than a panorama; – in the end, as blood-bespattered as an epic? (*T12* 404).

The answer given in the Epilogue is that, as 'a man interested in all problems of art, even the most vulgar', Low might be amused to hear about the genesis and growth of *The Wrecker*. He received into the bargain 'a prodigious quantity of theory', since 'some of us like theory', declared Stevenson, a century before the boom in literary theory which he could scarcely have imagined[34] (*T12* 404–5).

While some of the experience of Loudon Dodd was drawn from Stevenson's own life, the character was so closely modelled on Low that Stevenson at one time suggested to Burlingame that the illustrator of *The Wrecker*, W.B. Hole, be shown a photograph of Low to 'give him a cue' (*L6* 375–7). The fact that the characters in *The Wrecker* were so closely modelled on real people as to be 'portraits, almost undisguised' was partly, Stevenson explained to Burlingame, because the novel was 'in quite a new vein for me: being chiefly a study of manners'; and partly for 'convenience in collaboration, when it is so ready a thing to say to your collaborator: "O, make him so and so!" ' (*L6* 376). These two factors also contributed to the enormous size of *The Wrecker*. Stevenson's self-confessed lack of experience of 'stories in this vein of matter-of-fact' left him unprepared for the way they 'grow in the hands', leading him to complain of *The Wrecker*: 'the beastly tale rises in our hands like dough' (*L6* 382). The process of collaboration was also painfully slow, with Stevenson being dependent on a 'respected collaborateur' who could on occasion play the temperamental artist and withhold work he was dissatisfied with (*L6* 392). Such problems were intensified when Lloyd left for England in August 1890 in order to arrange the sale of Skerryvore and the shipment of its furniture to Samoa. Lloyd's departure led to 'the hell of collaboration half the world away' (*L7* 9). Stevenson explained the slow progress of *The Wrecker* to Burlingame by the fact that: 'I am denuded of my proofs, my collaborator having walked away with them to England; hence some trouble in catching the just note' (*L7* 33). Burlingame refused to proceed with the serial publication of *The Wrecker* until the novel was finished. This annoyed Stevenson who protested: '[*The Wrecker*] can't be done for a good many months:...Lloyd is off to England; he has to do the Cruise of the *Currency Lass* part in England (he cannot work at sea) and he is scarce there yet; it has then to come back to me; I have to do it, it has to go to you. That makes close on six months at the most moderate computation' (*L7* 34). It was this complicated process of literary production, with proofs having to be sent between New York, Samoa and England, in a period when mails were slow and unreliable, that caused Stevenson to describe inter-continental collaboration as 'hell'.

Stevenson considered *The Wrecker* 'a good yarn on the whole and of its measly kind', though he did not rate that 'measly kind' very highly, commenting: 'of course it [*The Wrecker*] didn't set up to be a book – only a long yarn with some pictures of the manners of today in the greater world – not the shoddy sham world of cities, clubs and colleges – but the world where men still live a man's life' (*L7* 180–1). It was 'a dark, violent yarn with interesting, plain turns of human nature', he told Colvin; and if Burlingame had not liked the Epilogue, then he did, as Stevenson had hoped, like the ending, which was 'rather strong meat' (*L7* 217, 189). The climax of *The Wrecker* was indeed strong meat, as the castaway crew of the *Currency Lass* butcher the crew of the *Flying Scud* that had come to rescue them. The trigger for this 'abomination', which makes the perpetrators themselves faint and vomit before drinking themselves unconscious, was the demand by Captain Trent of the *Flying Scud* for the bulk of the castaways' treasure chest in return for rescuing them. This murderous struggle for treasure, which erupts on the *Flying Scud* anchored off Midway Island, is like a dark reprise of the violence that erupted on and around the *Hispaniola* anchored off Treasure Island, the difference being that whereas Treasure Island was mountainous and 'romantic', Midway Island is low and 'ingloriously savage' (*T12* 357–8). Henley thought that in *The Master of Ballantrae* the (by comparison) 'almost respectable' crew of the *Hispaniola* had been transformed into the 'raving, loathsome miscreants who formed the crew of the *Sarah*' (*M* 350). In *The Wrecker*, the crew of miscreants has been transported to a 'miserable islet' in the North Pacific which did not even live up to its billing as coaling station of the Pacific Mail (*T12* 355–7).

A 'Masterpiece in Grime', the phrase used by Henley in his review of *The Master of Ballantrae* (*M* 350), hardly fits *The Wrecker*, which may be grimy, but is scarcely a masterpiece; arguably, however, the phrase might be applied to *The Ebb-Tide*. The latter was described by Stevenson in a letter to Gosse as 'a dreadful, grimy business' (*L8* 104), while to Henry James he wrote of it:

[T]he grimness of that story is not to be depicted in words. There are only four characters, to be sure, but they are such a troop of swine! And their behaviour is really so deeply beneath any possible standard, that on a retrospect I wonder I have been able to endure them myself until the yarn was finished.... If the admirers of Zola admire him for his pertinent ugliness and pessimism, I think they should admire this; but if, as I have long suspected, they neither admire nor understand the man's art, and only wallow in his rancidness like a hound in offal, then they will certainly be disappointed in *The Ebb-Tide*. Alas! Poor little tale, it is not *even* rancid (*L8* 107).

If a connotation of Stevenson's term 'rancid' was 'sexually explicit', in the way that the unbowdlerized version of 'The Beach of Falesá' had come close to being, then it is true that sex is hardly foregrounded in *The Ebb-Tide*. There is a suggestion that the previous captain and mate of the *Farallone*, whose death from smallpox had given the unsavoury trio of Herrick, Davis and Huish the chance to acquire the schooner, had caught the disease from girls too weak to repel them when the

Farallone had landed at a stricken island. In this variation of the 'Ship of Fools' motif, the ironically named Wiseman and Wishart had been too stupified by drink to realize that the 'barbaric keening' of the islanders was actually a 'death wail', and, mistaking the sounds of lamentation for a party, had proceeded to gatecrash (*T14* 50).

The story of Wiseman and Wishart is narrated by the member of the *Farallone*'s Kanaka crew whom Davis had named 'Uncle Ned', but who, when he finally speaks his mind, rejects this imposed name and insists on his name of 'Taveeta [David], all-e-same Taveeta King of Islael' (*T14* 49). Taveeta's narrative recounts 'the life and death of [Herrick's] two predecessors; of their prolonged, sordid, sodden sensuality as they sailed, they knew not whither, on their last cruise' (*T14* 51). This insane career of drunkenness and negligence, fuelled by the *Farallone*'s cargo of champagne, is repeated by Davis and Huish, with the pusillanimous and incompetent Herrick looking helplessly on. But when the *Farallone* reaches a low island once more, the possibility of chasing island women could hardly be more remote. Not only has this island's population been all but annihilated by smallpox; it is ruled by Attwater, a fanatical missionary and pearl fisher, who, being 'a plain man and very literal' in his Christianity, had married off his 'too pretty' servant girl to put her out of temptation's way (*T14* 95). The ambiguity in Attwater includes his sexuality, notwithstanding his claim to look forward to making an excellent marriage when he returns to England. One does not have to go all the way with Wayne Koestenbaum[35] to find something suggestive in the following exchange in the island cemetery:

... "I dislike men, and hate women. Here was one I liked though," and [Attwater] set his foot upon a mound. "He was a fine savage fellow; he had a dark soul; yes, I liked this one. I am fanciful," he added, looking hard at Herrick, "and I take fads. I like you."
    Herrick turned swiftly and looked far away.... "No one can like me," he said.
    "You are wrong there," said the other, "as a man usually is about himself. You are attractive, very attractive" (*14* 90–1).

Then, 'spreading out his arms like a crucifix', Attwater urges Herrick to: 'fall on your knees and cast away your sins and sorrows on the Redeemer' (*T14* 92).

Whatever Koestenbaum may wish to make of the reputedly dark continent of Stevenson's sexuality in general, and of his relationship with Lloyd Osbourne in particular, the mechanics of their literary collaboration is a fairly murky area, especially in Lloyd Osbourne's rather overheated account.[36] Stevenson first mentioned *The Pearlfisher, The Ebb-Tide*'s original title, in a letter from Honolulu in April 1889 to Charles Baxter, asking him to register title of the story he and Lloyd were working on, which he called 'the gaudiest yarn' (*L6* 289). This was in fact the third 'yarn' that Louis and Lloyd had attempted to co-write for the *New York Ledger* since the previous March, when S. S. McClure had brought the *Ledger*'s proprietor to Saranac Lake to discuss terms for a story (*L6* 148). The two other stories were ultimately abandoned. In May 1889 Lloyd was working on the first draft of *The Pearlfisher*, to 'break the ground' (*B* 249); in June he gave his unfinished manuscript to his sister Belle who was leaving for Sydney, while Lloyd and the rest of the Stevenson party set sail in the *Equator*. It was from 'Equator Town' in Tembinok's Apemama that Stevenson wrote to Colvin that he and Lloyd were hard at work on *The Wrecker*, which was to be the first of their 'South Sea Yarns', with *The Pearlfisher* (still in Sydney) the second, and *The Beachcombers* (which never materialized) the third (*L6* 330). After the *Equator* cruise, and a brief but decisive first encounter with Samoa, the Stevensons' visit to Sydney had to be cut short when Louis fell sick; they escaped from Sydney on the *Janet Nicoll*, having picked up Lloyd's manuscript of *The Pearlfisher*. On the *Janet Nicoll* cruise Stevenson did nothing on *The Wrecker*, he wrote to Colvin, but 'solved the problem of the far more important *Pearl Fisher* [sic], none of which had been yet done except by Lloyd; who is of course incapable of turning the ugliness of this rugged, harsh and really striking tale' (*L6* 405). Writing in August 1890 to Marcel Schwob, Stevenson commented that he had: 'two huge novels on hand – *The Wrecker* and *The Pearl Fisher*, in collaboration with my stepson – the latter, *The Pearl Fisher*, I think highly of, for a black, ugly, trampling, violent story, full of strange scenes and striking characters (*L6* 401). However, while Stevenson's struggles with *The Wrecker* fill his correspondence from late 1889 through to the novel's completion in November 1891, little is heard of its fellow 'South Sea Yarn' until February 1893 when Stevenson asked Baxter to prepare to dispose of the serial rights of *The Schooner Farallone*, which was 'the butt end of what once was *The Pearl Fisher*' (*L8* 29). The fact that this 'most grim and gloomy tale' was no longer a huge novel, but would come in at between 65 to 70,000 words, presented a problem. The original deal with the *New York Ledger*, brokered in 1888 by McClure, had been for £1000; five years later, in 1893, the *Ledger* had lost interest, but McClure 'in a rather handsome way' had maintained the original offer (ibid.). The problem was that the book which, as originally planned, would have been longer even than *The Wrecker*, was now very much shorter; in the event, however, McClure kept more or less to his word.

In February 1893 Stevenson told Baxter he was confident he would complete *The Schooner Farallone* in a month to six weeks (ibid.). In fact it was not until June, after 'thirteen days about as nearly in Hell as a man could expect to live through', that he finally finished what was by now called *The Ebb-Tide*, 'as grim a tale as was ever written, and as grimy, and as hateful' (*L8* 90–1). The pace at which Stevenson ground out *The Ebb-Tide* was so excruciatingly slow that he described it as a crucifixion: 'I break down at every paragraph, ... and lie here, and sweat, and curse over the blame thing, till I can get one sentence wrung out after another. Strange doom! after having worked so easily for so long!' (*L8* 68) Far from emulating Sir Walter Scott's prolificacy – 'not much Waverley Novels about this!' (*L8* 67) – Stevenson now felt closer to Flaubert's agonizingly slow writing method – 'This is Flaubert outdone' (*L8* 88). Part of the problem was the fact that *The Ebb-Tide* was written in the third person, a narrative form that Stevenson had not employed since *Prince Otto*, written ten years before. There was, he said, 'such a veil of words' over *The Ebb-Tide*, in contrast to the 'naked writing' he had increasingly come to prefer (*L8* 72). The tension between 'a vilely realistic dialogue and a narrative style pitched about ... "four notes higher" than it should have been, has sown my head with grey hairs', Stevenson confided to Gosse (*L8* 103). He was capable of spending 'a living half hour upon a single clause'; unfortunately, however, 'this sort of trouble ... produces nothing when done but alembication ...' (*L8* 88), he told Colvin, repeating his earlier complaint that: 'This forced, violent alembicated style is most abhorrent to me: it can't be helped: the note was struck years ago on the *Janet Nicoll* and has to be maintained somehow' (*L8* 70). 'Nearly dead with dyspepsia, over-smoking, and unremunerative over-work', moaned Stevenson, he 'crippled on' at what he called the 'ever-to-be execrated *Ebb-Tide*, or Stevenson's Blooming Error' (*L8* 88, 94). There is in Stevenson's letters at this time a recurrent note of exhaustion and near despair, as when he wrote to Colvin:

> The truth is of course that I am wholly worked out; but God, it's nearly done, and it shall go somehow according to promise. I go against all my Gods, and say it is *not worthwhile* to massacre yourself over the last few pages of a rancid yarn, that will never be worth a damn, and that reviewers will quite justly tear to bits (*L8* 90).

To Gosse he sounded a more stoic note: 'I grind away with a dogged, dour sensation – and an idea *in petto* [secretly] that the game is about played out. I have got too realistic, and I must break with these trammels – I mean I would, if I could; but the yoke is heavy (*L8* 103). In the increasingly pessimistic tone of Stevenson's letters of this period, religion figures either as a source of imagery for the agony of artistic production, or ironically in his treatment of the missionary type, for whom Stevenson had deeply ambivalent feelings. To his mother, a godly woman and the daughter of a Scotch minister, as the Revd Dr Hyde had put it, Louis wrote of *The Ebb-Tide*: 'I believe you will think it vile; though it does end in a conversion' (*L8* 79); but to Charles Baxter he wrote sarcastically: 'There is a peculiarity about this tale in its new form: it ends with a conversion! We have been rather tempted to call it *The Schooner Farallone*: A Tract by R.L.S. and L.O. It would make a boss [hollow] tract; the three main characters... are barrats, insurance frauds, thieves and would-be murderer; so the company's good' (*L8* 29).

Although Stevenson's great wish had been for *The Ebb-Tide* to appear in the *London Illustrated News*, he accepted its serialization in the first thirteen issues of Jerome K. Jerome's new twopenny weekly magazine *To-day*, starting in November 1893 (*L8* 67; 216 n.8). His feelings about it continued to be ambivalent. At first he told Colvin that did not want Lloyd's name to appear as co-author, since it was 'unfair on the young man to couple his name with so infamous a work' (*L8* 156); but when Colvin enthused over the last two chapters (written entirely by Stevenson), Louis changed his mind, and left it up to Colvin whether or not to credit Lloyd (*L8* 158). He remained diffident about its publication in book form, telling Colvin on 5 November 1893 that the book version could wait (*L8* 180). The following January he wrote apropos Baxter's proposal for a collected edition (the 'Edinburgh Edition'): '*The Ebb-Tide* is a matter on which you in England must judge. I am indifferent; if you think it is being successful in this magazine, you can publish it. If you think it is not, keep it for the works' (Stevenson had already earmarked it for a volume of 'Stories and Fantasies' in the projected edition) (*L8* 227). There has been a suggestion that Louis's decision after all to credit Lloyd may have had to do with concerns over the American copyright of the book. The Chace Act of 1891 (the first American international copyright law) had given foreign authors some protection, but only if they were typeset, printed and bound in the United States.[37] The American edition appeared first, published not by Scribner's, who showed little interest in *The Ebb-Tide*, but by a new and innovative Chicago publishing house, Stone and Kimball.[38] The first British edition was published on 21 September 1894 by Heinemann, though the authority of their text has been disputed.[39]

By the time he had completed *The Ebb-Tide*, Stevenson was suffering from 'over-exhaustion and fiction-phobia', he told Colvin, and, temporarily abandoning fiction, he resumed work on the family history which he had been writing intermittently since August 1891 (*L8* 94). The central focus of this history, with the working title: *Northern Lights: Memorials of a Family of Engineers*, was Louis's grandfather, Robert Stevenson, who had famously built the Bell Rock lighthouse. Hence Louis in his letters referred to the work simply as 'my Grandfather', and regarded it primarily as biography. In a letter to Gosse in June 1893, enquiring after his previous (mysteriously unanswered) letter criticising Gosse's biography of *his* father,[40] Stevenson announced:

> I have left fiction wholly, and gone to my Grandfather, and on the whole found peace.... I like biography far better than fiction myself; fiction is too free. In biography you have your little handful of facts, like bits of a puzzle and you sit and fit 'em together this way and that, and get up and throw 'em down, and say damn, and go for a walk. And it's real soothing; and when done done, gives an idea of finish to the writer that is very peaceful. Of course, it's not really so finished as quite a rotten novel; it always has and always must have the incurable illogicalities of life about it... (*L8* 104).

Louis's 'Grandfather' was never completed, but appeared posthumously as *Records of a Family of Engineers* in the Edinburgh Edition.

The pleasure Stevenson took in working on the biography of his grandfather was derived not only from its genre, but also from the opportunity it gave him to go back to his Scottish roots, with which he, like many another expatriate Scot, seems to have become obsessed. From Samoa he badgered his friends and family back in Scotland to follow up his hunches and leads about the complex history of the Stevenson family. He wrote to his cousin Bob, for the first time in over three years, to tell him about Stevenson of Stevenson, 'who was quite a great party and dates back to the wars of Edward First', and about the subsequent history of the Stevensons, firstly in Neilston, south-west of Glasgow, and later in Glasgow itself (*L8* 303). Louis admitted to Bob that his 'sham antiquarianism' (*L8* 364) derived in some measure from the fact that he was childless: 'I wish to trace my ancestors a thousand years... It is not love, not pride, not admiration; it is an expansion of the identity, intimately pleasing, and wholly uncritical; I can expend myself in the person of an inglorious ancestor with perfect comfort; ... I suppose, perhaps, it is more to me who am childless, and refrain with a certain shock from looking forwards' (*L8* 303). Stevenson's maternal ancestors were summoned up too, with Maggie Stevenson's grandfather, James Balfour, laird of Pilrig, meeting David Balfour in chapter three of *Catriona*. Such an admixture of family history in the fiction Stevenson wrote in Samoa is also evident in his wish to claim kinship (through the wife of the same James Balfour) with the Border Elliotts who are at the centre of *Weir of Hermiston*. Describing his involvement in a fracas at Vailima, Stevenson commented: 'I judged that I was much fallen off from my Elliott forefathers, who managed this class of business with neatness and despatch' (*L7* 240 and n.2). It is noticeable that after *The Ebb-Tide*, all the fiction that Stevenson was engaged on in the last part of his life was set largely or wholly in Scotland (although, as discussed above, Stevenson's late Scottish fiction is doubtless coloured by his Samoan experience).

While Samoa may appear only indirectly in Stevenson's late fiction, it dominated his non-fictional writing in a very explicit way. He continued to send letters about Samoan politics to *The Times* on such a regular basis that he attracted the attention of the authorities not only in Samoa, but also back in London. The British Consul in Samoa, Sir Thomas Cusack-Smith, wrote a despatch to the Foreign Office about Stevenson's dealings with Mataafa, and referring to Stevenson's letters to *The Times*, concluded acidly: '...while his language and some of his deductions are to be regretted his facts appear to be accurate upon a somewhat hasty perusal.... I fear Mr Stevenson's interest in Samoan affairs is commensurate with the amount of gratuitous advertisement he secures thereby' (*L8* 21 n.3). This despatch drew the Foreign Office comment: 'Mr Stevenson would do better if he stuck to novel writing and left politics alone' (ibid.). On 29 December 1892 the British High Commissioner of the Western Pacific, Sir John Thurston, issued the so-called Sedition (Samoa) Regulation 'for the maintenance of peace and good order in Samoa'. This piece of legislation seemed explicitly designed to muzzle Stevenson when it declared in section three: 'The expression "Sedition towards the Government of Samoa" shall embrace all practices, whether by word, deed, or writing, having for their object to bring in Samoa discontent or dissatisfaction, public disturbance, civil war...and generally to promote public disorder in Samoa' (*L8* 25). In February 1893 Stevenson sent a copy of the Regulation to *The Times*, with a short accompanying letter (not included, incidentally, in the 'Letters to *The Times* etc' section in Colvin's Edinburgh Edition) declaring that, despite these 'barbarous' tactics – 'a new experience for a British subject' – he would continue to report to *The Times* any further scandal, and 'endure my three months in Apia Gaol with as much patience as I may' (*L8* 24). Stevenson's letter, which appeared in *The Times* on 4 April 1893, six weeks after he had sent it, provoked widespread criticism of the Regulation (*L8* 26 n.1). The latter had by this time been subject to internal Foreign Office criticism, but bureaucratic incompetence in the Colonial Office made it appear as if the amendments Thurston was ordered to make to the Regulation were the result of Stevenson's letter. An enraged Thurston made a further attempt to vilify Stevenson, but, perhaps because of Stevenson's friends in high places (he has corresponded with Lords Rosebery and Ripon, respectively the Foreign and the Colonial Secretary), Thurston was firmly put in his place. However, if Lord Ripon had ridiculed the accusation that a writer of what he called Stevenson's 'established popularity and high distinction' was, in Thurston's phrase, 'a mischievous man with a morbid desire for notoriety' (ibid.), ironically it was precisely Stevenson's status as a novelist that in the end silenced him more effectively than any government legislation. Though he kept sending letters about Samoa to *The Times*, he felt bound in the end to write to James Francis Hogan, an MP who had raised in Parliament the question of the treatment of Mataafa in exile, an issue on which Stevenson had written to *The Times* in April 1894. In October 1894, less than two months before his death, Stevenson wrote to Hogan: 'Mataafa is now known to be my hobby. People laugh when they see any mention of his name over my signature, and *The Times*, while it grants me hospitality, begins to lead the chorus. I know that nothing could be more fatal to Mataafa's cause than that he should be made ridiculous, and I cannot help feeling that a man who makes his bread by writing fiction labours under the disadvantage of suspicion when he touches on matters of fact' (*L8* 374).

If Stevenson suspected that London readers of *The Times* were not taking his stream of letters about Samoan politics very seriously, he knew for certain that one particular London reader was heartily sick of reading Stevenson's blow-by-blow accounts of life in Samoa. In March 1894 Sidney Colvin wrote to Stevenson in an overtly racist manner:

[Do] any of our white affairs [interest you at all]? I could remark in passing that for three letters or more you have not uttered a single word about anything but your beloved blacks – or chocolates – confound them; beloved no doubt to you; to us detested, as shutting out your thoughts, or so it often seems, from the main currents of human affairs, and oh much less interesting than any...of our known and hereditary associations, loves and latitudes. Forgive this 'expectoration', as your German friends would call it; it comes from the heart; and please let us have a letter or two with something besides native politics, prisons, *kava* feasts, and such things as our Cockney stomachs can ill assimilate (*L8* 279 n.1).

In his reply Stevenson took up as a sarcastic refrain Colvin's phrase 'blacks or chocolates', before reasoning with him: 'Dear Colvin, please remember that my life passes among my 'blacks or chocolates'. If I were to do as you propose, ... it would cut you entirely off from my life. You must try to exercise a trifle of imagination, and put yourself, perhaps with an effort, into some sort of sympathy with these people, or how am I to write to you?' (*L8* 281–2) Colvin did apologize for being 'a beast' in his letters, with the excuse that: 'writing across half the planet is a horrid difficult job, at best: the glance of the eye is wanting, and the tone of the voice, to make all right when the words are cutting.... As to that particular *boutade* [outburst] about the natives and your correspondence, please forgive' (*L8* 282 n.6). To be fair, Colvin (who was quite capable of suppressing material) did include Stevenson's reproof over the 'blacks or chocolates' comment in the *Vailima Letters*, though he tried to pass off his comment as 'a petition, not meant to be so seriously taken'.[41] Stevenson, however, did seem to take the comment seriously. His journal-letters to Colvin became noticeably shorter and more business-like. Nevertheless, he could not resist imparting to Colvin with ironic diffidence one particular piece of information about 'native politics, prisons, *kava* feasts, and such things': 'You have heard a great deal more than you wanted about our political prisoners. Well, one day about a fortnight ago the last of these was set free. Old Po'e ... was one that I had had a great deal of trouble with. I had taken the doctor to see him, got him out on sick leave, and when he was put back again gave bail for him' (*L8* 357–8). Stevenson had indeed taken considerable trouble over Po'e, one of the chiefs who had supported Mataafa, and who had been imprisoned after the latter's defeat and exile. Stevenson had written to, and met with, Laupepa, the victorious King of Samoa, asking for clemency on the grounds of Po'e's great age and poor health; the release of Po'e was secured by Stevenson standing surety in the sum of one hundred dollars (*L8* 312 and n.1).

After their release, Po'e and his fellow prisoners requested a meeting with Stevenson, to which he reluctantly agreed, fearing the inroads it would make into his heavy writing schedule. He was surprised, however, by the plan which the ex-prisoners proposed. Since they had been set free without condition, whilst other chiefs released previously were still bound to work on the roads, they proposed to express their gratitude to Stevenson for his support during their captivity, and his part in securing their release, by building a road linking Vailima to the public road (*L8* 358). Such a willingness to engage in road-making – 'the most fruitful cause (after taxes) of all rebellions in Samoa, a thing to which

they could not be wiled with money nor driven by punishment'
(*L8* 359) – touched Stevenson and his family deeply. In his penultimate
letter to Colvin (and the last of the *Vailima Letters*), Stevenson recounted
how, on the completion of the road, he had organized a feast and written
a speech (translated into Samoan with the help of a missionary) for the
occasion. Louis's speech was in effect a sermon (for to the end of his life
he could not resist emulating his grandfather Lewis Balfour, minister of
Colinton); it appeared in various newspapers, and was reprinted as an
appendix to the *Vailima Letters* and subsequently in Colvin's edition of
the *Letters*. Besides expressing his gratitude and pleasure in the new
road, Stevenson wanted to present its construction as a lesson to the
Samoans: 'There is but one way to defend Samoa. Hear it before it is too
late. It is to make roads, and gardens, and care for your trees, and sell
their produce wisely, and, in one word, to occupy and use your country.
If you do not others will.'[42] Once more, Stevenson insisted on what he
perceived as parallels between Samoa and Scotland, in this case a parallel
between the looming annexation and depopulation of Samoa (following
the Hawaiian experience), and the depopulation of Scotland by the
Highland Clearances. This address, one of the last things Stevenson was
to write, could be seen to echo his very first paid publication, when it
ended – uncannily enough – with an excursus on 'Roads'.[43] 'Chiefs!',
Stevenson apostrophized his congregation, 'Our road is not built to last
a thousand years, yet in a sense it is. When a road is once built, it is
a strange thing how it collects traffic, how every year as it goes on, more
and more people are found to walk thereon, and others raised up to
repair and perpetuate it, and keep it alive; so that perhaps even this
road of ours may, from reparation to reparation, continue to exist and
be useful hundreds and hundreds of years after we are mingled in the
dust.'[44] This coincidence of Stevenson's literary career coming full circle
resonates with the sermon's lament for a lost Scottish past and its hopes
for a better Samoan future, a future to which the childless Stevenson
committed himself unreservedly: 'I do not speak of this lightly, because
I love Samoa and her people. I love the land, I have chosen it to be my
home while I live, and my grave after I am dead; and I love the people,
and have chosen them to be my people to live and die with'.[45]

6
Conclusion

It is clear from Stevenson's letters during the last two years of his life that he was coming under increasing strain. This was in part due to illness: an epidemic of influenza laid low the whole Stevenson family in 1893, leaving Louis isolated and having to communicate his agonies over *The Ebb-Tide* to Lloyd by means of notes (*L8* 77). The experience of illness was nothing new to Stevenson, and he experienced better health in Samoa than he had done for a decade. Nevertheless in the end he started to succumb to sheer exhaustion, due mainly to the constant pressure of having to grind out copy, in at best indifferent health. As he wrote to George Meredith in September 1893:

> For fourteen years I have not had a day's real health; I have wakened sick and gone to bed weary; and I have done my work unflinchingly. I have written in bed, and written out of it, written in hemorrhages, written in sickness, written torn by coughing, written when my head swam for weakness; and for so long, it seems to me that I have won my wager and recovered my glove. I am better now, have been rightly speaking since first I came to the Pacific; and still, few are the days when I am not in some physical distress. And the battle goes on – ill or well, is a trifle; so as it goes (*L8* 163–4).

He was also greatly distressed by Fanny's symptoms of mental illness. In April 1893 he finally admitted in a letter to Colvin, most of which the latter suppressed: 'Well, there's no disguise possible: Fanny is not well, and we are miserably anxious. I may as well say that for ... nearly eighteen months there has been something wrong; I could not write of it; but it was very trying and painful – and mostly fell on me (*L8* 39). The precise nature of Fanny's illness is not clear; as Stevenson wrote to Colvin: 'there's nothing you can say is *wrong*, only it ain't *right*; it ain't *she*; at first she annoyed me dreadfully; now of course, that one understands, it is more anxious and pitiful' (*L8* 39). The presenting symptoms were alarming, and culminated in 'a hell of a scene which lasted all night – I will never tell anyone what about, it could not be believed, and was so unlike herself or any of us – in which Belle and I held her for about two hours; she wanted to run away' (ibid.). There has been much speculation about the nature and causes of Fanny's illness, ranging from purely psychological explanations to the theory that she was suffering from Bright's disease;[1] and despite the animus against her in some Stevenson biographies (such as McLynn's), it has to be said that Fanny Stevenson had to live with the often stressful and occasionally dangerous consequences of her husband's life-choices. Whatever Fanny was suffering from, it took a considerable toll not only on her, but also on Louis, and left a residual anxiety never entirely dissipated. By 21 May 1893 Fanny was well enough to write a deeply sympathetic note to Baxter on the death of his wife (something Louis seems to have found difficult); on the same day Louis wrote to his mother about Fanny: 'I do believe she is all right now:...only with some old illusions not yet – probably never to be eradicated' (*L8* 80).

Concern for his family's future increasingly absorbed Stevenson as he began to feel financially over-committed (largely because of the expense of further work on Vailima which – ironically – he had been talked into by his family). He felt bound to keep writing even though he was obviously exhausted. Already in July 1893 he had written to Baxter: 'I perceive by a thousand signs that we grow old and are soon to pass away...I am myself very ready; or would be – will be – when I have made a little money for my folks'; and repeating the words of his literary father-figure, Sir Walter Scott, who was also driven by financial necessity to work himself into the grave, Stevenson continued: 'The truth is, I have never got over the last influenza yet, and am miserably out of heart...Lungs pretty right, stomach nowhere, spirits a good deal overshadowed;...I am not yet sure about the *intellects*; but I hope it is only one of my usual periods of non-work. They are more unbearable now, because I cannot rest. *No rest but the grave for Sir Walter!*'[2] (*L8* 140–1). Stevenson's death-wish became increasingly overt as he foresaw the possibility of a falling off of his powers and his reputation. He wrote to his old school friend Baildon on 30 January 1894: 'Yes, if I could die just now, or say in half a year, I should have had a splendid time of it on the whole. But it gets a little stale and my work will begin to senesce; and parties to shy bricks at me; and now it begins to look as if I should survive to see myself impotent and forgotten. It's a pity suicide is not thought the ticket in the best circles' (*L8* 243). Perhaps his bleakest remarks were reserved for what was to be his last letter to Fanny Sitwell:

> I shall never do a better book than *Catriona*, that is my high-water mark, and the trouble of production increases on me at a great rate – and mighty anxious about how I am to leave my family; an elderly man, with elderly preoccupations, whom I should be ashamed to show you for your old friend; but not a hope of my dying soon and cleanly...I was meant to die young, and the Gods do not love me.
>
> This is like an epitaph, bar the handwriting, which is anything but monumental, and I daresay I had better stop. Many are the annoyances of the sons of man, but mine surely is unusual; that I cannot *get died*....I cannot make out to be anything but raspingly, harrowingly sad...(*L8* 282–3).

The handwriting in the autograph of this letter[3] does indeed look painfully diminished; and unusually for Robert Louis Stevenson, as he styled himself even in letters to Fanny Sitwell, he signed himself here simply: 'Louis' (ibid.).

Stevenson's agonies over the production of *The Ebb-Tide* were to be repeated in the writing of *St Ives*. Invoking once more the decline of his literary father-figure, Sir Walter Scott, he wrote to Colvin in October 1894:

> I know I am at a climacteric for all men who live by their wits, so I do not despair. But the truth is I am pretty nearly useless at literature, and I will ask you to spare *St Ives* when it goes to you; it is a sort of *Count Robert of Paris*.[4]...No toil has been spared over the ungrateful canvas; and it *will not* come together, and I must live, and my family....That is rightly the root and ground of my ill. The jingling tingling damned mint sauce is the trouble always; and if I could find a place where I could lie down and give up for (say) two years, and allow the sainted public to support me, if it were a lunatic asylum, wouldn't I go there, just! (*L8* 371–3).

This was to reiterate what he had written the previous month to Colvin, who ironically was taking a 'nerve-cure' near Wiesbaden: 'I have been trying to get along with *St Ives*. I should now leave it aside for a year and I daresay should make something of it after all. Instead of that, I have to kick against the pricks, and break myself, and spoil the book, if there was ever anything to spoil:...I'm as sick of the damned thing as ever anyone can be; it's a rudderless hulk...' (L8 357). These letters from Stevenson set alarm bells ringing back in Britain. As Colvin relates in the Epilogue to *Vailima Letters*, he and Baxter telegraphed Stevenson about the success of the Edinburgh Edition 'in terms intended to ease his mind and to induce him to take the rest of which he seemed so urgently in need'.[5] 'It seems doubtful,' Colvin continued, 'if our words were fully understood: it is more doubtful still if that ever-shaping mind had retained any capacity for rest, except, as he had himself foretold, the rest of the grave. At any rate he took none, but on receipt of our message only turned to his old expedient, a change of labour'.[6] Stevenson did indeed misunderstand the cablegram from Baxter and Colvin, and read it as meaning that the (astonishingly lucrative) deal for *St Ives*, which Baxter had negotiated with Astor's *Pall Mall Magazine* and McClure's American syndicate, was off. This misunderstanding was only discovered by Colvin too late, when he read Maggie Stevenson's reply in February 1895 to his letter of condolence on Louis's death (L8 390 n.4). According to Stevenson's mother, it was this communication breakdown, rather than what it pleased Colvin to call Louis's 'ever-shaping mind', that drove Stevenson at the very end of his life to 'plunge into *Hermiston*', as Maggie put it; nevertheless, she continued, 'he seemed at the last to be working easily and with keen enjoyment' (ibid.). The tendency to romanticize the writing of *Weir of Hermiston* as the final flaring of the brief candle of Stevenson's literary life has already been touched on above. It is typified in Fanny's version, reported by Baxter to Lord Guthrie in 1914, twenty years after the event: '[Louis] had been at work on *Weir*, and in the evening [of the day of his death], came down much elated,... exclaiming "I've done the best piece of work in my life"' (L8 404 n.2). In his account of Stevenson's death, Lloyd Osbourne has Stevenson 'buoyant and happy' on the day of his death, filled with the sense of successful effort at the book 'he judged the best he had ever written'.[7] Osbourne's later version, written especially for the Tusitala edition of 1924, further elaborated his account of Stevenson's views on *Weir*: '[Stevenson said] it was a masterpiece; that never before had he written anything comparable with *Weir*, that it promised to be the greatest novel in the English language' (T16 xi). These lines seem as fabricated as the scene they are set in, as Frank McLynn has pointed out.[8] It may be that Stevenson was in fact as elated by his work on *Weir* as his family has suggested; but there is little evidence of this in his correspondence. More typical is his comment to Colvin: '[*The Ebb-Tide*] gives me great hope, as I see I *can* work in that constipated, mosaic manner, which is what I have to do just now with *Weir of Hermiston'* (*L8* 250).

A considerable part of Stevenson's literary endeavour during the last year of his life was engaged, not in producing new works, but in planning and preparing the first collected edition of his works: the Edinburgh Edition. This project was first proposed by Baxter, doubtless as what McLynn calls 'a brilliant money-making wheeze',[9] in order to take some of the all-too-evident pressure off Stevenson. The latter wrote to Baxter on 1 January 1894 saying he was delighted with his idea, and enclosing a plan for the contents of the collected edition (*L8* 225). He later wrote to Baxter: 'I wish to assure you of the greatness of the pleasure that this Edinburgh Edition gives me. I suppose it was your idea to give it that name. No other would have affected me in the same manner' (*L8* 289). Though if possible, Stevenson admitted sentimentally, he would almost have preferred the 'Lothian Road Edition', in memory of their drunken escapades down Edinburgh's Lothian Road, when nothing would have seemed more preposterous to those penniless youths than the idea that Louis would end up alive and well on the island of Upolu, with Baxter at home bringing out the Edinburgh Edition of his works (*L8* 290). The thought of drunken Edinburgh youths prompted in Stevenson the rather bizarre idea that he might dedicate the Edinburgh Edition to the wild boy of Edinburgh's literary history, Robert Fergusson; this, he immediately saw, would look like affectation (ibid.). In any case, the proper dedicatee of his collected works should be his wife, he decided, and for this purpose he proposed to use the poem 'To My Wife', with its famous reference to his 'precipitous city' (*L8* 291). In the event this poem was kept, as it had originally been intended, for *Weir of Hermiston*.[10] From his first letter to Baxter welcoming the idea of the Edinburgh Edition, Stevenson had tried to take an active role in planning it. However, the painfully slow and unreliable mail service made Stevenson's involvement problematic. His letter to Colvin in May 1894 began by declaring that he was entirely in agreement with the latter's proposals for the 'E.E.'; but immediately set about questioning the contents Colvin had proposed. He felt obliged to 'abominate and reject' the proposed reprinting of his juvenile *The Pentland Rising*, which would only take place (as in fact it did) over his dead body (*L8* 288, and n.4); other proposals he made for inclusion and exclusion were also in the event overridden (ibid., and n.5). The following month he wrote to Baxter: 'I . . . take back the restrictions announced in my last. It is to be your edition. Please yourselves. And this is not only from humility, . . . but from a sense of what is possible and what is not at so great an interval of posts' (*L8* 307). On the same day he wrote to Colvin, in an interestingly different tone: 'You are to please understand that my last letter is withdrawn unconditionally. You and Baxter are having all the trouble of this Edition, and I simply put myself in your hands to do what you like with me' (*L8* 309). The power struggle with Colvin continued over the question of whether the latter's name was to appear as editor of the Edinburgh Edition. Colvin had demurred at this proposal, perhaps from modesty, or perhaps, as Stevenson suggested to Baxter, from fear of ridicule (*L8* 307). In the end, however, Stevenson felt obliged to dissociate himself from any editorial responsibility for the Edinburgh Edition. Despite asking for proofs of 'the *Magnum Opus*' (*L8* 337), he received none. A month before his death, and in his last letter to Baxter, he wrote: 'I have nothing to do with the Edition; no proofs have ever reached me; so far as I can hear no attempts are being made that any should reach me; Colvin writes by this mail that he has been cutting and carving on my immortal text; I do not say that he is wrong: I do say that 'all excisions, alterations and additions' have not been made by me. They have been made by him and he must stand the responsibility' (*L8* 384). The phrase 'excisions, alterations and additions' referred to a slip Colvin wanted to (and did) insert into the first volume of the Edinburgh Edition, which claimed 'the sanction and approval of the author'. Stevenson's heated response to this proposal, in what was his last letter to Colvin (though it was not included in the *Vailima Letters*), ran as follows: 'Really, if you consider your letter of this month and the various corrections which you there indicate it must appear to the meanest capacity that you *are* the editor, and that I *did not* make all excisions, alterations and additions. I am afraid, my dear fellow, that you cannot thus play fast and loose ...' (*L8* 384). Ironically, given that Colvin made changes Stevenson did not request, the latter's final words to Colvin were precisely to request the correction of an 'unpardonable' grammatical error in *The Ebb-Tide*; this correction, fully sanctioned and approved by the author, was never made (ibid., and n.10).

In November 1894 the Edinburgh Edition began to be published, and Baxter set off for Samoa in order to deliver the first two volumes to Louis personally. He had only reached Port Said when he heard the news of Stevenson's death; he continued his journey and finally arrived in Samoa on 31 January 1895. Stevenson had written to Baxter in August 1894:

I have been so long waiting for death; I have unwrapped my thoughts from about life so long, that I have not a filament left to hold by; I have done my fiddling so long under Vesuvius, that I have almost forgotten to play, and can only wait for the eruption and think it long coming. Literally no man has more wholly outlived life than I (*L8* 353).

The eruption finally came on 3 December 1894, when Stevenson died from what the doctors who attended him called 'apoplexy combined with paralysis of the lungs', or in modern terminology, a cerebral haemorrhage (*L8* 408 n1). The following day he was buried, according to his wishes, on the summit of Mount Vaea. His body was carried to its final resting place only with immense difficulty. The Samoan chiefs, who had watched by his body all night, made another road for Tusitala; this time they cut a path straight up the steep mountainside with their knives and axes. It was a terrible climb up the mountain, Belle recorded, and was too much for Fanny and Maggie even to contemplate (*L8* 407). A large cement tomb was later built, with a bronze plate on either side: one plate bore the words in Samoan 'The Tomb of Tusitala', followed by Ruth's speech to Naomi[11] from the Samoan Bible; on the other was inscribed Stevenson's own famous poem 'Requiem', first sketched in August 1879 on the train to San Francisco, and given its definitive version in Hyères in 1884.[12] The only monument left on 4 December 1894 was, Belle records, a pile of stones on the grave, and 'a little white tin cross trimmed with artificial flowers and fastened with cheap white ribbon' (*L8* 407). This present, from a Samoan woman married (like Uma) to a beachcomber, had been tied with cocoanut sinnet to a twig stuck into the loose earth. Louis would have smiled at that, wrote Belle.

* * *

When news of Stevenson's death reached London, Henry James is said to have gone straight to Fanny Sitwell, crying: 'It isn't *true*, it isn't *true*, say it isn't true'.[13] Of his personal sense of loss, he wrote to Edmund Gosse: 'Of what can one think, or utter or dream save of this ghastly extinction of the beloved R.L.S.? It is too miserable for cold words – it's an absolute desolation. It makes me cold and sick – and with the absolute, almost alarmed sense, of the visible material quenching of an indispensable light.'[14] To Fanny he wrote with acute awareness of the inadequacy of the language of grief:

> My Dear Fanny Stevenson,
>   What can I say to you that will not seem cruelly irrelevant or vain? We have been sitting in darkness for nearly a fortnight, but what is

our darkness to the extinction of your magnificent light?... You are such a visible picture of desolation that I need to remind myself that courage, and patience, and fortitude are also abundantly with you. The devotion that Louis inspired – and of which all the air about you must be full – must also be much to you. Yet as I write this word, indeed, I am almost ashamed of it – as if anything could be 'much' in the presence of such an abysmal void. To have lived in the light of that splendid life, that beautiful, bountiful thing – only to see it, from one moment to the other, converted into a fable as strange and romantic as one of his own, a thing that has been and has ended, is an anguish into which no one can enter fully and of which no one can drain the cup for you.[15]

Already in this letter James hints at the process by which Stevenson's life was to be transmuted into fiction, a fiction that would eventually come close to supplanting the fiction he actually wrote, and certainly his serious, 'grown-up' fiction. This process, begun by Stevenson himself, for example when he all but commissioned Colvin to publish the *Vailima Letters*, culminated in Graham Balfour's *Life*, of which James wrote sadly to Gosse:

I see now that a really curious thing has happened.... Insistent publicity, so to speak, has done its work (I only knew that it was *doing* it, but G.B.'s book's a settler), and Louis, *qua* artist, is now, definitely, the victim thereof. That is, he has *superseded*, personally, his books, and this last replacement of himself so *en scène* (so largely by his own aid, too) has *killed* the literary baggage.[16]

Writing in 1948 in the Introduction to her edition of the letters of Henry James and Robert Louis Stevenson, Janet Adam Smith hoped that: 'This record of the relationship between two writers shows the encouragement that James received from having one critical and appreciative reader among his equals; and it may help to place Stevenson among the most conscious, conscientious and interesting novelists who have written in English. A generation that has never been bothered by hero-worship may perhaps be led to read *The Beach of Falesá* and *Thrawn Janet* with the same attention as *The Author of Beltraffio* and *The Turn of the Screw*, and find in reading them the same delight that once did Henry James'.[17] Far from the 'Life of Stevenson' falling away, however, to leave his 'immortal text' standing clear of biographical encumbrances, it was to develop over the next half century, starting with the works of Daiches and Furnas, into virtually a minor literary genre.[18] But finally, at the beginning of the twenty-first century, Stevenson's fiction, though it may not command the critical attention reserved for the likes of Henry James, has also begun to attract a degree of critical interest that is in marked contrast to the neglect it suffered during much of last century.[19]

Notes

Introduction and chronology

1. Stevenson to Edmund Gosse, 18 June 1893 (*L8* 104).
2. Janet Adam Smith (ed.), *Henry James and Robert Louis Stevenson: A Record of Friendship and Criticism* (London: Rupert Hart-Davis, 1948), p. 46. Here, as throughout, the italics are in the original, unless otherwise stated.
3. This observation is made in the Biography section of the R.L.S. website.
4. For the 'Covenanters', see notes to Chapter 3 below.

1   The English scene

1. 'Claire' seems to have been one of Stevenson's nicknames for Fanny Sitwell. Prior to the full publication of Stevenson's letters, G.S. Hellman ('The Stevenson Myth' in *The Century*, December 1922) and J.A. Steuart (*Robert Louis Stevenson: Man and Writer* (London: Sampson Low, Marston & Co., 1924)) had postulated, on the basis of the 'Claire' reference, a love affair with a blacksmith's daughter (Hellman) or a Highland girl turned Edinburgh prostitute (Steuart). J.C. Furnas demolished these theories in his *Voyage to Windward* (London: Faber and Faber, 1952), pp. 394–9.
2. Henley also gave 'worship' to his 'Madonna', Anna Boyle, in an unpublished letter of 1876, now held by the Beinecke Rare Book and Manuscript Library, Yale University. My thanks to Anna Fleming.
3. *The Concise Scots Dictionary* (ed. Mairi Robinson) (Aberdeen: Aberdeen University Press, 1985).
4. Sidney Colvin, *Memories and Notes* (London: Edward Arnold, 1921), p. 103; see also R.C. Terry (ed.), *Robert Louis Stevenson: Interviews and Recollections* (Basingstoke and London: Macmillan – now Palgrave Macmillan.
5. Michel Le Bris, *RL Stevenson: Les années bohémiennes* (NiL Editions, 1994), p. 387.
6. Ibid., pp. 386–7; Cf. *L1* 45.
7. Ibid. pp. 388, 404. Cf. J.C. Furnas (1952), pp. 82–7; James Pope Hennessy, *Robert Louis Stevenson* (London: Jonathan Cape, 1974), pp. 70–2; Jenni Calder, *R.L.S.: A Life Study* (London: Hamish Hamilton, 1980), pp. 70–6; Ian Bell, *R.L.S. Dreams of Exile* (Edinburgh: Mainstream Publishing, 1992), pp. 91–4; McLynn, *Robert Louis Stevenson* (London: Pimlico, 1994), pp. 70–2, 80–6.
8. Stevenson addressed his nurse Alison Cunningham as 'My second Mother, my first Wife' in his dedication to her of *A Child's Garden of Verses*. He also told Fanny Sitwell of an occasion in a Glasgow restaurant where Maggie and he enjoyed the thought that no one would guess they were mother and son (*L1* 304).
9. On Freud and *Jekyll and Hyde* see Chapter 3 below.
10. Andrew Lang, *Adventures Among Books* (London: Longmans, 1905), p. 43; see also Terry, op. cit., p. 58.

11. Ibid., p. 44; see Terry, op. cit., p. 58.
12. See below in this chapter for Stevenson's discussion of James's discussion of Besant's 1884 paper 'The Art of Fiction'.
13. Gosse gives the date as '1877, or late in 1876' in the extract from *Critical Kit-Kats* reprinted in Jenni Calder (ed.), *The Robert Louis Stevenson Companion* (Edinburgh: Paul Harris Publishing, 1980), p. 44; see also Terry (ed.) (1996), p. 54. Stevenson and Gosse had previously met briefly on a steamer in the Hebrides in 1870.
14. Ibid., p. 44; see Terry, op. cit, p. 54. Gosse slightly misquotes Shakespeare's *King John* III.iv.81.
15. Ibid., p. 45; see Terry, op. cit., p. 55.
16. Ibid.
17. For Henley's review, see Chapter 4 below.
18. Unpublished letter to Anna Boyle from Henley in February 1876. Now held by Beinecke. My thanks to Anna Fleming.
19. Unpublished letter to Anna Boyle; see previous note.
20. I am unable to elucidate Swearingen's claim.
21. *Meredith: The Critical Heritage* (ed. Ioan Williams) (London: Routledge and Kegan Paul, 1971), p. 450.
22. George Meredith, *The Amazing Marriage* (London: Constable, 1898), pp. 61–3.
23. On the connections between *Prince Otto* and the debate about 'realism' in literary theory see, Chapter 3 below.
24. *Admiral Guinea* and *Beau Austin*, dedicated to Lang and Meredith respectively.
25. Smith (ed.) (1948), p. 80.
26. Ibid.
27. Ibid.
28. Ibid., p. 94.
29. *The Norton Anthology of Theory and Criticism* (ed. Leitch *et al.*) (New York: W.W. Norton & Co., 2001), p. 853.
30. Ibid., p. 862.
31. Ibid., p. 856 n.4.
32. See for example White's 'The Historical Text as Literary Artifact' in Leitch *et al.* (eds), pp. 1709–29.
33. On Roger's Fry's recommendation that writers should 'fling representation to the winds', see Virginia Woolf, *Roger Fry: A Biography* (London: The Hogarth Press,1940), p. 172. I have discussed Stevenson's problematization of aesthetic theory in 'Stevenson's "Auld Alliance": France, Art Theory and the Breath of Money in *The Wrecker*', *Scottish Studies Review* (Autumn 2002).
34. Smith (ed.) (1948), p. 101.
35. Ibid., pp. 101–2.
36. Smith claimed (op. cit., p. 10) that Stevenson and James met at Colvin's house in the British Museum, though I can find no other reference to such meetings. It may be pertinent to note that even in the second edition of her *Robert Louis Stevenson: Collected Poems* (London: Rupert Hart-Davis, 1971), despite the fact that a decade earlier in *Voyage to Windward* (p. 212) Furnas had cited evidence for Stevenson's introduction to James in 1879, Smith still insisted that they had first met at Bournemouth in 1885, and that Stevenson's earlier doggerel about James was based solely on his knowledge of James 'through his works'.
37. Smith (ed.) (1948), pp. 126–7. James is citing Archer's 'R.L. Stevenson: his Style and Thought', *Time*, 1885.
38. Ibid., pp. 129–31.
39. Ibid., pp. 150–5.

40. Ibid., p. 131.
41. Ibid., p. 160.
42. Ibid., pp. 163, 176.
43. Ibid., pp. 180, 220.
44. Ibid., p. 18.

2 The French connection

1. For the precise date of this meeting – a matter of some controversy among Stevenson scholars – see below.
2. Though not explicitly using the phrases 'spots of time' or 'surprised by joy', Stevenson does refer to Wordsworth in 'Ordered South' (*T25* 65). As well as anticipating Joyce's 'epiphany', Stevenson's 'glad moment' seems also to have a family resemblance to what C.S. Lewis called (after Wordsworth) 'Joy'. See Lewis's *Surprised by Joy* (London: Geoffrey Bles, 1955); also William Gray, *C.S. Lewis* (Plymouth: Northcote House: 1998), chapter 1 *passim*.
3. The following day Stevenson wrote to his mother that the violets had been given to him, appropriately enough, by 'little Dowson' (the future nineties poet Ernest Dowson). He described 'the most inexpressible bliss' produced by the opium, but reassured his mother that he was 'not quite the figure for much opium' (*L1* 407).
4. See Louis Stott, *Robert Louis Stevenson and France* (Milton-of-Aberfoyle: Creag Darach Publications, 1994), p. 32.
5. On the relation of Stevenson's prose poems to Baudelaire's, see his letters to Fanny Sitwell in May 1875, and to Colvin in June 1875 (*L2* 138, 142–3). Stevenson's surviving prose poems are printed in an appendix to *L2*.
6. Leslie Stephen's letter is reproduced in the Tusitala *Letters* (vol. 1) (*T31* 161–3).
7. See Will Low, *A Chronicle of Friendships*, extract in Jenni Calder (ed.) (1980), pp. 56–60.
8. Though it was precisely a *woman* artist (Fanny Vandegrift) who was to change Stevenson's life. On the previous page Stevenson mentions the impact of 'that essentially modern creature, the English or American girl-student' on 'the institution of the painters' colony' in France (*T30* 101).
9. See Chapter 1 above.
10. See Calder (1980), pp. 99–101; McGlynn (1994), p. 108; Le Bris (1994), p. 595; Le Bris, *Pour Saluer Stevenson* (Paris: Flammarion, 2000), pp. 149–50; see also Margaret MacKay, *The Violent Friend* (London: Dent, 1970), p. 38; Alexandra Lapierre, *Fanny Stevenson* (London: Fourth Estate, 1996), pp. 161–3.
11. Connections between *An Inland Voyage* and WWI were made, replete with references to 'the Hun' and 'the Boche', in 'With R.L.S. Through the Land of War', by J.A Hammerton (Written in War Time), in *Robert Louis Stevenson: His Work and Personality* (ed. St. J.A[dcock]) (London: Hodder and Stoughton, 1924), pp. 160–83; see also Nicholas Rankin, *Dead Man's Chest* (London: Faber, 1987), pp. 104–8.
12. See Graham Greene's comments in *A Sort of Life* (London: The Bodley Head, 1971), pp. 198–9.
13. Letter of May 1871 to Izambard, written in Charleville; Cf. Graham Robb, *Rimbaud* (London: Picador, 2001), pp. 81–5.
14. First appeared in *London*, November 1878, and later in *New Arabian Nights* (London: Chatto and Windus, 1882); see *T1* 266.

15. 'Ces nouvelles «bohémiennes»', in the phrase of Le Bris (2000), p. 99.
16. Ibid., p. 88 (this repeats verbatim an entire page from Le Bris (1994), pp. 334–5).
17. Ibid., p. 96.
18. Ibid., pp. 96–7. My translation.
19. Quoted by Barry Menikoff in his '*New Arabian Nights*: Stevenson's Experiment in Fiction', *Nineteenth Century Literature*, 45 (1990) p. 359.
20. Roland Barthes's widely-discussed 'L'effet de réel' was published in *Communications 11* (1968).
21. For Borges on Stevenson see: 'Jorge Luis Borges, sur Stevenson (entretien avec M. Balderson)' in Michel Le Bris (ed.), *Robert Louis Stevenson* (Editions de L'Herne, 1995); also Nicholas Rankin, op. cit., pp. 1–5. Baudrillard quotes from 'A Humble Remonstrance' in the epigraph to *La Pensée Radicale* (Paris: Collection Morsure, 1994). I am indebted to Jonathan Gray for this reference.
22. For Stevenson's projected essay on de Banville and other 'Parnassien' poets, see his letter to Colvin of 14 January 1875 (*L2* 107 and n.1).
23. See the rondels published in *New Poems* (*T23* 145); also Smith (ed.) (1971), pp. 90, 463–4. Stevenson claimed to have preceded Lang, Henley, Dobson and others in experimenting with the rondel form (*T17* 112).
24. The essay was dropped from *Travels with a Donkey* , and only appeared post-humously (*S* 34). Stevenson consistently spells 'Cevennes' without the accent in both the book and his correspondence.
25. Cited by Rankin, op. cit., p. 116.
26. For the 'Covenanters', see the notes to Chapter 3 below.
27. Lloyd Osbourne wrote in his Preface to *Virginibus Puerisque* that he last saw Stevenson 'walking away down the long length of the platform, a diminishing figure in a brown ulster. My eyes followed him hoping that he would look back. But he never turned, and finally disappeared into the crowd. Words cannot express the sense of bereavement, of desolation that suddenly struck at my heart. I knew I would never see him again' (*T25* x).
28. Douglas Gifford, 'Stevenson and Scottish Fiction' in *Stevenson and Victorian Scotland* (ed. Jenni Calder) (Edinburgh: Edinburgh University Press, 1981), p. 64 (where he inaccurately claims that 'The Story of a Lie' is set in France). On 'Kailyard' literature see Chapter 3 below.
29. The poem referred to was posthumously published as 'Now bare to the beholder's eye' (*T23* 197–8).
30. Stevenson does not mention the comparison that Henley drew with George Meredith; see Chapter 1 above.
31. See Chapter 5 for discussion of *In the South Seas*.
32. On Stevenson's reaction to *La Bête Humaine* see below, Chapter 5.
33. See *Will du Moulin*; suivi de *M. Schwob/R.-L.Stevenson Correspondances* (ed. F. Escaig) (Paris: Editions Allia, 1992), p. xii.
34. Ibid., p. ix. My translation.
35. Ibid., p. 99.

3 Forever Scotland

1. *The Silverado Diary* (*T18* 256).
2. On the vicissitudes of Stevenson's reputation as a 'Scottish Writer' see Kenneth Gelder (ed.), *Robert Louis Stevenson: the Scottish Stories and Essays* (Edinburgh: Edinburgh University Press, 1989), p. 1f.

3. Reprinted in *Essays Literary and Critical* (*T28* 93–110); see also 'My First Book' (*T2* xxiii).
4. In the summer of 1894, before turning to *St Ives* and *Weir of Hermiston*, Stevenson had been working on *Heathercat*, as well as intermittently on *The Young Chevalier*.
5. See letters to Colvin and his father in December 1880 proposing to write *An Historical Description of the Highlands from 1700 to the Present Day* (*L3* 128–9; *S* 55).
6. cf. Patrick Walker, *Biographia Presbyteriana* (c.1732); Robert Wodrow, *The History of the Sufferings of the Church of Scotland, from the Restauration to the Revolution* (1721–2); James Kirkton, *The Secret and True History of the Church of Scotland, from the restoration to the year 1678* (1817). The 'Covenanters' were those who remained faithful to the 'Covenants' of 1638 and 1643 to uphold Presbyterianism in Scotland, when Charles I and (after the Restoration) Charles II and James II (VII of Scotland), sought forcibly to impose the Church of England's Episcopalianism and *Book of Common Prayer* in Scotland. This material has recently been reworked in James Robertson's novel *The Fanatic* (London: Fourth Estate, 2000).
7. As well as the 'bulky historical romance without a spark of merit, . . . now deleted from the world', also entitled *The Pentland Rising*, and the much attempted but never completed novel on Hackston of Rathillet (see 'My First Book' referred to above), Stevenson also produced out of the same material a short story 'The Plague-Cellar', finally published in *The Scotsman* in 1985; see Gelder (1989), pp. 16–21 and notes.
8. *The Pirate* (Border Edition) (London: Macmillan – now Palgrave Macmillan, 1901), pp. xxi–xxiii.
9. A key tenet of Calvinism is its emphasis on Original Sin, with the state of humanity after the Fall being one of 'total depravity'.
10. The 'hill-preachers' were 'Covenanting' ministers who were 'outed' when the Episcopalianism of the Anglican Church was imposed in Scotland after the Restoration of the Stewart monarchy. They took to holding secret open-air services ('conventicles') and were fiercely persecuted during the so-called 'killing-times', which ended with the 'Glorious Revolution' and accession of the Protestant William of Orange. The 'Cameronians' were an extreme wing of the Covenanters.
11. *The Merry Men and Other Tales* (*T8* xii). Cf. letter to Colvin of June 1881 (*L3* 189).
12. See Gelder (ed.) (1989), p. 283 n.2.
13. Compare, for example:

> Now my little heart goes a-beating like a drum,
>   With the breath of the Bogie in my hair;
> And all around the candle the crooked shadows come
>   And go marching along up the stair. (*T22* 22)

with: 'But there was . . . naething to be seen but the muckle shadows turnin' around the can'le . . . 'an' naething could he hear but the dunt-dunt-duntin' o' his ain heart' (*T8* 118).
14. Deacon William Brodie was by day a respectable 18th century Edinburgh cabinet maker (whose work later found its way into the Stevenson household at 17 Heriot Row). By night Brodie was a notorious villain, who was eventually

caught and hanged in 1788. Already at the age of 14 Stevenson had begun a play about Brodie, which in 1878 was 'fished out' and rewritten in collaboration with Henley as *Deacon Brodie, or The Double Life*. The play was first performed in 1882, and published in 1892 (see *S* 36–8).

15. In his *Nightmare: the Birth of Horror* (London: BBC Books, 1996), Christopher Frayling has sought, on the basis of previously unpublished extracts from Graham Balfour's papers in the National Library of Scotland, to demythologize the Balfour/Osbourne story of the miraculous literary resurrection of *Jekyll and Hyde* three days after Stevenson burned the original version of his dream-inspired 'bogey tale', following Fanny's criticisms. For 'the legend of the burned manuscript' there is, says Frayling (p. 151), '*no credible historical evidence*'. However, in an unpublished letter to Henley, Fanny talks of Louis writing 'nearly a quire of utter nonsense', which he said was 'his greatest work', but which she says *she* will burn after she has shown it to Henley. References in the letter suggest that this must have been *Jekyll and Hyde* rather than 'The Travelling Companion', which Stevenson himself later burned. I am grateful to Anna Fleming for a copy of this letter, now held by the Beinecke Rare Book and Manuscript Library, Yale University.

16. See Daiches in Calder (ed.) (1981), p. 17.

17. On the notorious tag denoting the self-contradiction endemic in Scottish culture, see Hugh MacDiarmid, 'The Caledonian Antisyzygy and the Gaelic Idea', *Selected Essays of Hugh MacDiarmid* (ed. Duncan Glen), (London: Jonathan Cape, 1969).

18. Jenni Calder wants to limit David's attachment to Alan personally, and not to the world he represents; see 'Story and History: R.L. Stevenson and Walter Scott', *Cahiers Victoriens & Edouardiens*, 40 (1994) 21–34.

19. Cf. Cluny Macpherson's remark in *Kidnapped* (*T6* 166).

20. *Rob Roy* (Border Edition) (London: Macmillan – now Palgrave Macmillan, 1906), pp. xciii–xcv.

21. In 1751, rather than 1752, as Stevenson points out in his Dedication of *Kidnapped* to Charles Baxter (*T6* xi).

22. See letters to Gosse and to his father in November and December 1881 (*L3* 248–9, 257).

23. See Donald McFarlan (ed.), *Kidnapped* (Harmondsworth: Penguin, 1994), p. 225 n.27.

24. See *Kidnapped; or the Lad with the Silver Button: The Original Text* (ed. Barry Menikoff) (San Marino: Huntington Library Press, 1999), p. 178 (italics added); also pp. liv–lvi.

25. Ibid., p. lxiii.

26. *Rob Roy*, p. xcv.

27. Cf. 'A Gossip on Romance' in *Memories and Portraits* (*T29* 119–31).

28. On literature, psychoanalysis and letters, see the discussion generated by Lacan's Seminar on Poe's 'The Purloined Letter' in J.P. Muller and W.J. Richardson (eds), *The Purloined Poe* (Baltimore: Johns Hopkins University Press, 1988).

29. *Rob Roy*, pp. xcvi–xcviii.

30. *The SaturdayReview*, LXXVI (1893), quoted by Emma Letley in her edition of *Kidnapped* and *Catriona* (Oxford: OUP, 1986), p. 488 n.405.

31. Letley (ed.), p. xxii.
32. Ibid., pp. xix–xx.
33. 'Abbotsford' was the impressive house Sir Walter Scott had constructed close to the River Tweed in the Scottish Borders.
34. See Douglas Gifford, 'Stevenson and Scottish Fiction: The Importance of *The Master of Ballantrae*' in Calder (ed.) (1981), pp. 8–9.
35. See Appendix to *The Master of Ballantrae* (ed. Adrian Poole) (Harmondsworth: Penguin, 1996), p. 226.
36. See Gifford in Calder (ed.) (1981), p. 75.
37. Introduction to *The Master of Ballantrae* in *Robert Louis Stevenson: the Scottish Novels* (introduced by Jenni Calder and Roderick Watson), (Edinburgh: Canongate Books, 1995), pp. vii, xii.
38. Poole (ed.) (1996), p. 227.
39. *St Ives*, Preface and Chapters XXXI to XXXV by Jenni Calder, with Research and Foreword by R.J. Storey (Glasgow: Richard Drew Publishing, 1990).
40. Op. cit., pp. xxii–xxiii.
41. The term 'Kailyard' ('cabbage patch' in Scots) was first used by the critic J.H. Millar in 1895 in *The New Review* to describe the novelists J.M Barrie, S.R Crockett and John Watson ('Ian Maclaren'). By 1903 Millar was using the term in his *Literary History of Scotland* in a pejorative sense to describe a school of rural sentimentality with stock characters representing solid virtues and inhabiting an 'arcadia of village life, far removed from the ills of 19th century Scotland, its industrial development, poverty and high mortality rate. . . . The world created by the Kailyard novelists is little more than a projection of 18th century Romantic views about nature and its beneficial effects on humankind' (Trevor Royle, *The Mainstream Companion to Scottish Literature* (Edinburgh: Mainstream Publishing, 1993), p. 166). George Douglas Brown's *The House with Green Shutters* (1901) represents a reaction against the Kailyard school.
42. J.M. Barrie in *An Edinburgh Eleven*, reprinted in Calder (ed.) (1980), p. 71.
43. See *Scottish Literature* (ed. Gifford, Dunnigan and MacGillivray) (Edinburgh: Edinburgh University Press, 2002), pp. 484–5 (section co-written by Douglas Gifford and Lindsay Lunan).
44. See Gifford in Calder (ed.) (1981), p. 68; also p. 64.
45. See Gifford *et al.* (eds) (2002), p. 485 (section co-written by Douglas Gifford and Gordon Gibson).
46. Ibid., p. 448 (section co-written by Douglas Gifford and Lindsay Lunan).
47. Centenary Edition of *Weir of Hermiston* (ed. Catherine Kerrigan) (Edinburgh: Edinburgh University Press, 1995), pp. xxxiii–xxxiv.
48. *The Stickit Minister and Some Common Men* (London: T. Fisher Unwin, 1895), p. 15.
49. Colvin and/or Henley are inaccurate in that Weir's sister was 'in gentler manner hanged', as Stevenson puts it in the relevant passage in *Edinburgh: Picturesque Notes* (T26 157). The Major Weir story is revisited in James Robertson's *The Fanatic* (see note 6 above).
50. Letter of James to Gosse in 1901, quoted in Smith (ed.) (1948), p. 46.
51. Kerrigan (ed.) (1995), p. 117 and note.

4   America

1. Stevenson's earliest recorded reference to Whitman is in a letter to his cousin Bob in December 1867 (*L1* 119).
2. See W.G. Lockett, *Robert Louis Stevenson at Davos* (Hurst and Blackett, 1934), p. 127.
3. See Havelock Ellis (in collaboration with J.A. Symonds), *Sexual Inversion* (1897).
4. John Carey includes a passage from 'Across the Plains' in his *Faber Book of Reportage* (London: Faber, 1987). In the Introduction he dismisses the question, which clearly troubled Colvin, of whether reportage is 'literature', preferring to ask 'why intellectuals and literary institutions have generally been so keen to deny it that status' (p. xxxvi).
5. See Mehew's comments *L3* 1.
6. Calder (ed.) (1980), p. 47.
7. *From Clyde to California: Robert Louis Stevenson's Emigrant Journey*, (edited and introduced by Andrew Noble) (Aberdeen: Aberdeen University Press: 1985), pp. 51–2. Noble's edition makes available the full version of *The Amateur Emigrant* first published by James D. Hart in *From Scotland to Silverado* (1966). An edition by Roger G. Swearingen of the complete unrevised manuscript of *The Amateur Emigrant* was privately printed in two volumes in 1976 and 1977.
8. Ibid., p. 73.
9. Ibid., p. 21.
10. Despite William Archer's view, based on what he called Stevenson's 'arrantly Socialist' essay 'Beggars', that Stevenson was a 'Fabian *malgré lui*' (*M* 385), Stevenson published in 1887 in *The Contemporary View* 'The Day after Tomorrow', an essay sceptical of the socialist state he felt Britain was unconsciously becoming. The essay culminates in an imagined battle between the rival communes of Poole and Dorchester! (*T26* 122–3).
11. Though Stevenson twice deleted a reference to his status as, in Stevenson's eyes, a 'gentleman' from the version he intended for publication; Cf. Noble (ed.), pp. 77, 78.
12. Furnas, p. 151.
13. Christopher Isherwood, *Goodbye to Berlin* (London: Hogarth Press, 1939), p. 13.
14. Noble (ed.), p. 142.
15. Ibid. p. 285 n.17.
16. Dennis Kearney; Cf. ibid., pp. 285 n.17, 287 n.7.
17. Cf. Lewis Mumford's observation that the steamship companies had learned from the slum landlords that maximum profit was to be derived from exploiting the working class poor; quoted in Noble (ed.), p. 20.
18. See McLynn, p. 163, where he gives credence to the claim of Katherine Osbourne, Lloyd's estranged wife, that Belle had herself proposed marriage to Louis before his marriage to her mother. Calder (1980), pp. 137–8, offers a different interpretation.
19. 'Mr Stevenson's Methods in Fiction', *National Review*, January 1890 (i.e. before the first Sherlock Holmes story appeared in 1891); quoted in *L8* 49, n.1.
20. Cf. Gelder (ed.) (1889), p. 283 n.2.
21. Cf. McLynn, p. 158.
22. John E. Jordan (ed.), *Robert Louis Stevenson's Silverado Journal* (Book Club of California, 1954); extracts appear in *T28*.
23. Noble (ed.), p. 222.

24. Joseph Strong, Belle's 'drunken, feckless and irresponsible' husband, came to be highly regarded as one of the leaders of the Hawaiian school of painting; Cf. *L3* 6, n.3.
25. Masson (ed.), *I Can Remember Robert Louis Stevenson* (Edinburgh: Chambers, 1922), p. 194.
26. It may well have been providential that Japp came to Braemar, liked *The Sea Cook*, and took it back to London to find a suitable publisher, who in the event was James Henderson, from a village neighbouring Japp's in Scotland. However, the idea that Japp came 'charged by...Mr Henderson to unearth new writers for *Young Folks*' seems to be a piece of autobiographical invention (*S* 65).
27. For a discussion of the change of title, and the introduction of Stevenson's *nom de plume*, see J.A. Pierce, 'The Belle Lettrist and the People's Publisher; or, The Context of *Treasure Island*'s First-Form Publication', *Victorian Periodicals Review*, 31:4 (1998) 356–68.
28. Cf. Robert Louis Stevenson, *Treasure Island* (ed. J. Seeleye) (Harmondsworth: Penguin, 1999), p. xx.
29. Ibid., pp. xxxi–xxxiii. On *Treasure Island* and California, see also Anne Roller Issler, *Stevenson at Silverado* (revised) (Fresno: Valley Publishers, 1974), pp. 102–3.
30. Seelye (ed.), pp. xvi–xix.
31. Ibid., pp. xiii–xv, xxiv–xxv.
32. A possibility suggested by Louis's uncle, Dr George Balfour; see *B* 240.
33. *Odes* IV.vii.16.
34. *The Master of Ballantrae* (ed. Poole) (Penguin, 1996), p. 227.
35. Ibid., p. 228.
36. McLynn, p. 299.
37. Calder (ed.) (1980), p. 73; see also Terry (ed.) (1996), p. 192.
38. Ibid., p. 75; see Terry, op. cit., p. 194.
39. Ibid., p. 81; see Terry, op. cit., p. 195.
40. Cf. Graham and Hugh Greene (eds), *The Penguin Book of Victorian Villanies: The Great Tontine etc.* (Harmondsworth: Penguin, 1985).

5   In the South Seas

1. *In the South Seas* (*T20* 123).
2. See Brenda Maddox, *The Married Man: A Life of D.H. Lawrence* (London: Minerva, 1995), p. 314.
3. See Rod Edmond, *Representing the South Pacific: Colonial discourse from Cook to Gauguin* (Cambridge: CUP, 1997), p. 161.
4. The date of 28 July given in *In the South Seas* is, according to Mehew (*L6* 205 n.1), a misprint for 20 July, a mistake perpetuated in every subsequent version. Neil Rennie corrected it his 1998 Penguin edition.
5. See Ruth Blair's edition of *Typee* (Oxford: OUP, 1996), pp. vii–viii.
6. Robert Louis Stevenson, *In the South Seas; A Footnote to History* (New York: Charles Scribner's, 1898), p. ix.
7. Ibid., p. x.
8. Rod Edmond calls Stevenson's Pacific writing 'the product of complex transactions between an already extensively textualized Pacific and his own distinctive experience...' (op. cit., p. 160).

9. Joseph Conrad, *Heart of Darkness* [1902] (Harmondsworth: Penguin, 1983), p. 41; Marlow's opening monologue begins on p. 29.
10. Fanny Stevenson's Prefatory Note to *The Merry Men and Other Tales* (*T8* xii).
11. Masson (ed.) (1922), p. 223.
12. Horace, *Odes*, IV.ix.25; reference in *L7* 196 n.5.
13. H.J. Moors, *With Stevenson in Samoa* [1910] (Glasgow: Collins, no date), pp. 16–18.
14. Ibid., p. 21.
15. Cited in *L7* 2–3.
16. See McLynn (1994), pp. 383–90.
17. The phrase occurs in Stevenson's poem 'The Woodman' in *Songs of Travel* (*T22* 162); also Smith (ed.) (1971), pp. 277, 514–15.
18. See Elaine Showalter, *Sexual Anarchy* (London: Virago, 1992), discussed in Edmond (1997), pp. 177–9. Eve Kosofsky Sedgwick's *Between Men: English Literature and Male Homosocial Desire* (New York: Columbia University Press, 1985) was used by Wayne Koestenbaum to discuss the collaboration of Stevenson and Lloyd Osbourne in his *Double Talk: The Erotics of Male Literary Collaboration* (London: Routledge, 1989), pp. 145–51.
19. The MS. of *The Beach of Falesá* is reproduced in Barry Menikoff, *Robert Louis Stevenson and 'The Beach of Falesá': A Study in Victorian Publishing* (Stanford University Press, 1984); for the marriage contract see p. 124 (and p. 101 for a photograph of the holograph).
20. Menikoff (1984), pp. 85–6.
21. Furnas's edition of *The Beach of Falesá* appeared in 1956, and Calder's Penguin edition of *Dr Jekyll and Mr Hyde and Other Stories* in 1979. Calder acknowledges Furnas's edition as 'the first printing of the story as Stevenson wrote it', and the blurb to the Penguin edition claims that the text is here published in 'its original, uncensored form'.
22. Menikoff, op. cit., p. 76.
23. Ibid., p. 75.
24. Ibid., p. 5.
25. R.L. Stevenson, *South Sea Tales* (ed. Roslyn Jolly) (Oxford: OUP, 1996), p. xxxv.
26. Menikoff, op. cit., p. 5.
27. Ibid., pp. 23, 27.
28. Thus Paul Ricoeur describes Marx, Freud and Nietzsche in his *Freud and Philosophy* (New Haven: Yale University Press, 1977), p. 33.
29. Menikoff, op. cit., p. 76.
30. Ibid., p. 118; see also Calder, *Tales of the South Seas* (Edinburgh: Canongate, 1996), p. 166. Calder's Canongate edition reproduces Menikoff's text, while her Penguin edition retains the Cassell text, apart from the reinstated full marriage contract. Jolly reproduces Cases's yarn in an end-note.
31. Menikoff, op. cit., pp. 25–31.
32. On Stevenson's rebuttal of the Rodin/Zola comparison, see Chapter 2 above.
33. Low's reply to Stevenson's 'A Letter to a Young Gentleman who Proposes to Embrace the Career of Art', entitled 'A Letter to the Same Young Gentleman', appeared in the same number of *Scribner's Magazine* (September 1888).
34. Cf. my essay: 'Stevenson's "Auld Alliance": France, Art Theory and the Breath of Money in *The Wrecker*', *Scottish Studies Review* (Autumn 2002).

35. Cf. Koestenbaum (1989).
36. Cf. *B* 248–50; *S* 187; and Hinchcliffe and Kerrigan's Centenary Edition of *The Ebb-Tide* (Edinburgh: Edinburgh University Press, 1995), pp. xviii–xix, 156.
37. See Hinchcliffe and Kerrigan (eds), pp. 157–8.
38. Ibid., p. 159 n.3. In 1894 Stone and Kimball paid a large sum for first American rights to all Stevenson's subsequent writings, and suffered irreparable financial loss when he died later that year.
39. Ibid., p. 158.
40. It is probable that, given Stevenson's critical tone, Gosse chose not to acknowledge this letter (*L7* 104–6). Gosse's biography of his father, *The Life of Philip Henry Gosse, F.R.S., by his Son* (1890), is not to be confused with his later, and celebrated, *Father and Son* (1907).
41. *Vailima Letters* (London: Methuen, 1899), p. 328 n.1 (Letter 38).
42. Ibid., p. 361.
43. Freud's famous analysis of 'The Uncanny' in terms of repetition and death is perhaps nowhere better exemplified than in Stevenson's fable 'The Song of the Morrow', written probably in the same period as 'Roads'.
44. Ibid., p. 366.
45. Ibid., p. 363.

6 Conclusion

1. Bright's disease was diagnosed by Dr George Trousseau in Honolulu where Fanny joined Louis after he fell ill on his final trip there in October 1893 (*L8* 179). For a sympathetic reading of Fanny's problems see Alexandra Lapierre, *Fanny Stevenson* (London: Fourth Estate, 1996), pp. 456–64. Frank McLynn gives a more hostile reading, see op. cit., pp. 442–7, 456–62.
2. Stevenson slightly misquotes Lockhart's *The Life of Sir Walter Scott*, where the ailing Scott says: 'no repose for Sir Walter but in the grave' (London: Everyman Edition, p. 637).
3. In the National Library of Scotland.
4. Scott's last novel, considered to show a decline in his powers.
5. *Vailima Letters*, pp. 355–6.
6. Ibid.
7. Balfour reprinted Lloyd Osbourne's account of Stevenson's death his *Life*, pp. 369–70.
8. McLynn, p. 502.
9. Ibid., p. 485.
10. See *L8* 291 n.8; Cf. Smith (ed.) (1971), pp. 326, 538.
11. 'Whither thou goest, I will go; and where thou lodgest, I will lodge: thy people shall be my people, and thy God my God: where thou diest, I will die, and there will I be buried' (*Ruth* 1:16–17).
12. 'Requiem' is in *Underwoods* (*T22* 83); for different versions see Smith (ed.) (1971), pp. 478–9.
13. Smith (ed.) (1948), p. 10.
14. Ibid., p. 11.
15. Ibid., pp. 248–9.

16. Ibid., p. 46.
17. Ibid., p. 47.
18. Cf. the Biography section of the R.L.S. website.
19. See, for example, William B. Jones (ed.), *Robert Louis Stevenson Reconsidered: New Critical Perspectives* (Jefferson, North Carolina: McFarland, 2003).

Bibliography

Primary texts

In the three decades following the Edinburgh Edition of 1894–96, edited by Sidney Colvin in (at times strained) discussion with Stevenson himself, there were various editions of Stevenson's works. The most popular of these (and the one used in the present study) is the Tusitala edition (London: Heinemann, 1924) edited by Lloyd Osbourne and Fanny Stevenson; this includes short essays by Osbourne (of some interest, but of at times dubious accuracy) about Stevenson at different stages of his life. A Centenary Edition of Stevenson's works, published by Edinburgh University Press, is slowly appearing, though at present its completion looks unlikely; the present study has referred to *The Ebb-Tide* (eds P. Hinchcliffe and C. Kerrigan) and *Weir of Hermiston* (ed. C. Kerrigan) in this edition. The most recent volume in Centenary Edition is *The Collected Poems* (ed. R.C. Wilson), which appears to supplement rather than replace the text used in the present study, Janet Adam Smith's ground-breaking *Collected Poems*, first published in 1950.

An indispensable guide to Stevenson's works in prose is Roger G. Swearingen, *The Prose Writings of Robert Louis Stevenson* (Basingstoke and London: Macmillan – now Palgrave Macmillan, 1980).

The letters of RLS first appeared in the *Vailima Letters* (ed. Sidney Colvin) (London: Methuen, 1895), and from 1899 in various editions of *Selected Letters* edited by Colvin, finally appearing as the last five volumes of the Tusitala edition. Letters between Stevenson and Henry James are included in Janet Adam Smith (ed.), *Henry James and Robert Louis Stevenson: A Record of Friendship and Criticism* (London: Rupert Hart-Davis, 1948). The definitive edition of Stevenson's letters is *The Letters of Robert Louis Stevenson* in 8 volumes (ed. Bradford A Booth and Ernest Mehew) (New Haven and London: Yale University Press, 1994–95). From the latter, Ernest Mehew has also selected and edited a single volume *Selected Letters* (New Haven and London: Yale University Press, 1997, paperback 2001).

There are many editions of individual works by Stevenson. Those referred to in the present study are as follows (in order of publication):

Dr Jekyll and Mr Hyde and Other Stories (ed. Jenni Calder) (Harmondsworth: Penguin, 1979.).

From Clyde to California: Robert Louis Stevenson's Emigrant Journey (ed. Andrew Noble) (Aberdeen: Aberdeen University Press: 1985),

Treasure Island (ed. Emma Letley) (Oxford: OUP, 1985).

Kidnapped and Catriona (ed. Emma Letley) (Oxford: OUP, 1986).

Robert Louis Stevenson: the Scottish Stories and Essays (ed. Kenneth Gelder) (Edinburgh: Edinburgh University Press, 1989),

St Ives, Preface and Chapters XXXI to XXXV by Jenni Calder, with Research and Foreword by R.J. Storey (Glasgow: Richard Drew Publishing, 1990).

Kidnapped (ed. Donald McFarlan) (Harmondsworth: Penguin, 1994).

Robert Louis Stevenson: the Scottish Novels (introduced by Jenni Calder and Roderick Watson) (Edinburgh: Canongate Books, 1995).

The Master of Ballantrae (ed. Adrian Poole) (Harmondsworth: Penguin, 1996).

Tales of the South Seas (ed. Jenni Calder) (Edinburgh: Canongate Books, 1996).

South Sea Tales (ed. Roslyn Jolly) (Oxford: OUP, 1996).

In the South Seas (ed. Neil Rennie) (Harmondsworth: Penguin, 1998).

Robert Louis Stevenson: Selected Poems (ed. Angus Calder) (Harmondsworth: Penguin, 1998).

Kidnapped; or the Lad with the Silver Button: the Original Text (ed. Barry Menikoff) (San Marino: Huntington Library Press, 1999).

Treasure Island (ed. J. Seeleye) (Harmondsworth: Penguin, 1999).

R.L. Stevenson on Fiction: an Anthology of Literary and Critical Essays (ed. Glenda Norquay) (Edinburgh: Edinburgh University Press, 1999).

The Strange Case of Dr Jekyll and Mr Hyde and Other Tales of Terror (ed. Robert Mighall) (Harmondsworth: Penguin, 2002.).

Biographical works (in order of publication)

Graham Balfour, *The Life of Robert Louis Stevenson* [1901] (One Volume Edition: London: Methuen, 1906).

W.E. Henley, Review of Balfour's *Life* [see previous entry] in the *Pall Mall Magazine*, December, 1901, extracts in Calder (ed.) (1980) and Terry (ed.) (1996).

Andrew Lang, 'Recollections of Robert Louis Stevenson' in *Adventures Among Books* (London: Longman, 1905), extracts in Terry (ed.) (1996).

Will H. Low, *A Chronicle of Friendships* [1908], extracts in Calder (ed.) (1980) and Terry (ed.) (1996).

H.J. Moors, *With Stevenson in Samoa* [1910] (Glasgow: Collins, no date), extracts in Terry (ed.) (1996).

J.M. Barrie, *An Edinburgh Eleven* [1913], extracts in Calder (ed.) (1980).

Sidney Colvin, *Memories and Notes of Persons and Places* [1913] (London: Edward Arnold, 1921), extracts in Calder (ed.) (1980 and Terry (ed.) (1996).

Edmund Gosse, *Critical Kit-Kats* [1913], extracts in Calder (ed.) (1980) and Terry (ed.) (1996).

G.S. Hellman, 'The Stevenson Myth' in *The Century*, December 1922.

Rosaline Masson (ed.), *I Can Remember Robert Louis Stevenson* (Edinburgh: Chambers, 1922).

J.A. Steuart, *Robert Louis Stevenson: Man and Writer* (London: Sampson Low, Marston & Co., 1924).

Robert Louis Stevenson: His Work and Personality (ed. St. J.A[dcock]) (London: Hodder and Stoughton, 1924).

W.G. Lockett, *Robert Louis Stevenson at Davos* (Hurst and Blackett, 1934).

David Daiches, *Robert Louis Stevenson* (Glasgow, 1947)

J.C. Furnas, *Voyage to Windward: The Life of Robert Louis Stevenson* (London: Faber and Faber, 1952).

Margaret MacKay, *The Violent Friend: the Story of Mrs Robert Louis Stevenson* (London: Dent, 1970).

James Pope Hennessy, *Robert Louis Stevenson* (London: Jonathan Cape, 1974).

Anne Roller Issler, *Stevenson at Silverado* (revised) (Fresno: Valley Publishers, 1974).

Jenni Calder, *RLS: A Life Study* (London: Hamish Hamilton, 1980).
Jenni Calder (ed.), *The Robert Louis Stevenson Companion* (Edinburgh: Paul Harris Publishing, 1980).
Nicholas Rankin, *Dead Man's Chest* (London: Faber, 1987).
Ian Bell, *Robert Louis Stevenson: Dreams of Exile* (Edinburgh: Mainstream Publishing, 1992).
Frank McLynn, *Robert Louis Stevenson* (London: Pimlico, 1994).
Louis Stott, *Robert Louis Stevenson and France* (Milton-of-Aberfoyle: Creag Darach Publications, 1994).
Michel Le Bris, *RL Stevenson: Les années bohémiennes* (NiL Editions, 1994).
Michel Le Bris (ed.), *Robert Louis Stevenson* (Editions de L'Herne, 1995).
Alexandra Lapierre, *Fanny Stevenson* (London: Fourth Estate, 1996).
Christopher Frayling, *Nightmare: the Birth of Horror* (London: BBC Books, 1996).
R.C. Terry (ed.) *Robert Louis Stevenson: Interviews and Recollections* (Basingstoke and London: Macmillan – now Palgrave Macmillan, 1996).
Michel Le Bris, *Pour Saluer Stevenson* (Paris: Flammarion, 2000).

Critical works (in alphabetical order)

Brantlinger, Patrick, *The Reading Lesson: the Threat of Mass Literacy in Nineteenth-Century British Fiction* (Bloomington: Indiana University Press, 1998).
Calder, Jenni (ed.), *Stevenson and Victorian Scotland* (Edinburgh: Edinburgh University Press, 1981).
Calder, Jenni, 'Story and History: R.L. Stevenson and Walter Scott', *Cahiers Victoriens & Edouardiens*, 40 (1994).
Daiches, David, 'Stevenson and Scotland' in Calder (ed.) (1981).
Edmond, Rod, *Representing the South Pacific: Colonial discourse from Cook to Gauguin* (Cambridge: CUP, 1997).
Gifford, Douglas, 'Stevenson and Scottish Fiction' in Calder (ed.) (1981).
Gifford, Dunnigan and MacGillivray (eds), *Scottish Literature* (Edinburgh: Edinburgh University Press, 2002).
Gray, William, 'Stevenson's "Auld Alliance": France, Art Theory and the Breath of Money in *The Wrecker*', *Scottish Studies Review* (Autumn 2002).
James, Henry, 'Robert Louis Stevenson' [1887] in *The House of Fiction* (ed. Leon Edel) (London: Rupert Hart-Davis, 1957); also in Janet Adam Smith (ed.), *Henry James and Robert Louis Stevenson* (London: Rupert Hart-Davis, 1948).
Jones, William B. (ed.), *Robert Louis Stevenson Reconsidered: New Critical Perspectives* (Jefferson, North Carolina: McFarland, 2003).
Koestenbaum, Wayne, *Double Talk: the Erotics of Male Literary Collaboration* (London: Routledge, 1989).
MacDiarmid, Hugh, 'The Caledonian Antisyzygy and the Gaelic Idea', in *Selected Essays of Hugh MacDiarmid* (ed. Duncan Glen), (London: Jonathan Cape, 1969).
Maixner, Paul (ed.), *Robert Louis Stevenson: The Critical Heritage* (London: Routledge, 1971).
Menikoff, Barry, 'New Arabian Nights: Stevenson's Experiment in Fiction', *Nineteenth Century Literature*, 45 (1990).
Menikoff, Barry, *Robert Louis Stevenson and 'The Beach of Falesá': A Study in Victorian Publishing* (Stanford: Stanford University Press, 1984).

Noble, Andrew (ed.), *Robert Louis Stevenson* (London: Vision Press, 1983).

Pierce, J.A., 'The Belle Lettrist and the People's Publisher; or, The Context of *Treasure Island's* First-Form Publication', *Victorian Periodicals Review*, 31:4 (1998).

Sandison, Alan, *Robert Louis Stevenson and the Appearance of Modernism* (Basingstoke and London: Macmillan – now Palgrave Macmillan, 1996).

Showalter, Elaine, *Sexual Anarchy: Gender and Culture at the Fin de Siècle* (London: Virago, 1992).

Veeder, W. and Hirsch, G. (eds), *Dr Jekyll and Mr Hyde After One Hundred Years* (Chicago: University of Chicago Press, 1988).

Index

N.B. When someone is only mentioned as the recipient of a letter from Stevenson, a reference is not normally given in the index.